MW01274030

Identities, Trust, and Cohesion in Federal Systems: Public Perspectives

Edited by

JACK JEDWAB AND JOHN KINCAID

Queen's Policy Studies Series
School of Policy Studies, Queen's University
McGill-Queen's University Press
Montréal & Kingston | London | Ithaca

School of Policy Studies Publications Program
Robert Sutherland Hall
138 Union Street
Kingston, ON K7L 3N6
www.queensu.ca / sps /

Library and Archives Canada Cataloguing in Publication

        Identities, trust, and cohesion in federal systems : public perspectives / edited by Jack Jedwab and John Kincaid.

(Queen's policy studies series)
Includes bibliographical references and index.
Issued in print and electronic formats.
ISBN 978-1-55339-535-5 (softcover).--ISBN 978-1-55339-536-2 (PDF).--ISBN 978-1-55339-537-9 (HTML)

        1. Federal government--Case studies. 2. Comparative government--Case studies. 3. Case studies. I. Kincaid, John, 1946-, editor II. Jedwab, Jack, 1958-, editor III. Queen's University (Kingston, Ont.). School of Policy Studies, issuing body IV. Series: Queen's policy studies

JC355.I34 2018   321.02   C2018-906016-6
                                            C2018-906017-4

Contents

Contributors

Sarah Arras is a PhD researcher at the Department of Political Science at the University of Antwerp in Belgium. Her research focuses on EU regulatory agencies and interest group involvement.

Paul C. Bauer is a Max Weber fellow at the European University Institute. Previously he worked and studied at the universities of Bern, Konstanz, Pompeu Fabra, and Sciences Po Bordeaux. He investigates questions in the areas of political sociology and research methodology, and his research has been published in the *Public Opinion Quarterly*, *Political Science Research and Methods*, *European Sociological Review*, *Political Behavior*, and *Swiss Political Science Review*.

A. J. Brown is professor of public policy and law in the Centre for Governance and Public Policy at Griffith University, Brisbane, Australia. He is also a board member of Transparency International Australia, fellow of the Australian Academy of Law, and fellow of the Regional Australia Institute. He has worked or consulted in or for all levels of government and in all branches of government in Australia, including as a state ministerial policy advisor. He also researches, consults, and teaches widely in public policy, public sector management, public accountability, and public law. A leading commentator on Australian federalism, intergovernmental relations, and devolution, he is the foundation lead researcher of the Australian Constitutional Values Survey, conducted every two years since 2008. His books include *Restructuring Australia: Regionalism, Republicanism and Reform of the Nation-State* (Federation Press, 2004) and *Federalism and Regionalism in Australia: New Approaches, New Institutions?* (ANU E-Press, 2007). In 2008, he was a delegate to the Australia 2020 Summit. In 2011, he was a member of the Australian Government's Expert Panel on Constitutional Recognition of Local Government. He is currently leading an Australian Research Council Discovery Project on the future of federalism.

Richard L. Cole (1946–2017) was professor emeritus of Urban Affairs and Political Science and former dean of the School of Urban and Public Affairs at the University of Texas at Arlington. He published extensively on federalism, intergovernmental relations, public policy, and urban affairs.

Mireia Grau Creus is head of the Research Area of the Institut d'Estudies de l'Autogovern (Institute of Self-Government Studies) of the Government of Catalonia. She has published several articles and chapters on intergovernmental relations and self-government in Spain, such as "The Catalan Parliament's Contribution to the Consolidation and Development of Sewlg-Government and Defence of Catalan National Identity" in Guy Laforst and André Lecours, eds., *The Parliaments of Autonomous Nations* (2016) and "A Step Backwards or a Step Forwards? The Politics and Policies of Decentralization under the Governments of the Partido Popular" in *South European Society and Politics* (July 2005).

Jacob Deem is a PhD candidate at Griffith University's Centre for Governance and Public Policy in Brisbane, Australia. He has a keen interest in federalism and issues of multi-level governance. His research focuses on the principle of subsidiarity. In particular, he investigates whether public attitudes of citizens in Australia, Canada, Germany, and the UK explain variations in subsidiarity's realization in those countries.

Laura Flamand is research professor in political science at the Center for International Studies, El Colegio de México. She is the co-author of *Seguro popular y federalismo: Un análisis de política pública* (CIDE 2015), and her work has appeared in *Política y Gobierno, Foro Internacional,* and *Journal of Public Governance and Policy,* among other journals and edited volumes. She holds a PhD in political science from the University of Rochester, New York, and a BA in government and public administration from El Colegio de Mexico. Her work "The New Role of Subnational Governments in the Federal Policy Process: The Case of Democratic Mexico" was awarded the *New Voices in the Study of Democracy in Latin America* fellowship from the Woodrow Wilson Center for International Scholars in 2005, and her research has been supported by grants and fellowships from the U.S. National Science Foundation, the United Nations Program for Development, the World Bank, and the McArthur, Ford, and Hewlett foundations. Her scholarly work explores the effects of democratization on the operation of federal systems with emphasis on both politics and policy, especially in Argentina, Brazil, and Mexico. She is an expert in policy analysis and evaluation in Mexico, especially in the environmental, health, and social arenas.

Markus Freitag is professor of political sociology at the University of Bern. His research focuses on aspects of political and social participation. He has published extensively in journals such as *British Journal of Political Science, Comparative Politics, Comparative Political Studies, Electoral Studies, European Journal of Political Research, European Political Science Review, European Union Politics, European Sociological Review, Governance, International Political Studies, Journal of Conflict Resolution, Political Studies, Publius: The Journal of Federalism, Political Psychology,* and *West European Politics.*

Jack Jedwab is president of the Association for Canadian Studies and the Canadian Institute for Identities and Migration. He is chair of the Canadian National Metropolis Conference on Immigration and Integration. He holds a PhD in Canadian History from Concordia University.

John Kincaid is the Robert B. and Helen S. Meyner Professor of Government and Public Service and director of the Meyner Center for the Study of State and Local Government at Lafayette College, Easton, Pennsylvania, USA. He also is senior editor of the Global Dialogue on Federalism, an elected fellow of the National Academy of Public Administration, editor of *Federalism* (4 vols. 2011), and coeditor of *Courts in Federal Countries: Federalists or Unitarists?* (2017).

Pascal Sciarini is professor of Swiss and comparative politics at the University of Geneva. His main research topics are decision-making processes, direct democracy, Europeanization, and political behaviour. His work has appeared in several journals, such as *British Journal of Political Science, Comparative Political Studies, Electoral Studies, European Journal of Political Research, Journal of Politics, Journal of European Public Policy,* and *West European Politics.* His most recent, coauthored book is *Political Decision-making in Switzerland: The Consensus Model under Pressure* (Palgrave Macmillan 2015). He is also coeditor of the *Handbook of Swiss Politics* (2007, 2014).

Henrik Scheller, PhD, is senior expert for public finance at the German Institute of Urban Affairs, Berlin. Previously, he was a professor at the chair "Politics an d Governance in Germany and Europe" at the University of Potsdam, Germany. He has published several books on federalism: *Föderale Politikgestaltung im deutschen Bundesstaat — Variable Verflechtungsmuster in Politikfeldern* (Federal policy-making in the German federal state — variable patterns of joint decision-making in different policy areas, 2008) and *Fiskalföderalismus* (together with George Anderson, 2012). He is coeditor of the *Jahrbuch für Öffentliche Finanzen*.

Dave Sinardet is professor of political science at the Free University of Brussels (VUB) and at the Université Saint-Louis Bruxelles. His research interests include nationalism, federalism, and multilingual democracy, on which he has published widely. He is also an expert in Belgian politics.

María Fernanda Somuano has been associate professor at the Center for International Studies at El Colegio de México since 2001 and coordinator of the MA in political science since 2010. Her main research areas are political participation and citizenship in Mexico and Latin America, subnational democratization processes, social movements, civic culture, public opinion, and values in new democracies. Her most recent book publications are *Confianza y cambio político en México* with Reynaldo Ortega (El Colegio de México, 2015) and *Democracy in Mexico: Attitudes and Perceptions of Citizens at National and Local Level* coedited with Salvador Martí I Puig, Reynaldo Ortega, and Claire Wright (Institute of Latin American Studies, University of London, 2014).

Peter Thijssen is professor in political sociology at the Department of Political Science, University of Antwerp, Belgium, and member of the research group Media, Movements and Politics (M²P). His research focuses on political participation and public opinion. Currently he is working on a research project on the politics of solidarity.

1

Introduction and Comparative Observations

Jack Jedwab and John Kincaid

How do citizens in federal systems perceive and weight their multiple identities and attachments? How do their identities influence their trust in the various orders of government and affect the cohesion of a federation as a whole? Do cohesive federations depend on public trust and strong attachment to the national or central government? Under what conditions are attachment and identification with the various orders of government in conflict or compatible?

Based on extensive analyses of public opinion data in eight federal countries, this collection of essays offers valuable insights into debates about the relationships between identities, institutional trust, and cohesion in eight federal systems: Australia, Belgium, Canada, Germany, Mexico, Spain, Switzerland, and the United States. The essays consider how the citizens of these federations understand the challenges of plural identities, trust in multiple governments, and federal cohesion (cf. Moreno and Colino 2010). The comparative perspective offers valuable opportunities to comprehend how expressions of identity, trust, and cohesion correlate with centralized, decentralized, and/or asymmetrical models of federalism. The anthology aims at filling a gap in the literature because there is little cross-country comparative research on public opinion and attitudes toward these key dimensions of federal governance.

The book's first four chapters examine what some analysts have de-

Identities, Trust, and Cohesion in Federal Systems: Public Perceptions, edited by Jack Jedwab and John Kincaid. Montréal and Kingston: McGill-Queen's University Press, Queen's Policy Studies Series. © 2018 The School of Policy Studies, Queen's University at Kingston. All rights reserved.

scribed as multinational/multilingual federations, with the first two, Canada and Spain, addressing secessionist pressure and the second two, Belgium and Switzerland, having so far achieved unity while accommodating diversity. Canada is the only case in the volume that has experienced official public referenda on secession. In 2014, Catalonia held a non-binding referendum that supported independence from Spain. Another referendum was scheduled for 1 October 2017. Belgium became formally federal in 1993, with Flanders and Wallonia having reached, for now, a *modus vivendi*, showing no immediate propensity to break up the country. Switzerland has not faced secessionist threats and is often held up as a successful example of federal accommodation of a multilingual, multi-religious, multinational federal society (e.g., Livingston 1952).

The last four chapters analyze more territorially homogeneous federations. The first two of those—the United States and Mexico—are not only neighbours but also experiencing particular trust stresses in public trust of various governments in their federal systems, although with differences as to which governments are most and least trusted by Mexicans and Americans. The last two countries, Australia and Germany, are not experiencing particular trust stresses but are experiencing debates about federalism reform related to system performance.

Dimensions of Federalism

Federalism is, ideally, a democratic mode of governance in which the authority to govern is distributed and shared between a general or central government and regional governments variously called autonomous communities, cantons, *Länder*, provinces, and states. Both the general and constituent governments act directly on the citizens in different and sometimes overlapping spheres. There is more than one form of federal governance, and there are about twenty-eight federal and quasi-federal countries (Iraq, Nepal, plus twenty-six others in Hueglin and Fenna 2015) in the world—depending on how one defines federalism. Variations are often attributable to such things as the original terms of the federation agreement and evolving demographic realities, notably as regards the dominant expression of identity within a given country along with territorial concentrations of "national," ethnic, and/or language groups. These groups figure prominently among several considerations that can determine whether the distribution of power and/or authority is principally the purview of the general or central government or of other orders of government. Assessment of the order of government responsible for decision-making in a particular area is usually the litmus test for whether the federation is centralized or decentralized.

Federalism is often seen as an important means to accommodate cultural and linguistic diversity (Watts 2008; Moreno and Colino 2010), but providing self-rule for specific "nations" within the federation can also weaken the commitment to shared rule needed to sustain the federal polity (Norman 2006; Erk and Anderson 2009). A unique contribution of these essays is their reliance on public opinion data to help elucidate these relationships. The federations examined here also display important similarities and differences in their institutional structures and modes of governance.

Federal systems of governance are influenced by, among other things, diverse cultural and regional circumstances. Some federations are more centralized than others, some are more decentralized or non-centralized, and still others are characterized by varying degrees of asymmetry (Tarleton 1965; Watts 2008). Each of these features of governance can be justified by governing authorities as essential to making federalism work by achieving some degree of cohesion. The differences between these varieties of federalism are also reflected in the areas the contributors to this volume prioritize in their respective assessments of effective governance. Certain contributors stress the importance of identities, particularly the recognition of national minorities—as in Belgium, Canada, Spain, and Switzerland. Political recognition is seen as a precondition to intergroup harmony and, thus, to sustaining unity within the federation. Other contributors emphasize the degree of trust in government as the key element in building cohesion and preserving unity. Some consider connections between trust in government and recognition of identities and discuss them in tandem as they assess the effectiveness of federalism.

The population composition of the eight federations is fairly diverse and also characterized by regional concentrations of specific groups in four of the cases. The tremendous population diversity of the United States does not have territorial expressions comparable to Catalonia in Spain and Quebec in Canada. In some federations, regional expressions of identity are more salient and, therefore, more important for comprehending the particular governance challenge. Cohesion or harmony within a federation can be influenced by the importance citizens attach to cultural identity markers such as language, nationality, ethnicity, religion, and race. The importance of group identity can give rise to calls for constitutional recognition by minorities—national or otherwise—within the federation. The manner in which such calls are addressed can be central to harmonious intergroup relations, which can be regarded as a condition of cohesion. The intersection of regional and cultural expressions of identity may represent an even more significant challenge in this regard. The contributors employ various data sets to consider how identity formation is managed, trust in government is enhanced, and cohesion is attained.

Federations rarely remain static. They have evolved with time as changing social and economic conditions have given rise to reinterpretation, negotiation, and modification of the powers and rights prescribed in the federation's original constitutional pact and/or agreement (Kincaid and Tarr 2005).

Different models of federalism are analyzed in this collection of country studies so as to gain insight into some of the common and uncommon governance challenges that are encountered in the countries examined. The contributors make effective use of empirical data to draw evidence-based conclusions about ongoing issues facing federalist governance. The essays break some new ground in this regard.

The Country Cases

While the countries examined in this volume are all federal or quasi-federal, there is considerable diversity among them and, therefore, quite different public opinion dynamics and sources of attachment or detachment and objects of, as well as reasons for, public trust and mistrust. The country cases were selected to reflect different types of developed federal systems and to illustrate different federal challenges. Resources limited to eight the number of cases that could be included in the project, and the cases are limited to major Western federal systems. We hope this book will stimulate further research along the lines of identities, trust, and cohesion not only in developed federations but also in newer and less developed federal systems, some of which face serious, even federation-threatening, challenges.

Canada

Evoking such terms as grievances, discontent, and alienation, Canadian discourse around federalism sometimes sounds like a troubled marriage. While the terminology may sometimes seem vague, it is the discourse to which Canadians have become accustomed when describing the problems of federalist governance. Jack Jedwab employs various data sets to examine the relationship between attachment to and identification with Canada and the level of grievance felt with certain aspects of federalist governance. He contends that some degree of grievance is inevitable in a federation with important differences in resource endowment and demography between regions/provinces. It is observed that outside of the majority French province of Quebec, heightened grievance in other provinces does not necessarily imply diminished attachment to Canada. While the rest of Canada does harbour grievance, it does not translate into detachment from Canada. This is not the case in Quebec, where francophones are somewhat more likely than other Canadians to regard identities as competing choices, such that a strong sense of grievance may reinforce attachment to the province and erode attachment to Canada. Identity-based claims within federations can be the most difficult to reconcile. In Canada and Spain, the desire for constitutional recognition of specific "national" cultural characteristics of one or more member states remains an ongoing challenge for fostering members' sense of solidarity and thus preventing breakup.

Spain

In her discussion of public attitudes in Spain's quasi-federation, Mireia Grau Creus looks at whether the desire for decentralization or centralization was motivated by identity issues or economic considerations. For more than two decades after 1978, decentralization enjoyed consistent support from most citizens, and autonomous communities such as Catalonia and the Basque Country were seen as key pillars of making democracy work in Spain. Support for centralism declined while support for decentralization grew simultaneously with the expansion of regional self-government and the rise of dual identities (i.e., of people feeling as much Spanish as from their autonomous community). Until recently, the desire for decentralization was the prevailing trend among the Spanish population and was related to economic and social welfare considerations.

However, harmony between citizens and their decentralized institutions began to decline in the early 2000s, especially in 2005, and dramatically deteriorated during the post-2008 economic crisis. Support for decentralization shrunk while support for centralization increased, and recentralization became a top political issue. Although there were some changes in national identities as well, they were not of the same intensity as preferences about territorial decentralization. In the autonomous regions, the expansion of self-government sustained support, and Catalonia's increased support for independence put the cohesion of Spain at risk. Many Catalans opposed the ruling against major aspects of Catalan self-government issued by the Constitutional Court of Spain in 2010. Hence, the re-centralization trend seems linked to the highly controversial Catalan-led wave of self-government reforms initiated in 2004 and to the vast economic crisis or, perhaps, the argument that attributes the responsibility for the crisis to the self-governing autonomous communities that are said by their critics to foster duplication, inefficiencies, heightened economic costs, and spendthrift behaviour.

The author asks, though, whether attitudinal surveys showing support for decentralization after 1978 may have been mistaken because the most common indicators employed in surveys have been linked to grasping citizens' preferences on rather abstract features of decentralization, such as institutional setting and powers, that mean very little to people's day-to-day reality. These indicators do not seem to tap perceptions and attitudes toward the concrete effects of decentralization. Nevertheless, concludes the author, the future of Spain's decentralized system and of Spain itself is uncertain.

Belgium

Belgium became formally federal in 1993 and is based on territorially unilingual regions and communities, except for Brussels. Belgium is unique for the absence of national political parties and national public media. Peter Thijssen, Sarah Arras, and Dave Sinardet point out that, between 2007 and 2011, Belgium was in a deadlock because elite representatives of the two main language communities—Dutch and French—disagreed about the direction of Belgium's ethno-federal system. Recently, considerable attention has been given to a paradoxical side effect of federalism that could lead to a devolutionary spiral because the recognition of territoriality embodied in Belgium's process of becoming federal in 1993 risks strengthening group identities that could diminish interaction between groups and reduce support for the federal polity. As a result, ethno-linguistic groups might become increasingly assertive and, consequently, greater responsibility could devolve to the subnational governments. The authors contend that this would ultimately hollow out the *raison d'être* of the overarching federation. They note that elites in the consociational tradition used to be pacifiers of community differences, but, in recent years, they have more and more chosen a confrontational stance on community-related subnational issues.

The authors test a number of hypotheses, finding, among other things, that Walloons are more supportive than Flemings of devolving more powers to the regional governments but that support for devolution is greater among less-educated rather than more-educated Flemings and Walloons. Support for devolution is strongest among Belgians who identify primarily with a region and/or community; however, federation has not strengthened regional and/or community identification. Most Belgians feel Belgian in the first place. Likewise, each group's knowledge of the other group's language and media programming has not decreased since federation. Belgians who have regular relations with members of the other ethno-linguistic group want less devolution of more competences to the regions and communities.

Consequently, from elite and media discourse, Belgium may appear to be completely divided; however, the authors' data show that Belgian society generally does not reflect such a deep division. While the elites are running in one direction, most Belgians are standing pat or running in a different direction.

Switzerland

Theoretically, political trust is vital for the healthy functioning of democratic political systems and an important element of the citizen-state relationship. Paul Bauer, Markus Freitag, and Pascal Sciarini contend that political trust among Swiss citizens varies both with regard to institutions in the different orders of government (i.e., federal, cantonal, local) as well as with respect to the federal system's development over time. They point out that Switzerland is a highly decentralized country in which the constituent political entities (i.e., cantons) wield far-reaching political authority. It is also a culturally diverse federal polity in which the cantons are a powerful presence. When asked which order— commune, canton, linguistic region, country, and Europe—they identify with most, Swiss citizens say "country" first and "canton" second. This ranking holds for citizens from all three linguistic regions.

The authors find that, compared to most other European countries, including France, Germany, and Italy, trust in political institutions is generally high in Switzerland. Similarly, cantonal and cultural-linguistic subpopulations trust their different national and subnational institutions to a great extent, although overall citizens display slightly more trust in their local governments first and cantonal governments second. Over time since 1995, trust has increased in local and cantonal authorities as well as in the federal Parliament, while trust in political parties has been in decline. There is some regional variation though. Trust in local and cantonal governments is highest in German-speaking cantons and lowest in French-speaking cantons, while trust in cantonal authorities is highest for individuals belonging to the Italian-speaking region. Institutional trust in Switzerland is believed to reflect the perceptions that political institutions perform relatively well and that Switzerland has achieved unity while preserving diversity. Another factor contributing to high levels of political trust is the emphasis on direct democracy as referenda increase the feeling of belonging to a unified Swiss nation. Furthermore, attitudes toward the federal, cantonal, and local governments are not in conflict. In sum, the extension of strong popular rights serves to strengthen federalism, and there have been no calls for major federalism reform since implementation of the new 1999 Constitution.

United States of America

Analyzing the United States, John Kincaid and Richard Cole point out that while public trust in the federal government has dropped to a new nadir, Americans express fairly high levels of trust in their local and state governments. Further, there has been a growing gap between low trust in the federal government and higher trust in local and state governments. Americans also express high levels of attachment first to the English language, then to their country, their state, their city, their ethnic and ancestral group, the world, their neighbourhood, and their religious group, in that order. Americans are more religious than the citizens of most other countries, and they display fairly high ancestral attachments compared to citizens of Canada, Germany, and Spain. Americans express more ambivalent attitudes about immigrants, although survey responses are coloured by long-standing controversies over illegal immigration, which has been a flashpoint for polarization. Even so, majorities of Americans support immigration and are receptive to the contributions made by immigrants to American society.

The country has, however, experienced a very high level of political polarization between the two political parties—Democrats and Republicans—which is most evident among elites and party activists but increasingly evident among citizens as they are led to sort themselves out between the parties. The election of Donald Trump to the presidency in 2016 was one reflection of this polarization and the disgruntlement underlying it. Polarization has had some significant impacts on the operation of the federal system, including gridlock in Congress, which has elevated the federalism roles of the president and Supreme Court. There has, however, been no public clamour to reform the federal system or devolve more powers to state and local governments. The last presidential candidate to champion a "New Federalism" was Ronald Reagan in 1980.

Mexico

Maria Fernanda Somuano and Laura Flamand observe that Mexicans exhibit very little confidence in their governments. Among North Americans, Mexicans are the least trusting of their governments (cf. Kincaid et al. 2003; Cole, Kincaid, and Rodriguez 2004; Kincaid and Cole 2011). Mexico also consistently ranks at the bottom of the list of Latin American countries regarding citizen satisfaction with democracy, and Mexicans' satisfaction with democracy has been declining. The authors examine the sources of this generalized and persistent distrust. They contend that the key explanations for such low trust are the perceived ineffectiveness of public safety policies and governments' inadequate responsiveness to the needs of the citizens. Levels of trust vary markedly across different parts of Mexico, and the basis for trust may diverge. In Mexico City, the degree of trust in government is higher where citizens are members of political parties, unions, and non-governmental organizations. In other parts of the country, perceived lower degrees of corruption result in higher levels of trust in the national government. Yet other considerations affecting trust include the perceived state of the economy. The authors conclude that because Mexicans tend to trust the federal government more than their state or municipal authorities, recentralizing tendencies may enjoy wide popular support and further weaken the possibility of state and local governments checking the powers of the federation, although states have been somewhat more assertive since 2000.

The authors also suggest that, for democracy to blossom in Mexico in the next twenty years, governance needs to be strengthened system-wide. There must be decisive enforcement of the rule of law, increased accountability of public servants and politicians (i.e., by consolidating the checks and balances across branches and orders of government), and citizen empowerment. In the realm of federalism, state and local governments need to be transformed in at least two crucial areas: fiscal responsibility, given that they tend to spend mostly federal transfers and not own-source income; and civil service, because a large number of state and municipal public officials lack the professional qualifications and expertise to perform their jobs.

Australia

A. J. Brown and Jacob Deem examine changes in the degree of satisfaction with democracy and trust in Australia's federal political institutions against a backdrop of a stable federal political culture supportive of a federal system. Employing results from the Australian Constitutional Values Surveys, the authors document recent declines in public satisfaction with the way democracy works in Australia and a gradual decline in satisfaction with the current three-level federal system despite an unchanging landscape of federal political culture in which, according to the authors' measures, about two-thirds of Australians are federalists. Comparison of these results using attitudes toward each order of government identified declining ratings of the federal government's effectiveness as an important factor in falling democratic satisfaction. Given the nature of the perceived institutional and structural deficiencies of the system, the extent to which the federal government is relied upon to make the entire system "work" leaves many citizens with no institution in which to place their faith. At the same time, while specific support is low, diffuse support is high. Like US citizens, Australian citizens' national attachment is very strong, but at the subnational level, unlike the United States and even more so Canada, Australians' local attachment competes with and may outrank state attachment—a pattern more akin to Germany.

But Brown and Deem observe that, while confidence in the current federal system may be declining, most citizens do not see federalism itself as at fault. Rather, public concerns appear to stem from the performance, nature, and configuration of Australia's state and local governments, particularly the states, and of some states more than others—but as a result of their size and structure more than their incumbent governments or policies. The results suggest a public openness to reforms of federalism, including abolishing the states and creating new regional governments.

Germany

Henrik Scheller finds that in Germany the public strongly desires equality of living conditions, solidarity, social cohesion, and cooperation between the orders of government, while elite and academic discourse is shaped by calls for wide-ranging federalism reforms oriented toward the American model of dual federalism and competition (cf. Kenyon and Kincaid 1991). Germany's federal experience has always been characterized by discrepancies between public and elite attitudes toward federalism—something also found more recently in Belgium. The public prefers a pragmatic and cooperative approach to solving major challenges faced by the *Länder* and the federal republic. Consequently, elite demands for an extensive disentanglement of federal and *Land* competences and financial responsibilities risk weakening the legitimacy of the federal system.

Germans already feel ambivalent about their federal system. Their approval of it is far from unanimous; they have a low level of identification with their *Länder*; and there is much debate over which order of government should play a greater role in future decision-making, especially economic policies. Germans would like to see a larger governing role accorded to the federal and local orders of government. This preference can be found most frequently in eastern Germany and in Bavaria and Saarland in western Germany. However, many Germans also want a bigger role for the European Union (EU). In Hamburg, Berlin, Schleswig-Holstein, and Hesse, respondents preferred a greater role for the EU than for their national government. A 2008 survey found that people identified most strongly with their immediate community (39 percent) followed by the federal government (32 percent), the European Union (14 percent), and their *Land* (11 percent). A majority of the public approves of national regulation in a wide variety of policy areas, including equal standards nationwide and also within the European Union. A key point, though, is that the desire for more power for a particular order of government does not consistently coincide with strong identification and satisfaction with the *Länder*, the federal government, or the EU.

There is strong support in principle for the country's fiscal equalization system. Given their desires for uniformity and cooperation, a clear majority of Germans oppose reform calls to give *Länder* more freedom to set their own tax rates. Similar to Australia, there also is sizable public support for reconfiguring the *Länder*, especially to create *Länder* having more equal economic resources. Consequently, concludes Scheller, Germans want more unity than diversity, making a constitutional reform promoting cooperation and more equity conceivable and preferable to a competitive federalism model.

Decentralization and National Identity

Does attachment to the general or central government diminish in decentralized federations? In Belgium, a side effect of decentralization appears to be stronger attachment to the regional and community governments and weaker ties with the federation government, at least among many elites. The politics of recognition and the politics of redistributing powers are underlying elements of this outcome. The contributors caution about the possible hollowing-out of the justification for federalist governance where decentralization is regarded as a means to build group cohesion.

Spain's quasi-federalism has often been praised for its decentralized approach to plurinationalism. During the decentralizing decades following 1978, many citizens came to exhibit strong attachments to their autonomous community without undercutting their attachment to Spain. But the global economic crisis that began in December 2007 triggered a decline in support for decentralization and regional self-rule in much of Spain while simultaneously fuelling increased secessionist feeling in Catalonia. The central government employed its spending power to shape autonomous-community public policies, and observers viewed this as a form of recentralization that became especially unpopular in Catalonia and has remained contentious to this day.

Decentralization may result in reduced attachment to the central government if two orders of government within the federation are perceived to be in competition. In Canada, it is in the predominantly French province of Quebec where federal and provincial attachments are seen to be competing by a significant segment of the francophone population. Many francophones view Canada in dualistic or bi-national terms, perhaps even as "two solitudes" (MacLennan 1945); hence, many think they face competing choices. Quebec francophones who are the most dissatisfied with Canadian federalism may seek constitutional recognition of Quebec's national identity and greater decentralization of powers to the province. A sizable minority favours secession.

There is an important intersection between the call for national identity recognition and greater decentralization. Many people desirous of such recognition assume that increasing self-rule powers will follow from recognition, but it remains unclear whether past or future transfers of powers from the federal to the regional governments strengthen or weaken cohesion in the federal system. It is less evident, for example, that devolution will bolster the attachment of Quebec francophones to Canada. This could be an elusive goal. At best, identity recognition and/or structural change may only stave off the appetite of some Quebec francophones for secession. In Switzerland, by contrast, there appears to be a stable balance between national and cantonal identity and a cohesive identity with Switzerland.

Despite differences in degrees of decentralization and in the presence of diverse national, ethnic, religious, and linguistic groups across the eight case-study countries, the majority of people in all eight federations identify with their country or nation-state first, even though some minority groups do not do so. It also appears from these studies that decentralization per se does not necessarily increase nor decrease subnational identities. Decentralization can endorse pre-existing subnational identities; in turn, subnational identities sometimes create political pressures that help drive decentralization. Addressing subnational identity concerns through decentralization, however, does not necessarily increase attachment to the country or nation-state. If one takes a social constructivist view of national identity (Emerson 1960; Anderson 1991), decentralization creates semi-autonomous political spaces where subnational political and cultural elites can build "national" institutions and seek to strengthen a "national" identity within a constituent region.

Trust, Identity, and Cohesion

Another theme in the country case studies is the extent to which federal systems do or do not heighten trust in governance and political institutions. Social characteristics of federations, especially territorially based heterogeneity, are important contexts for opinion formation (Livingston 1956). Theoretical and empirical studies suggest that political trust is a vital resource for the functioning of democratic political systems and an important dimension in the citizen–state relationship. Trust theories hold that the viability of democracy depends substantially on the ability of political institutions to elicit public trust and reinforce trust within civil society. Trust promotes democracy; withdrawal of trust weakens it (Hetherington 2005; Tilly 2005).

Results from the Australian Constitutional Values Surveys provide insight into the degree of satisfaction with democracy and varying levels of trust in a federation's different orders of government. Falling trust may not be all negative, for example, if it indicates growing proportions of "critical citizens" (Norris 1999). But too much disenchantment poses a risk for the goals and stability of a democratic society (Doorenspleet 2012). While the tensions in Australian public trust do not culminate in serious challenges to national cohesion, they nonetheless may affect the long-term structure of the federal system. Therefore, it is important to identify the reasons behind fluctuations in trust and, especially in Australia's case, to see if the current federal structure of governance is working as a bulwark of overall trust, identity, and cohesion or whether it is undermining these or is simply irrelevant to them.

In the United States, there is a very high level of mistrust of the federal government and relatively high levels of trust in the state and local governments across the nation, but there is no agitation for restructuring the federal system, and federalism reform is not on politicians' agendas. Americans have a high level of attachment to their country and their constitutional system, and they are inclined to believe that dysfunctionality is not due to a flawed system but to misbehaving politicians who abuse the system.

In Switzerland, the federal, cantonal, and local political institutions are regarded as operating quite successfully in maintaining citizens' trust. However, individuals belonging to the country's three cultural regions (Italian-speaking, German-speaking, and French-speaking) evaluate different institutions differently on average. In short, there are some variations in institutional trust on the basis of cultural identification. When compared with other European countries, the degree of public trust in Switzerland's political institutions is generally good.

By contrast, in Mexico, there is a generalized and time-persistent level of distrust toward all political institutions. A national survey reveals that in Mexico satisfaction with democracy is positively and significantly correlated with the extent to which national and local leaders are trusted; however, stronger national attachments do not result in higher levels of trust and confidence in the national government. Rather the public's trust is more closely aligned with the effectiveness of government policies and, notably in Mexico, when it comes to the federal role in public safety—an understandable public sentiment in light of Mexico's drug wars.

Some research suggests that consociational democracy may be better for holding segmented societies together (e.g., Armingeon 2002) while federalism may be less conducive to social-trust creation (Freitag and Bühlmann 2009) and to fostering minority attachment to the national state (Elkins and Sides 2007). However, no clear pattern emerges from comparative federalist studies when examining the relationship between identity, trust, and social cohesion. It remains uncertain how each affects the other and to what degree they are interdependent. The inability to establish firm empirical relationships between the three might stem from the manner in which the terms are defined. As important as the concepts of trust and social cohesion are, there is a need to better determine how and whether they are useful in measuring the effectiveness of federalist governance. If not, it may be necessary to develop a conceptual framework that improves the comprehension of what makes federalism work.

At the same time, the case studies suggest that levels of trust in the various orders of government are not significant factors in public support for federalism or federal principles. In no country does trust per se generate public pressure to abolish federalism. Instead, dissatisfaction and low levels of trust are sometimes associated with citizen support for federalism reform, as in Australia and Germany. Threats to cohesion of the federal system arise mainly from variations in intensities of "national" identities rather than trust itself. Hence threats to cohesion are found in only three—Belgium, Canada, and Spain—of the eight cases examined in this volume.

Public Disenchantment with Federal Democracy

It is clear from our case studies that federal systems are not immune to the contemporary Western public's disenchantment with democracy. Although, overall, federal forms of government have stronger records of democratic performance and rights protection than non-federal governments (Norris 2008; Kincaid 2010), most of the cases in this volume evidence public dissatisfaction with democracy and the performance of governments. As a number of observers have noted, sustaining trust in democratic leadership is "permanently problematic" (Kane and Patapan 2012, 83). However, a democracy cannot flourish if citizens are overly compliant. Democracy works better when citizens share a culture of skepticism (Cleary and Stokes 2006) by which they recognize their leaders are fallible and, thus, understand the need for constraining institutions, including those associated with federalism.

Norris (1999) hypothesized that, because of power sharing, citizen confidence in important political institutions would be greater in federal than unitary systems, but she found the opposite, though she attributed the outcome to a failure to measure decentralization within federations. Fitzgerald and Wolak (2014) found in Western Europe that citizens in both federal countries characterized by decentralization and majoritarian countries characterized by a concentration of power displayed higher trust in local authorities and lower trust in central authorities. Matsubayashi (2007) found that citizens in highly decentralized systems express higher levels of system support.

Clearly more systematic comparative research is needed on the extent, if any, to which federal democratic systems are more or less conducive to public satisfaction with democracy and trust of governments as compared to non-federal systems. There also is a need to determine whether or how public disenchantment and mistrust affect the viability and performance of federal systems. All of the federal systems in this volume that have low levels of public satisfaction and trust nevertheless continue to function and have done so through, in some cases, long periods of dissatisfaction and distrust. Governments in Switzerland appear to enjoy the highest levels of trust, but are the citizens of Switzerland appreciably better off than the citizens of the other federations analyzed in this volume? The higher levels of trust in Switzerland may contribute to higher levels of cohesion compared to the strains found in Belgium, Canada, and Spain, but, from a historical perspective, how can we be sure that contemporary trust in Switzerland is not a function of, rather than a causal factor in, the ability of the peoples of Switzerland to learn how to live together peacefully over several hundred years, during which time they gradually tightened their federal ties (Baker 1993)?

More research is needed, as well, on the causes and consequences of differential trust across the orders of government. Presumably these matters are more important in federal than in non-federal systems. What causes citizens to trust the government of the federation more than regional and/or local governments, or vice versa? Hetherington and Nugent (2001), who found support for devolution to be highest among US respondents who most distrusted the federal government, concluded that citizens shift support from one order of government to another not because of governments' perceived capabilities but because of distrust of the other order of government. Jennings (1998), however, suggested that trust has two dimensions—instrumental (i.e., performance) and relational (i.e., representativeness and accountability of leaders). The former is more relevant to trust in the distant federal government; the latter influences trust in state and local governments. A partial explanation may be that because citizens have less direct experience and interaction with distant governments, such as the federal government, their trust in distant governments is based more on stereotypes and generalized trust (Lubell 2007).

What are the institutional and governance consequences of such differential trust? One study in the United States suggested that "trust in state governments dampens support for the federalization of state policy domains" (Mikos 2007, 1701). The Australia case in this volume suggests that distrust of the states could result in public support for abolishing the states and creating new regional governments. In Spain, there appears to be growing support for secession in Catalonia, as Catalans feel more distant from and distrustful of Madrid even while many other citizens of Spain support recentralization.

Overall, the case studies suggest that federalism per se is not a source of public disenchantment; instead, disenchantment arises from issues associated with the performance of institutions and the behaviour of political elites, although disenchantment can be exacerbated in heterogeneous federations where public evaluations of performance also include government behaviour toward "national" groups within constituent regions.

Do Elites Represent the People?

Another striking finding from this volume's case studies is the disconnect between elites and the people. This disconnect is examined directly in the cases of Belgium and Germany.

The authors of the Belgium study note that, in the past, elites operating in the consociational tradition acted as pacifiers of community differences. Today, they are much more confrontational and subnationalistic as they champion greater autonomy for their respective communities. Judging from elite and media discourse, Belgium appears to be divided very deeply; yet opinion polls show that Belgian society does not reflect that division and that popular attachment to the regions and communities has not become stronger since federalization in 1993.

In Germany, the general public prefers a cooperative and pragmatic approach to federalism instead of the normative concepts advanced by most elites. The elites tend to promote a disentanglement of competences and greater competition among the orders of government. Various elites propose to reduce equalization transfers, increase *Land* tax powers so as to generate more independent sources of *Land* revenue, tighten debt restrictions on the *Länder* and municipalities, and even alter *Land* boundaries. By contrast, the public displays strong desires for equality of living conditions, solidarity, social cohesion, and cooperation among the orders of government. Germans support nationally driven uniform policies in education—from kindergartens to universities—and in many other policies. A deeply rooted consciousness of solidarity seems to be a fundamental feature of Germany's political culture.

The Australia case study suggests that federal reform in tune with public sentiments, especially making institutions more federal, could bolster public trust in governance overall. Although confidence in Australia's current federal system is falling, most citizens do not see federalism per se as being at fault.

Dissatisfaction with democracy and distrust of governments in most of the other cases suggest likewise an elite/public disconnect in those federations. Consequently, there is a need for more research on such disconnects, including the institutional and governance consequences of disconnects between the people and national elites, the people and regional or local elites, and the people and all elites—federal, regional, and local. One possible consequence of such disconnects could be the rise of radical populists on the left and the right, even in federal democracies such as Australia, Austria, Spain, Switzerland, and the United States.

Are the Constituent Regional Governments Important for Citizens?

Another interesting finding from the analyses is the relatively low level of public enthusiasm for regional governments; namely, autonomous communities, cantons, provinces, and states. In Australia, there is strong support for abolishing the states and replacing them with a larger number of regional governments. In Belgium, despite the emphases of political elites on the predominance of the regional and community governments, most Belgians identify with Belgium more than with their regional government. Furthermore, Belgians who have regular encounters with members of the other ethno-linguistic group want less devolution of powers to the regional governments. Except for francophones, Canadians are most attached to their country first and then to their province, but less than half of Canadians support giving more power to the provinces. Only in Quebec is there a greater tendency to put the province first. In Germany, citizens identify most with their local community and least with their *Land*. Throughout the country, residents believe *Land* governance and politics play a notably subordinate role. In Mexico, citizens trust the federal government more than their state and local governments and do not envision their states being engines of government reform. More than two-thirds of Americans feel very attached to their country, but only 40 percent feel attached to their state. Their attachment to local government is lower yet, even though they trust local governments the most. Only in Switzerland does there appear to be more robust citizen identification with the cantons, although this identification holds second place after "country."

These findings raise important questions for future research because, in principle, the constituent regional governments are the building blocks of a federation and the bulwark of federalism. Do weak or lukewarm attachments to these governments create a climate conducive to centralization (Riker 1964; Levy 2007)? Should federalists worry about this? One preliminary perspective is to consider that a World Bank study ranks Switzerland as the world's third most decentralized country, followed by the United States in ninth place, Canada in place twelve, Germany at twenty, Belgium at twenty-three, Spain at forty-six, Australia at fifty-five, and Mexico at eighty-one (Ivanyna and Shah 2012). Do attachments to the constituent governments really matter very much one way or the other in most federations or to most citizens of a federation who do not identify with a territorialized 'national' group? Are such attachments important in their own right?

Likewise, do variations in how citizens evaluate their regional and local governments make a significant difference for federal governance? In Switzerland, for example, public trust in the cantonal and local governments is significantly higher in the German-speaking than in the French-speaking cantons. However, it is not clear that this difference makes a big difference for Swiss federalism. In other, less cohesive multinational federations, such differences could make a big difference in federalism.

Is the Federation Government the Linchpin?

Most of the case studies suggest that the federation government is the most crucial influence in citizens' views of trust, identity, and cohesion. This may be linked to the extent that in most of the case-study federations, with the partial exceptions of Canada and Spain, diffuse support for the country and political system as a whole is high even while specific support for current governments is low. The federation government is the one government that encompasses the whole country and political system.

Consequently, in Australia, citizens' views of the quality of democracy are based more on what is occurring in the Commonwealth government than on state and local governments. The authors of the Australia study show that most citizens, despite their specific dissatisfactions, retain high levels of federal political culture and believe that Australia needs a multi-levelled system. In Belgium, there is actually more public support for a Belgian entity among citizens than among most elites. Germans express a strong preference for national regulation across a large variety of policy fields and appear to be open to creating constituent political entities that are more equal in economic resources so as to reduce the sizable disparities existing between the country's *Länder* today. Although Mexicans display comparatively low levels of trust in all their governments, they trust their federal government somewhat more than their state and municipal governments, and they see the federal government as being somewhat more efficient and responsive to public preferences. Mexico's northern neighbours trust their local and state governments much more than their federal government, but Americans do not clamour for reductions of federal power. Only in Switzerland is public support relatively balanced among the orders of government, thus making the federation government a less decisive force.

Canada and Spain may not be full exceptions to this pattern. One comparative study of Canada, Germany, Spain, and the United States found that the most significant factor in citizens' beliefs that their constituent region is treated equitably and not subordinately is trust in the federation government (Kincaid and Cole 2016).

Other Research Directions

Other important areas meriting research include the impacts of demographic variables, economic crises, civil-society interest groups, and political parties on public attitudes toward federalism and federal systems of government. Some of the cases suggest that generational and educational variables may be important. Economic crises were shown to have attitudinal consequences in Spain and Switzerland, or at least in the case of Spain, such that the financial crisis of 2007–2009 created a window of opportunity for centralists to blame the autonomous communities for economic inefficiencies. More attention needs to be given to the impacts of high courts on public attitudes. Although they act episodically, they can play highly influential roles in steering the course of federalism (Aroney and Kincaid 2017). The case studies do not specifically examine the roles of interest groups or pressure groups, but such groups play important political roles in all eight federations. The case studies in this volume also suggest that political parties are, under certain circumstances, crucial factors in public attitudes toward federalism and federal governance (Detterbeck, Renzsch, and Kincaid 2015).

Better measures of public attitudes toward dimensions, features, and processes of federalism are needed in order to advance research. How do citizens perceive the realities of decentralization, the responsibilities of the various orders of government, attributions of accountability, and cooperative or conflictual processes of intergovernmental relations? There also is a need to plumb the relations between identity and trust, the relative importance of identity and trust for federal cohesion, and the interactions between trust, identity, and system performance. Most important would be the inclusion of attitudinal items relevant to federalism in international cross-country surveys, all of which are weighted toward the presumption that all countries have unitary governments.

References

Anderson, Benedict. 1991. *Imagined Communities: Reflections on the Origin and Spread of Nationalism*. London and New York: Verso.

Armingeon, Klaus. 2002. "The Effects of Negotiation Democracy: A Comparative Analysis." *European Journal of Political Research* 41 (1): 81–105.

Aroney, Nicholas, and John Kincaid, eds. 2017. *Courts in Federal Countries: Federalists or Unitarists?* Toronto: University of Toronto Press.

Baker, J. Wayne. 1993. "The Covenantal Basis for the Development of Swiss Political Federalism: 1291–1848." *Publius: The Journal of Federalism* 23 (2): 19–41.

Cleary, Matthew, and Susan Stokes. 2006. *Democracy and the Culture of Skepticism: Political Trust in Argentina and Mexico*. New York: Russell Sage Foundation.

Cole, Richard L., John Kincaid, and Alejandro Rodriguez. 2004. "Public Opinion on Federalism and Federal Political Culture in Canada, Mexico, and the United States, 2004." *Publius: The Journal of Federalism*

34 (3): 201–21.

Detterbeck, Klaus, Wolfgang Renzsch, and John Kincaid, eds. 2015. *Political Parties and Civil Society in Federal Countries*. Don Mills, ON: Oxford University Press.

Doorenspleet, Renske. 2012. "Critical Citizens, Democratic Support and Satisfaction in African Democracies." *International Political Science Review* 33 (3): 279–300.

Elkins, Zachary, and John Sides. 2007. "Can Institutions Build Unity in Multiethnic States?" *American Political Science Review* 101 (4): 693–708.

Emerson, Rupert. 1960. *From Empire to Nation*. Boston: Beacon Press.

Erk, Jan, and Lawrence Anderson. 2009. "The Paradox of Federalism: Does Self-Rule Accommodate or Exacerbate Ethnic Divisions?" *Regional and Federal Studies* 19 (2): 191–202.

Fitzgerald, Jennifer, and Jennifer Wolak. 2014. "The Roots of Trust in Local Government in Western Europe." *International Political Science Review* 37 (1): 130–46.

Freitag, Markus, and Marc Bühlmann. 2009. "Crafting Trust: The Role of Political Institutions in a Comparative Perspective." *Comparative Political Studies* 42 (12): 1537–66.

Hetherington, Marc J. 2005. *Why Trust Matters: Declining Political Trust and the Demise of American Liberalism*. Princeton: Princeton University Press.

Hetherington, Marc J., and John D. Nugent. 2001. "Explaining Public Support for Devolution: The Role of Political Trust." In *What is it About Government that Americans Dislike?* edited by John R. Hibbing and Elizabeth Theiss-Morse, 134–51. Cambridge: Cambridge University Press.

Hueglin, Thomas O., and Alan Fenna. 2015. *Comparative Federalism: A Systematic Inquiry*. Toronto: University of Toronto Press.

Ivanyna, Maksym, and Anwar Shah. 2012. *How Close Is Your Government to Its People? Worldwide Indicators on Localization and Decentralization*. Policy Research Working Paper 6138, The World Bank, March. http://elibrary.worldbank.org/doi/pdf/10.1596/1813-9450-6138.

Jennings, M. Kent. 1998. "Political Trust and the Roots of Devolution." In *Trust and Governance*, edited by Valerie Braithwaite and Margaret Levi, 218–44. New York: Russell Sage Foundation.

Kane, John, and Haig Patapan. 2012. *The Democratic Leader: How Democracy Defines, Empowers and Limits its Leaders*. Oxford: Oxford University Press.

Kenyon, Daphne A., and John Kincaid, eds. 1991. *Competition among*

States and Local Governments: Efficiency and Equity in American Federalism. Washington, DC: Urban Institute Press.

Kincaid, John. 2010. "Federalism and Democracy: Comparative Empirical and Theoretical Perspectives." In Federal Democracies, edited by Michal Burgess and Alain-G. Gagnon, 299–324. London: Routledge.

Kincaid, John, and Richard L. Cole. 2011. "Citizen Attitudes Toward Issues of Federalism in Canada, Mexico, and the United States." Publius: The Journal of Federalism 41 (1): 53–75.

———. 2016. "Citizen Evaluations of Federalism and the Importance of Trust in the Federation Government for Opinions on Regional Equity and Subordination in Four Countries." Publius: The Journal of Federalism 46 (1): 51–76.

Kincaid, John, Andrew Parkin, Richard L. Cole, and Alejandro Rodriguez. 2003. "Public Opinion on Federalism in Canada, Mexico, and the United States in 2003." Publius: The Journal of Federalism 33 (3): 145–62.

Kincaid, John, and G. Alan Tarr, eds. 2010. Constitutional Origins, Structure, and Change in Federal Countries. Montréal and Kingston: McGill-Queen's University Press.

Levy, Jacob T. 2007. "Federalism, Liberalism, and the Separation of Loyalties." American Political Science Review 101 (3): 459–77.

Livingston, William S. 1952. "A Note on the Nature of Federalism." Political Science Quarterly 67 (1): 81–95.

———. 1956. Federalism and Constitutional Change. Oxford: Clarendon Press.

Lubell, Mark. 2007. "Familiarity Breeds Trust: Collective Action in a Policy Domain." Journal of Politics 69 (1): 237–50.

MacLennan, Hugh. 1945. Two Solitudes. New York: Duell, Sloan and Pearce.

Matsubayashi, Tetseya. 2007. "Population Size, Local Autonomy, and Support for the Political System." Social Science Quarterly 88 (3): 830–49.

Mikos, Robert A. 2007. "The Populist Safeguards of Federalism." Ohio State Law Journal 68 (3): 1669–1731.

Moreno, Luis, and César Colino, eds. 2010. Diversity and Unity in Federal Countries. Montréal and Kingston: McGill-Queen's University Press.

Norman, Wayne. 2006. Negotiating Nationalism: Nation-Building, Federalism, and Secession in the Multinational State. Oxford: Oxford University Press.

Norris, Pippa, ed. 1999. Critical Citizens: Global Support for Democratic

Government. Oxford: Oxford University Press.

————. 1999. "Institutional Explanations for Political Support." In *Critical Citizens: Global Support for Democratic Government,* edited by Pippa Norris, 217–35. Oxford: Oxford University Press.

————. 2008. *Driving Democracy: Do Power-Sharing Institutions Work?* Cambridge: Cambridge University Press.

Riker, William H. 1964. *Federalism: Origin, Operation, Significance.* Boston: Little, Brown.

Tarlton, Charles D. 1965. "Symmetry and Asymmetry as Elements of Federalism: A Theoretical Speculation." *Journal of Politics* 27 (4): 861–74.

Tilly, Charles. 2005. *Trust and Rule.* New York: Cambridge University Press.

Watts, Ronald L. 2008. *Comparing Federal Systems.* Montréal and Kingston: McGill-Queen's University Press.

2

Federalist Governance, Provincial Grievances, and Attachment to Canada

Jack Jedwab

Introduction

Canada celebrated its 150th anniversary in 2018. Reaching this milestone did not come without important challenges to the country's unity and to the preservation of its federal system of governance. Considerable negotiation over the political and fiscal arrangements has given rise to member provinces' perceptions about unequal treatment in the way resources are allocated, the extent to which they have influence around decisions made by the federal government, and the degree to which federal authorities interfere in matters that are the sole purview of the provinces. In the majority-francophone province of Quebec, these preoccupations are intertwined with a desire for recognition of the province's distinct character. These considerations have often been at the centre of efforts to assess the effectiveness of federalist governance in Canada.

It is often assumed that the harmonization of federal–provincial relations requires that the federal government address traditional grievances on the part of the provinces with respect to governance. For purposes of ensuring effectiveness in governing the country, it is important to pay attention to provincial concerns. However, changes in federalist governance by way of more decentralization or increased asymmetry are

Identities, Trust, and Cohesion in Federal Systems: Public Perceptions, edited by Jack Jedwab and John Kincaid. Montréal and Kingston: McGill-Queen's University Press, Queen's Policy Studies Series. © 2018 The School of Policy Studies, Queen's University at Kingston. All rights reserved.

unlikely to have a meaningful impact on levels of attachment to and/ or identification with Canada. Outside of Quebec, there is no particular problem when it comes to national attachment or identification. While many Quebecers prefer greater authority for their province, any changes to federalist structure this may require are unlikely to thicken attachment to Canada but may marginally quell the desire for separation of the province from Canada. The Canadian public's perceptions of the effectiveness of federalist governance is critical to the discussion that will follow.

Public perceptions about federal effectiveness are not necessarily based on how the Canadian federation operates. Yet these perceptions can often form the basis for elected officials' determination of whether federalist governance is effective. Hence their considerable importance, especially when it comes to issues of attachment to country and province where measuring public perception is the most common method for assessment.

Based on a detailed data analysis of public opinion, it is contended that the degree of effectiveness of federalist governance does not have significant influence on the level of attachment to Canada. Only in the case of the majority-francophone province of Quebec does the desire for recognition within the federation of the things deemed specific to its identify affect perceptions about federal effectiveness. The data analysis nonetheless suggests uncertain outcomes as regards attachment to Canada were changes to be introduced to federalist governance.

Although there is considerable literature on the workings of Canadian federalism and on Canadian identity respectively, relatively few studies explicitly consider if and how changes to federalist governance might influence attachment to or identification with Canada. That issue will be examined here.

Canadian federalists can take some comfort from a survey finding that more than two-thirds of the population agrees that "a federal form of government in which power is divided between a national government and state/provincial and local governments is preferable to any other kind of government" (Jedwab 2012a). Despite this relatively favourable view of federalism, there is fairly frequent talk among provincial politicians about grievances and specifically discontent with and/ or alienation from the federation. Specific attention will be directed at public perceptions of what are seen as traditional grievances on the part of the provinces vis-à-vis the federation and whether more aggrieved Canadians possess greater or lesser attachment to Canada and province respectively.

Since 1867, there have been important debates about how the architects of the federation originally envisioned the Canadian model of federalist governance. Historians generally concur that the country's founders preferred a more centralized form of government. In 1867, the federal Parliament's power to disallow provincial statutes, and the residual federal responsibility over peace, order, and good government, suggested such a preference. But, in the ensuing decades, the Judicial Committee of the Privy Council put a distinctly provincial/regional stamp on Canada's Constitution. What emerged was something far more decentralized than the founders desired. Additionally, with the evolution of the population's economic and social needs, areas of provincial responsibility took on increasing importance (i.e., health and education). Although negotiations around jurisdiction and finances were an ongoing source of federal–provincial tension, McLachlin (2013) describes the contemporary Canadian governance model as cooperative federalism.

Respect: What Does it Mean to the Provinces?

Among the litmus tests employed to assess satisfaction with federalism is the extent to which member provinces feel respected within the federation. When asked in an open-ended question to elaborate on what they mean by not being treated with respect, participants gave responses which varied by province and region. Albertans most often refer to an insufficient return on their important economic contributions to Canada. Atlantic Canadians say they don't get adequate support from the federal government. Quebecers say their distinct character is ignored. Ontarians complain that their economic needs are not given proper attention because they are seen as wealthy by the rest of the country. Manitobans and residents of Saskatchewan say that the federal government directs too much attention to the more populous provinces. British Columbians say there is too much focus on the eastern part of the country (i.e., Ontario and Quebec).

Loleen Berdahl (2010) argues that discontent with the federal government is rooted in perceptions of how provinces are treated. Tracking responses of Canadians around the perceived level of respect for their province by the federal government, Mendelsohn, Parkin, and Pinard note that in 2003 nearly three-quarters of Ontarians agreed that their province was treated with respect compared with some 40 percent of those in Atlantic Canada, Quebec, and Western Canada (Mendelsohn,

Parkin, and Pinard 2004). Nearly a decade later, with relatively few exceptions, the figures are fairly similar. Surveys conducted by Leger Marketing reveal that majorities in Alberta and to a lesser degree British Columbia no longer feel their provinces are being treated with disrespect by
the federal government. A 2010 study done by the Canada West Foundation, however, found improvement among Albertans in their perception
of the province's treatment by the federal government (Berdahl 2010).
It is worth noting that in the case of Alberta, the political representation
of the province in the federal Parliament rose considerably from 2006 to
2015 when, after fourteen years in the political opposition, the Conservatives were returned to power. Berdhal contends that feelings of alienation
on the part of western Canadians have been fuelled by discontent with
the federal government often expressed by a perception of "economic
exploitation by central Canada" (Berdahl 2010, 3).

Mendelsohn and Mathews (2010) reported that Ontarians increasingly felt their province was not being treated with respect by the federal
government. If, however, in 2010 their data pointed to a decline in the
perception of respect among Ontarians, in surveys conducted in 2012
there was a return to the higher rates for the level of respect reported
earlier. The economic impact of the 2008 recession on Ontario may help
explain the rise in dissatisfaction. By 2012, there was a sizeable increase
in the number of people who believed that their province was not getting enough money from the federal government.

Despite most Canadians' preference for a federalist form of governance, there is divergence between the provinces over the perception of
advantage and disadvantage from federalism. The data analysis reveals
that perceived disadvantage is not necessarily a function of a province/
region's economic condition. With few exceptions, the provinces of Atlantic Canada are considered the country's most economically vulnerable region, and yet, as observed in Table 2.1, views around advan-
tages/disadvantages are roughly similar to those held by a generally
wealthier Alberta. In 2012, Albertans and Atlantic Canadians were both
twice as likely to see advantage as disadvantage arising from federalist governance. Ontarians, Manitobans, and residents of Saskatchewan
were three times more likely to see advantage over disadvantage. British Columbians were somewhat less likely than other provinces to see
advantages from federalism, and Quebecers were divided on the issue.

Examining other grievances, in the 2012 ACS-Leger survey respondents in the Atlantic provinces, along with those in Manitoba and
Saskatchewan, were far more likely to agree that their provinces did

Table 2.1

Percentage in Agreement by Regions and Provinces in Canada with the Statement "Federalism has more Advantages than Disadvantages for my Province," 2012

	Atlantic Canada	Quebec	Ontario	Manitoba/ Saskatchewan	Alberta	British Columbia
Total agree	48	47	54	56	56	44
Total disagree	24	**41**	**19**	18	30	32
I don't know/ prefer not to answer	28	**12**	26	26	14	23

Note: Leger Marketing compiled a national sample of 1,500 respondents with a probabilistic margin of error of 3.9%, 19 times out of 20.

Source: Leger Marketing for the Association for Canadian Studies, November 2012, https://acs-aec.ca/pdf/polls/Federalism%20Data%20November%202012.htm

not receive a fair amount of money from the federal government than they were to express the view that the federal government interfered in provincial decision-making. Other provinces were nearly equally aggrieved by the lack of federal funds and federal interference in provincial decision-making. Frustration over the lack of respect for the province was most often expressed by Quebecers and Atlantic Canadians. Ontarians, Albertans, and British Columbians were much less likely to attest to their province being disrespected by the federal government.

Cumulating the three grievances cited in Table 2.2 below, we observe that Atlantic Canadians appear to be the most displeased, followed by Quebecers and residents of Manitoba and Saskatchewan. Citizens of Ontario and Alberta appear to be the most content. This finding may appear counterintuitive to some observers who will assume that Quebec is by far the country's most aggrieved province, a view undoubtedly influenced by the importance of support for secession in that province. Only among Quebecers, however, does the perception of disadvantage at the hands of the federal government translate into a desire for secession.

Table 2.2

Percentage of Canadians for Country and by Regions and Provinces that Agree with Selected Grievances Regarding Federalist Governance

Percentage that ...	Canada	Atlantic	QC	ON	MB/SK	AB	BC
Agree that the Federal government does not transfer the fair amount of money to my province	52	62	53	47	70	48	55
Agree that the Federal government interferes in provincial decision-making	51	53	55	50	40	49	56
Disagree that my province is treated with the respect it deserves within Canada	40	56	57	23	52	35	45
Cumulative Grievance Score	143	171	165	120	162	132	156

Note: Leger Marketing compiled a national sample of 1,500 respondents with a probabilistic margin of error of 3.9%, 19 times out of 20.

Source: Jack Jedwab, "Federalism 2010," and Jack Jedwab, "Data on the State of the Federation in 2012," 21 January 2012.

Empowerment

Savoie (2000) has insisted that all things Canadian are regional. Conrad (2006) contends that the results of federal elections provide support for this affirmation. As an example, she points to the June 2004 election, which saw an important number of Quebecers vote for the Bloc Québécois, a party dedicated to seeking national independence for their province. In 2005, much of the electorate in the four western provinces awarded seats to a reinvented Conservative party that combines a rhetoric of western alienation with a neo-liberal economic agenda and a neo-conservative social policy. On the other hand, during the federal Conservatives' time in power, Roger Gibbins urged Albertans to "abandon the litany of regional discontent, putting aside the past grievances and turning resolutely to the future, perhaps in partnership with other Western Canadian and territorial governments" (Gibbins 2005, 3). In 2015, the federal Liberals returned to power with an important majority of seats across much of the country.

Our analysis reveals that residents of those provinces who feel they have the most influence on federal decision-making tend to feel the least aggrieved. Ontarians are most likely to believe they have strong influence on federal government decisions, a feeling that has remained constant since the beginning of this century. A 2003 survey for the Centre for Research and Information on Canada (CRIC) revealed that only two in ten Ontarians felt their influence on decision-making was insufficient. In 2012, some three in ten Ontarians felt their influence on decision-making was insufficient, which was 20 percent below the national average (one in two Canadians did not believe that people in their province had strong influence on federal government decisions).

Mendelsohn and Mathews (2010) observed that from 2000 to 2010 a growing share of Canadians felt their province did not have enough influence on federal government decisions. That was not the case for Alberta. Whereas in 2004 Albertans were less likely than Quebecers to feel they had influence on federal government decision-making, by 2012 they were far more likely to believe their influence was greater (Jedwab 2012b). As noted earlier, the change might be explained by the shifting degree of representation of elected officials from the two provinces in the ruling federal political party at the time of the survey. Quebecers elected relatively few federal Conservatives, while nearly all Albertan representatives were Conservative.

A 2003 CRIC survey found a sizeable majority in the Prairies and in the Atlantic provinces felt a considerable lack of influence on the federal government. This remained the case in 2012. By that year, Quebec and British Columbia neared other regions of the country in their perceived lack of influence when it came to federal government decision-making. In 2012, about half the Canadian population surveyed agreed that the centre of power is shifting away from Central Canada and toward the West.

As residents of Canada's largest province, Ontarians are by far the least likely to favour increased powers for their provincial government. Indeed, Ontarians are almost equally divided over whether the federal or provincial governments should have more power. This contrasts markedly with the more than 70 percent of Quebecers who think their provincial government should have more power. Relatively few residents of the Prairies and Alberta favour giving the federal government more power. Yet Albertans are divided between giving more power to the provinces and maintaining the status quo. For their part, British Columbians (42 percent) favour more powers for the provincial government, while roughly one in six support according greater power to the federal government.

Empathy and Equalization

Smith (1998) points out that with differences in size, resources, and population, if the smaller units of the federation are to be able to compete on an equal footing with the larger ones, some intervention on the part of the federal government is necessary. Berdahl (2010, 2) contends that how a province feels it is being treated is often connected to whether it believes another province is receiving superior treatment by the federal government.

A 2013 ACS-Leger survey reveals that there is consensus across the country that "some regions of Canada are favoured over others." Approximately 80 percent in the eastern part of the country (the Atlantic provinces, Quebec, and Ontario) agree with this view compared with some 90 percent in western Canada (Alberta and British Columbia). Paradoxically, the provinces agree to a nearly similar extent that they are treated unequally (Jedwab 2009a). Ontarians and Albertans are least as likely than residents of other provinces to think their provinces are treated better.

Quebecers who advocate separation have often contended that the rest of Canada does not care about the concerns of their province. That sentiment, however, seems to be shared by residents of other provinces when asked whether the rest of the country cares about them. A 2009 ACS-Leger survey revealed that most Canadians simply think no one cares about their province other than its own residents (see Table 2.3). It found indeed that "Western Canadians feel East Canadians don't care about them, but most Eastern Canadians disagree. A majority of Ontarians feel the rest of Canada doesn't care but other regions disagree. Only in Quebec and the Atlantic provinces is there a greater tendency for most to agree that they don't care" (Jedwab 2009a).

Given the perception of unequal treatment and the view that various parts of the country don't care about one another, it might be assumed that the nearly 150-year federated relationship is troubled. But there

Table 2.3

Percentage of Canadians by Regions and Provinces that Agree with the Statement "People in other parts of Canada do not care about ..."
Selected Statements on Federation

Percentage Agree	Atlantic Canada	QC	ON	MB/SK	AB	BC
People in other parts of Canada do not care about Western Canada	31	31	41	66	72	61
People in other parts of Canada do not care about Ontario	34	27	58	42	40	39
People in other parts of Canada do not care about Quebec	48	61	57	53	57	54
People in other parts of Canada do not care about Atlantic Canada	70	59	50	51	48	46

Note: Leger Marketing compiled a national sample of 1,500 respondents with a probabilistic margin of error of 3.9%, 19 times out of 20.

Source: Jack Jedwab, "The State of the Canadian Union: Are attitudes towards Federalism in flux? Part 1–3," 28 July 2009.

remains an important degree of empathy across the country when it comes to the need to ensure that the most vulnerable provinces obtain support from the wealthier ones. As observed in Table 2.4 below, there are roughly similar levels of agreement across the country that, as part of the federation, people in my province should be responsible for helping those provinces that are most vulnerable (a view held by nearly seven in ten Canadians).

Table 2.4

Percentage of Canadians by Regions and Provinces that Agree "As part of the federation people in my province should be responsible for helping those provinces that are most vulnerable"

	Total	Atlantic	QC	ON	MB/SK	AB	BC
Net agree	69	64	66	71	71	71	69
Net disagree	22	27	26	18	23	25	21
I don't know/ I prefer not to answer	9	9	8	12	7	5	9

Note: Leger Marketing compiled a national sample of 1,500 respondents with a probabilistic margin of error of 3.9%, 19 times out of 20.

Source: Leger Marketing for the Association for Canadian Studies, June 2014.

In his brief overview of the "Historical Background and Development of Federal-Provincial Financial Relations," J. Harvey Perry (1951) examined the rules governing financial relations between the two orders of government. He used the term "fiscal need" to describe the process of consciously dividing available revenues to support the weaker members of the family of governments (Perry 1951, 23–4). In Canada, those provinces that benefit from what are referred to as "equalization" payments from the federal government are often called "have-not" provinces. More specifically, they are defined as provinces that cannot provide public services and fund public infrastructure at a national average level out of the taxes, royalties, and fees generated in the province; consequently, they need equalization payments from the federal government to make up the difference.

Breton contends that "equalization is primarily aimed at improving the condition of the weaker parts of the federation" (Report of the Royal Commission 1985, 508). Canada is a vast and sparsely populated country, and its abundance of natural resources is unevenly distributed across the provinces. Beyond that, the major economic differences between the provinces are attributable to diverse patterns of economic development, industrial location, urbanization, land use, and migration. There is a substantial degree of disparity in living standards between Canada's provinces. Coulombe (2013) describes this as a serious challenge for a highly decentralized federation. In 2013, Alberta had the highest per capita gross domestic product. Saskatchewan and Newfoundland had the next highest per capita GDP. The other Atlantic provinces and Quebec had the lowest per capita GDP.

Considering that Alberta's population in 2011 was approximately 3.6 million, thereby representing less than 10 percent of the country, its nearly 18 percent of national GDP is an indicator of the disparity in wealth between the provinces. By contrast, with some 24 percent of the country's population, Quebec is only somewhat ahead of Alberta in terms of its 19 percent contribution to the national GDP.

The equalization program aims at addressing fiscal disparities between provinces and allowing less prosperous provincial governments to provide residents with public services that are reasonably comparable to those in other provinces, at reasonably comparable levels of taxation. Coulombe (2013) points out that equalization can alleviate only a fraction of the disparity in provincial fiscal capacities.

Equalization payments are unconditional; the receiving provinces can spend according to their own priorities. The purpose of the program was entrenched in the Canadian Constitution in 1982, whereby "Parliament and the government of Canada are committed to the principle of making equalization payments to ensure that provincial governments have sufficient revenues to provide reasonably comparable levels of public services at reasonably comparable levels of taxation" (Subsection 36 (2) of the Constitution Act, 1982).

For 2015–16 Quebec secured the most overall funding from equalization payments, while on a per capita basis the province of Prince Edward Island received the most. As observed in Table 2.5, other provinces that received equalization payments in 2014–15 were Nova Scotia, New Brunswick, Ontario, and Manitoba (i.e., six of the country's ten provinces).

That a province receives equalization funds from the federal government does not imply that its citizens agree that federalism offers more advantages than disadvantages. Here again much depends on the perceived degree of entitlement felt within the province. This perception may also lead to some reticence for residents of a province to acknowledge receiving more than they give to the federation. It is also worth noting that many Canadians do not feel sufficiently informed about the matter to render an opinion.

A 2014 ACS-Leger survey revealed that most Atlantic Canadians be-

Table 2.5

Federal Transfers (Equalization Portion) to Provinces, 2005–6 to 2015–16

(millions of dollars)	2005–6	2010–11	2015–16
Canada	10,907	14,372	17,341
Newfoundland	861		
Prince Edward Island	277	330	361
Nova Scotia	1,344	1,391	1,690
New Brunswick	1,348	1,581	1,669
Atlantic Canada	3,830	3,302	3,720
Quebec	4,798	8,552	9,521
Ontario	—	972	2,363
Manitoba	1,601	1,826	1,738
Saskatchewan	89		
Alberta	—	—	—
British Columbia	590	—	—

Source: Department of Finance Canada Federal Transfers to Provinces and Territories, https://www.fin.gc.ca/access/fedprov-eng.asp.

lieve they get more from the federation (38 percent) than they give (32 percent). Although Quebecers receive a considerable amount in equalization payments, some 38 percent of the province's residents think they give more than they get. Still, there are more Quebecers who acknowledge getting more than they give from the federation. For their part, 49 percent of Ontarians think they give more than they get (24 percent), while Albertans think they give more (68 percent) than they get (13 percent), and British Columbians (49 percent) think they give more than they get (21 percent).

Federalist Governance, Identification, and Attachment to Canada

It is often assumed that grievances over federalist governance undercut identification with and/or attachment to Canada and strengthen provincial and/or regional identification and/or attachment. It's a relationship that has rarely been examined in Canada. Efforts to provide some empirical basis or other measurement for attachment to or identification with Canada are often guided by the assumption that stronger national identities are important for building social cohesion. Mendelsohn and Mathews (2010) observed that Ontarians have long lacked a strong sense of provincial identity. They demonstrate that changes in Ontarians' sense of regional discontent are not accompanied by greater attachment to the province, as relatively few Ontarians identify with their province more than with Canada. Ontarians continue to have the strongest sense of Canadian identity in the country but are increasingly similar to other Canadians when it comes to believing that their province is treated unfairly within the federation.

Assessing the relative importance of identities is often determined by the formulation of the question that serves as a basis for measurement. The most common means used to capture the importance of such identities is to weigh their relative importance or to rank them in order of what they regard as most and least significant. Behind the idea of ranking them is the assumption that identities are in competition. By contrast, weighing identities generally implies that they are complimentary and/or intersecting. As illustrated in Table 2.6 below, with the exception of Quebec, the level of attachment to Canada is higher than is the case for other markers of identity. That said, the intensity with which attachment is expressed can vary considerably. In general, country and language yield higher rates of the "very attached" response among Canadians than do province and city or town.

As regards attachment to Canada, some 87 percent of the population reported that they were either very (61 percent) or somewhat (26 percent) attached to the country. Francophone Quebecers constitute an exception as 64 percent report being very (30 percent) or somewhat (34 percent) attached to Canada. Overall, with few exceptions, Quebecers' level of attachment to Canada has been quite stable over the past twenty-five years. From 1991 to 2013, on average some 69 percent of the province's population reported they are either very or somewhat attached to the country. Attachment to Canada on the part of Quebecers declined between 2006 and 2009 but since 2010 has returned to the earlier levels (see Figure 2.1). Despite differences in attachment to Canada, Quebecers have a roughly similar level of attachment to their province as do other Canadians.

Table 2.6

Percentage of Canadians that Are Very Attached to Selected Markers of Identity

	Canada	Province	City or Town	Language
Very attached	56	40	33	58
Somewhat attached	31	42	45	31
Not very attached	8	13	14	7
Not attached at all	4	3	6	2
I don't know	1	1	1	1
I prefer not to answer	1	1	1	0

Note: Leger Marketing compiled a national sample of 1,500 respondents with a probabilistic margin of error of 3.9%, 19 times out of 20.

Source: Leger Marketing for the Association for Canadian Studies, October 2014.

Figure 2.1

Very, Somewhat and Total Attached to Canada for Quebec, 1991–2015

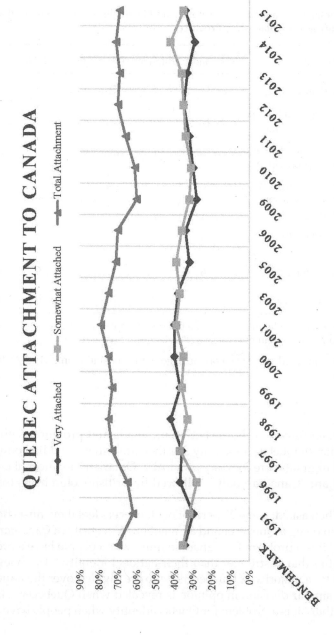

QUEBEC ATTACHMENT TO CANADA

Very Attached   Somewhat Attached   Total Attachment

Source: Maurice Pinard, CRIC, PCO, Leger Marketing surveys for the Association for Canadian Studies, 1991–2015.

Table 2.7

Percentage of Canadians for Country and by Regions and Provinces that Identify as Canadian or by Province

Identification as …	Canada	Atlantic	QC	ON	MB/SK	AB	BC
Canadian only	31	25	7	45	31	26	37
Canadian first but also from your province	27	26	22	25	33	35	31
Equally Canadian and from your province	19	25	20	15	19	24	18
From your province first but also from Canada	14	11	37	5	6	9	6
From your province only	3	1	13	0	2	0	0
None of the above	6	8	2	8	9	6	8
I prefer not to answer	1	4	0	1	0	0	0

Note: Leger Marketing compiled a national sample of 1,500 respondents with a probabilistic margin of error of 3.9%, 19 times out of 20.

Source: Jack Jedwab, "Data on the State of the Federation in 2012," 21 January 2012.

When forced to choose between Canada and province, with the exception of Quebec a majority say they are either Canadian only or Canadian first before they say provincial. Ontarians are most likely to say they are "Canadian only," followed by British Columbians (see Table 2.7).

When asked, some 27 percent of Quebecers feel they must choose between being a Quebecer and a Canadian. A majority of Canadians agree that "it is a problem for Canadian unity when people have a provincial identity that is stronger than their national identity." That view is not held by a majority of Quebecers, who are divided over the issue.

A similar division in opinion is revealed when Quebecers are asked whether "it is a problem for Quebec identity when people have a stronger Canadian identity." Overall 43 percent of Quebecers agree with this view. While the province's francophones are evenly divided over the issue, approximately one in four of the province's non-francophones concur (Jedwab 2014b).

In the event of a clash between their province's interests and Canada's national interest, when asked to make a choice Quebecers would put the provincial interest overwhelmingly on top. On the same question, Canada's interests prevail easily among Ontarians, Prairie residents, Albertans, and British Columbians. To a lesser degree, Canada is the first choice among Atlantic Canadians when asked to choose between country and province.

As observed in Table 2.8 below, in contrast with requiring Canadians to choose between Canadian and provincial identities, the assessment of attachment suggests there is less inherent conflict between them. In effect, those most attached to Canada also exhibit strong attachment to their province. In effect, when identities are weighed, it is more common to find that individuals with a strong sense of national identity possess strong provincial and community identities. The nearly two-thirds who are "very attached" to Canada are also very attached to their province compared to the less than half of those saying they are not at all attached

Table 2.8

Percentage of Canadians by Levels of Attachment to Canada Reporting Levels of Attachment to Province

Attachment to Province	Attachment to Canada			
	Very attached	Somewhat attached	Not very attached	Not at all attached
Very attached	65	57	51	46
Somewhat attached	28	31	30	35
Not very attached	5	10	16	8
Not at all attached	2	2	3	11

Note: Leger Marketing compiled a national sample of 1,500 respondents with a probabilistic margin of error of 3.9%, 19 times out of 20.

Source: Leger Marketing for the Association for Canadian Studies, June 2014.

to Canada saying they are not at all attached to their province.

Identity, Attachment, and Grievance

Can it be assumed that changes in governance or structural modifications within the federation will make citizens feel a greater sense of attachment to Canada and hence thicken national identity? In Quebec in particular, it is often assumed that extending more power to the provincial government will make citizens more comfortable with federalism, thus weakening the desire for separation. But is it safe to assume that diminishing the desire for sovereignty implies strengthening identification or attachment to Canada? In other words, will a transfer of power among those feeling aggrieved in Quebec, or for that matter elsewhere in the country, generate a stronger sense of identification with or attachment to Canada? (See Figure 2.1.)

Looking at the relationship between identification and grievance, there appears to be relatively little difference in the respective degree of frustration with the federal government among those defining themselves as Canadian only, Canadian first, and Canadian and province equally (see Table 2.9). However, when provincial identification prevails (something felt mostly by francophone Quebecers), the degree of grievance is far more pronounced. Finally, those identifying with their "province only" (almost exclusively francophone Quebecers) are considerably more aggrieved. The view that a province is not being treated with respect is where the widest gulf emerges between those who identify with Canada and those for whom Canada is either subordinate to the province or rejected completely.

Data that looks at the relationship between attachment and grievance gives rise to a somewhat similar interpretation in the scale measurement of identity. When it comes to the perception of fairness in the transfer of funds from the federal to the provincial government, there is virtually no difference in opinion between those who are very attached to Canada and those not very attached to the country (see Table 2.10). Only among those not attached at all (almost all francophone) is there a marked difference, with more insisting the transfer of funds is unfair. On the matter of perceived federal government interference in provincial decision-making, those who are not very attached to Canada are somewhat more likely to identify this as a problem than those reporting attachment. Again, those least attached to Canada were most preoccupied by perceived federal interference in provincial decision-making.

Table 2.9

Correlation: Percentage that Identify as Canadian or by Province that Agree with Selected Grievances Regarding Federalist Governance

% Agree	Canadian only	Canadian first but also from your province	Equally Canadian and from your province	From your province first but also from Canada	From your province only
Disagree that my province is treated with the respect it deserves in Canada	65	57	56	31	7
Agree that the federal government interferes in provincial decision-making	48	47	49	64	87
Agree that the federal government does not transfer the fair amount of money to my province	51	48	53	61	83

Note: Leger Marketing compiled a national sample of 1,500 respondents with a probabilistic margin of error of 3.9%, 19 times out of 20.

Source: Leger Marketing for the Association for Canadian Studies, November 2012.

The biggest gap between the most and least attached is found over the extent to which they disagree that their province is being treated with the respect it deserves in Canada.

By far, those least identifying with Canada and those least attached to the country are Quebec francophones. Indeed, the respondent's language, rather than region of residence, is the principal determinant

Table 2.10

Correlation: Percentage of Canadians by Level of Attachment to Canada that Agree with Selected Grievances Regarding Federalist Governance

	Attachment to Canada			
	Very attached	Somewhat attached	Not very attached	Not attached at all
Agree that the federal government interferes in provincial decision-making	52	51	64	76
Disagree that my province is treated with the respect it deserves in Canada	56	41	27	13
Agree that the federal government does not transfer the fair amount of money to my province	56	58	58	74

Note: Leger Marketing compiled a national sample of 1,500 respondents with a probabilistic margin of error of 3.9%, 19 times out of 20.

Source: Leger Marketing for the Association for Canadian Studies, November 2012.

of their grievance with federalism. This is confirmed in Table 2.11 below, which reveals that the level of attachment to Canada on the part of anglophone Canadians has little bearing on their reported degree of grievance. The only issue where there appears to be some variation in the level of attachment to Canada is in anglophone Canadians' response to the perceived respect for the province.

In the case of anglophone Canadians, it appears relatively safe to assume that changes in federalist governance would not have much impact on attachment to or identification with Canada. In the case of Quebec francophones, lower rates of attachment correspond with far higher degrees of grievance, which suggests that changes to governance might have some impact on attachment. We will explore this question further below.

Table 2.11

Correlation: Percentage of Canadians by Mother Tongue French and English by Level of Attachment to Canada that Agree with Selected Grievances Regarding Federalist Governance

Attachment to Canada and percentage that agree/disagree with selected grievances	French				English		
	Very attached	Somewhat attached	Not very attached	Not Attached at all	Very attached	Somewhat attached	Not very attached
Disagree that my province is treated with the respect it deserves in Canada	26	62	82	96	36	39	28
Agree that the federal government interferes in provincial decision-making	47	54	74	77	50	47	48
Disagree that the federal government does not transfer the fair amount of money to my province	41	27	14	8	27	24	22

Note: Leger Marketing compiled a national sample of 1,500 respondents with a probabilistic margin of error of 3.9%, 19 times out of 20.

Source: Leger Marketing for the Association for Canadian Studies, November 2012.

Quebec

A 2012 Abacus poll that found a majority of Canadians identify the conflict between Quebec and the rest of Canada as the most serious threat to the country's unity (Coletto 2012). Traditionally, most analysts of Quebec opinion on Canadian unity divide the population into federalists versus sovereignists (i.e., those favouring Quebec's independence from Canada). Within the federalist–sovereignist dichotomy, analysts identify various gradations of support for either option that range from unconditional federalists and sovereignists and a group in between that have been described interchangeably as conditional, soft, or undecided federalists or sovereignists. Since 1980, most surveys of Quebecers put support for remaining a part of Canada at about 60 percent and their desire for sovereignty at 40 percent after redistribution of the undecided. However, there has been some important volatility to this pattern, as evidenced in the 1995 Quebec referendum, which the federalist side narrowly won with 50.6 percent versus 49.4 percent for sovereignty (and a proposed new partnership with the rest of Canada).

As noted earlier in this essay, a 2012 survey on the sense of grievance toward the federal government revealed that Quebec is not the most aggrieved part of the country. Yet, outside of Quebec, a greater degree of grievance does not meaningfully result in weakening attachment to Canada or conversely in strengthening provincial attachment (despite the temporary presence of regional political parties that have attempted to mobilize opinion on the basis of provincial identity). Outside of Quebec, opinion leaders have rarely insisted that citizens must choose between their national and provincial identities.

As noted above, over one in four Quebecers feels they must choose between such identities. Indeed, they often construe them as choices between national identities. (It is worth noting that relatively few Quebec non-francophones share the view that they must choose and that the identities necessarily clash.) Advocates of Quebec separation along with many federalist francophones describe Quebec as a nation in the sociological rather than the geopolitical sense. Our survey findings suggest that Quebec francophones who feel more attached to Canada are less aggrieved. Yet there is no certainty that changes in federalist governance will modify Quebecers' perceptions over a particular grievance. That's because the data do not tell us what Quebecers regard as being more respectful toward their province or how much is too much when it comes to federal interference in provincial jurisdiction. Hence, even with evidence that removing a grievance will boost attachment to Canada, it remains unclear as to how to go about doing so.

It is uncertain whether francophone Quebecers who unconditionally favour separation can be persuaded to reconsider their view by addressing grievances or dissatisfaction with federal governance. It also remains unclear whether weak attachment/low identification with Canada is fuelling the sense of grievance. Possessing very low attachment to Canada, such individuals are no more likely to be persuaded of the benefits of Canadian federalism than unconditional federalists with high attachment to Canada are likely to be convinced of the merits of separation.

Quebecers with high attachment to Canada regard federal interference in provincial affairs as irritants, but such grievances are not considered important enough to them to endorse the country's breakup. It is worth noting that surveys reveal that if Quebecers were forced to choose between sovereignty and the status quo, nearly two-thirds would choose the latter (Ekos Politics 2014).

Recognizing Quebec

Since its inception in 1867, the varying interpretations of federalist governance as articulated by the leaders of the provinces have been difficult to reconcile. McLachlin (2013) notes that Confederation was the result of a need to accommodate three diverse groups that signed the original pact: the English Canadians in Ontario, the French Canadians in Quebec, and the eastern colonies. There remains ongoing debate about whether the 1867 confederation deal was a pact between the four founding provinces (Ontario, Quebec, Nova Scotia, and New Brunswick) and/or a compact of British and French founding peoples. Most Canadian historians contend that the deal was intended as a pact between provinces as opposed to between peoples (Cook 1969). Yet many Quebecers insist it was a pact between two founders, and some analysts have also added Canada's Aboriginal peoples as a third founder (Tully 2001).

Deep linguistic and religious differences divided the country at its inception. In the new nation of Canada that united French Catholic and Anglo-Protestant colonies, French Canadian politicians were very aware that they would be a minority in the new Parliament of Canada; therefore, they insisted that the provincial legislatures be vested with enough power to safeguard the French language and culture, the civil law, and the Roman Catholic religion in Quebec. The right to preserve difference was essential to maintaining Canadian unity.

In 1963, the Royal Commission on Bilingualism and Biculturalism was asked to "inquire into and report upon the existing state of bilingualism and biculturalism in Canada and to recommend what steps should be taken to develop the Canadian Confederation on the basis of an equal partnership between the two founding races, taking into account the contribution made by the other ethnic groups to the cultural enrichment of Canada and the measures that should be taken to safeguard that contribution" (Laurendeau and Dunton 1964, 328).

On the basis of the recommendations of the report, the Government of Canada introduced the Official Languages Act in 1969, which recognized English and French as the country's two official languages. Two years later, the federal government introduced a policy of multiculturalism within a bilingual framework. In October 1971, then Prime Minister Pierre Elliott Trudeau stated that:

> It was the view of the royal commission, shared by the government ... that there cannot be one cultural policy for Canadians of British and French origin, another for the original peoples and yet a third for all others. For although there are two official languages, there is no official culture nor does any ethnic group take precedence over any other. (Trudeau 1971)

In the aftermath of the defeat of the sovereignty option in the 1980 referendum, the Government of Canada took steps to patriate the Constitution from the British Parliament. The Canadian Constitution was updated in 1982 with an amending formula and a Charter of Rights and Freedoms. Quebec was not a signatory to the Constitution, and, in the late 1980s, discussions were held to bring the province into the Constitution with a recognition of its distinct characteristics. In the late 1980s, some of the country's provincial premiers rejected the Meech Lake Accord, which would have recognized Quebec as a distinct society (Watts 1991). A variation on that proposal—the Charlottetown Accord—was put to the population in a national referendum in 1992 and failed to secure majority support in every province, with the exception of New Brunswick (Vipond 1993). The successive failures at recognizing Quebec's distinct identity in the Constitution served as a catalyst for the highly divisive outcome of the 1995 referendum on Quebec sovereignty.

As the Canadian federation has evolved, so too has the debate over national identity. Iacovino (2013, 2) contends that "for some federalism is meant to transcend differences while others see it as the expression of a normative acknowledgment of difference—unity in diversity." He adds that there are competing visions around the constitutive bases of Canadian federalism. In contrast to Quebec's view, Iacovino (2013, 2–3) contends that "federalism in Canada is formally organized around principles of provincial equality, a Charter of Rights and Freedoms as a lynchpin of citizenship, bilingualism based on the personality principle and multiculturalism."

Gagnon and Tully (2001) insist that Canada is a multinational federation that includes the Quebec nation and the Aboriginal nations. There is no official acknowledgement by the Government of Canada of its tri-national/multinational character, and, perhaps more importantly, no federal institutions reflect this form of multinational governance. As Lecours (2014) notes, there are multiple ways in which the government of Canada acknowledges and accommodates Quebec's distinct character within the federation.

Given Canada's regional and demographic diversity, there is more than one way to describe the Canadian model or vision underlying the federation. As observed in the survey results below (see Table 2.12), the selected vision of Canada is influenced by one's language background. While there is no apparent consensus, most people describe Canada as a multicultural country with two official languages. For their part, many Quebecers are equally inclined to describe Canada as a country of three founding nations or peoples (i.e., British, French, and Aboriginal).

Some observers may question how Aboriginal peoples that are often depicted as colonized inside Canada are described as founders of the country. Others will object that there are at least fifty Aboriginal nations in Canada. Yet the idea that seemingly resonates most among Quebec francophones is more in line with how many think Canada should have been rather than how it was at the time of Confederation.

In the rest of the country, the multicultural/dual-language vision competes with the idea that Canada is a country of some 34 million equal citizens (that vision is in a virtual tie for dominance on the prairies). The once-popular idea of Canada as a federation of equal provinces no longer resonates with an important share of Canadians. It does, however, receive the support of one in six Atlantic Canadians. For some Canadians, these respective visions are not necessarily in contradiction. In Canada, citizens can stick to their preferred vision of the country without it ever encountering any meaningful challenge. As noted pre-

Table 2.12

Percentage of Canadians for Country and by Regions and Provinces that Agree with the Statement "Which of these visions best reflects your preferred image of Canada?"

June 2013	Total	Atlantic	QC	ON	MB/SK	AB	BC
Canada is a multicultural country with two official languages	43	48	41	45	39	43	41
Canada is a country of 34 million equal citizens	30	28	14	32	40	40	36
Canada is a country of three nations: the Quebec nation, the English-Canadian nation, and the First Nations (Aboriginals)	17	8	37	12	11	7	13
Canada is a country of ten equal provinces	10	16	8	11	10	10	10

Note: Leger Marketing compiled a national sample of 1,500 respondents with a probabilistic margin of error of 3.9%, 19 times out of 20.

Source: Leger Marketing for the Association for Canadian Studies, June 2013.

viously, many Canadians define the country not only on the basis of how it is seen but also on how they wish it to be.

When asked to elaborate on the meaning of their province not being treated with respect by the federal government, Quebecers refer to the failure to recognize the province's culturally distinct character. Would the recognition of Quebec as a distinct society or nation in the Canadian Constitution strengthen attachment to Canada? In a 2011 ACS-Leger survey, most Quebec francophones (48 percent) do not think it would have this effect; a similar view is held by a significant majority of non-francophones. Still, the fact that 44 percent of francophones would feel more attached to Canada if such recognition were extended to them is not insignificant and suggests that doing so might diminish the desire for separation. But the actual impact of such recognition remains difficult to estimate.

There also is uncertainty that transfers of powers to Quebec by the federal government would make more Quebecers feel at ease within the federation by diminishing the associated grievance. Polling by CROP for l'Idée Fédérale revealed that 42 percent of Quebecers disagree (versus 39 percent agreeing) that if the federal government refused to transfer new powers to Quebec, it would confirm the impossibility of the province developing within the Canadian federation. Yet other survey evidence suggests cause for reticence on the part of the federal government when it comes to structural modifications in governance as a means of reducing grievances. The same 2011 ACS-Leger survey found that most Canadians and most Quebecers do not think "there are any constitutional changes that can ever satisfy the majority of Quebecers" (Jedwab 2011). This aside, there is little interest in Quebec and elsewhere in Canada in reopening constitutional negotiations. More than seven in ten Canadians oppose the idea, and some two in three Quebecers oppose the idea (Jedwab 2012c).

Conclusion

Various data sets have been employed above to examine whether grievances with federalist governance on the part of the provinces undercut attachment and/or identification to Canada. The data suggest that in general it is only in Quebec among francophones that the expressed level of grievance meaningfully diminishes attachment. It is unclear however whether the sense of grievance generates detachment from Canada or whether the feeling of detachment fuels the grievance. As we have observed, it is possible to be unhappy about federalist governance without feeling detached from Canada. Indeed, while Quebec exhibits the lowest rate of attachment to Canada, on certain indicators, it is not the country's least aggrieved province.

The way frustrations with the Canadian federation are expressed may sometimes make the federal–provincial relationship feel like a troubled marriage. Applying the marriage analogy seems appropriate when provincial leaders speak about the need for greater autonomy, ask for more respect for their jurisdiction, call for special recognition of their unique characteristics, and/or insist they are not getting their fair share of money. It represents a set of grievances that is not simple to resolve.

The difficulty in formally recognizing the special characteristics of a member/partner in the federated family of members can make for a serious obstacle to preserving unity and harmony. For nearly fifty years, it is the majority French-speaking province of Quebec that has sought some form of distinctive recognition within Canada. This issue has been at the centre of a divisive debate for many francophone Quebecers over whether to remain in the federation or to seek a divorce. Although Quebec often articulates grievances around federalism in the same way as the other provinces, it is the threat of divorce among Quebecers that has no parallel elsewhere in the country.

Outside of Quebec a weak sense of attachment is very rare, and so it is difficult to offer reliable conclusions about corresponding levels of grievance. Undoubtedly, there is grievance—however unevenly distributed—elsewhere in Canada, but that does not translate into any meaningful degree of detachment from the country. It is uncommon for federal and provincial attachments to be viewed as competing in provinces outside of Quebec. For their part, many francophone Quebecers have long thought of federal and provincial attachments as competing choices. As noted above, if in the event of a conflict Quebecers were asked to choose between provincial and federal interests, the former would win out by a rather substantial margin.

It is highly uncertain that addressing these grievances will strengthen attachment to Canada on the part of francophone Quebecers. Their reported level of attachment to Canada has remained virtually unchanged over the past twenty-five years. Some may insist that this is because the federal government has not found meaningful responses. But there has never been any empirical support for this affirmation. The francophone Quebecers who are the most displeased with Canadian federalism seem more desirous of identity recognition than they are for changes in governance. Presumably the two are related. A transfer of some jurisdiction from the federal government to Quebec purportedly augments provincial capacity to promote identity. Again, it is difficult to know whether any such modification will achieve the desired outcome for strengthening unity in the federal system. It is far less evident that it will bolster Quebec francophone attachment to Canada. At best, identity and/or structural change may stave off the desire for more francophones to seek a divorce. But the relationship can be sustained without Quebec francophones feeling very attached to Canada. Many of them will simply see the Quebec–Canada relationship as a marriage of convenience, a condition that federalists in Quebec and elsewhere in Canada must accept.

References

Berdahl, Loleen. 2010. "Whither Western Alienation? Shifting Patterns of Western Canadian Discontent with the Federal Government." Canada West Foundation. October. http://cwf.ca/pdf-docs/publi cations/Whither-Western-Alienation.pdf.

Coletto, David. 2012. "Alberta, Federalism and the Politics of Regional Jealousy." Abacus Data. http://abacusdata.ca/2012/12/19/alberta -federalism-and-the-politics-of-regional-jealousy/.

Conrad, Margaret. 2006. "Regionalism in a Flat World." *Acadiensis* 35 (2): 138–44.___https://journals.lib.unb.ca/index.php/Acadiensis/article /view/10604/11225.

Cook, Ramsay. 1969. *Provincial Autonomy, Minority Rights, and the Compact Theory, 1867–1921*. Ottawa: Information Canada.

Coulombe, Serge. 2013. "Terms-of-Trade Changes, the Dutch Disease, and Canadian Provincial Disparity." Working Paper 2013–01, Institute of Intergovernmental Relations, School of Policy Studies, Queen's University, Kingston, ON. http://www.queensu.ca/iigr/ sites/webpublish.queensu.ca.iigrwww/files/files/WorkingPapers/ NewWorkingPapersSeries/WorkingPaper012013Coulombe.pdf.

Ekos Politics. 2013. "Quebec Liberals Headed to a Win." *iPolitics*. http://www.ekospolitics.com/wp-content/uploads/full_report_ april_4_2014.pdf.

Gibbins, Roger. 2005. "The Rich Kid: Where does Alberta Fit in the Can adian Family Now?" *Literary Review of Canada* 13 (4): 3–5.

Graves, Frank. 2012. "Canada Evolving: Sources of Stability and Change in the Canadian Social Fabric." Presentation at the State of the Federation, Kingston, ON, 1 December. http://www.ekospolitics.com/ wp-content/uploads/values_and_identity_december_1_2012.pdf.

Iacovino, Raffaele. 2013. "Collective Identity and Federalism: Some Reflections on Belonging in Quebec." *Canadian Issues* 31–5.

Jedwab, Jack. 2009a. "The State of the Canadian Union: Are Attitudes Towards Federalism in Flux? Part 1–3." 28 July. http://www.acs-aec. ca/pdf/polls/12487931265929.doc.

———. 2009b. "Federalism." 18 November. http://www.acs-aec.ca/ pdf/polls/12768872801610.htm.

———. 2009c. "Federalism and Canadian Identities: Updating the Portrait of Canada." 18 February. http://www.acs-aec.ca/pdf/ polls/12349705214964.doc.

———. 2010a. "Federal Measures: Designing a Global Index to Assess the Effectiveness of Federal Systems of Governance." Draft copy presented to the Privy Council.

———. 2010b. "The Canadian Grievance Index: A F-e-d-e-r-a-l Story." 11 February. http://www.acs-aec.ca/pdf/polls/12659046254337. ppt.

———. 2011. "Is Canada Entering a Post-Constitutional Era?" 7 November. http://www.acs-aec.ca/pdf/polls/Checking%20our%20 Constitution.doc.

———. 2012a. "Data on the State of the Federation in 2012." 21 January. http://www.acs-aec.ca/pdf/polls/Federalism%20Data%20Novem ber%202012.htm.

———. 2012b. "The Grievance Index 2012." 21 January. https://acs-aec.ca/pdf/polls/The%20Grievance%20Index%202012.pdf

———. 2012c. "Reopen Constitutional Talks: It's not what Quebecers want." *Montreal Gazette*, 21 April. http://www.montreal gazette.com/news/Reopen+constitutional+talks+what+Quebecers +want/6498552/story.html.

———. 2012d. "Pride in Canadian Symbols and Institutions." 26 November. http://www.acs-aec.ca/pdf/polls/Pride%20in%20Canadi an%20Symbols%20and%20Institutions.ppt.

———. 2014a. "What Keeps Canada Together? No Clear Majority, but Charter of Rights and Healthcare Still Tops." 1 July. https://acs-aec. ca/pdf/polls/What%20keeps%20Canada%20Together%20(7).pdf.

———. 2014b. "Benchmarking Attachment to Canada Historic Trends, Current Comparisons with Other Expressions of Identity." 3 July. https://acs-aec.ca/pdf/polls/Attachment%20to%20Quebec%20 and%20Canada%20June%202014%20v2.2.pdf.

Laurendeau, André, and Dunton, Davidson. 1964. "The Work of the Royal Commission on Bilingualism and Biculturalism." *The Empire Club of Canada Addresses*, Toronto, ON, 9 April, 328–38. http:// speeches.empireclub.org/60261/data

Lecours, André. 2014. "Multinationalisme et accommodement: une analyse du succès canadien." *l'Idée Fédérale*. July. https://ideefeder ale.ca/etude-multinationalisme-et-accommodement/.

Matthews, J. Scott, Matthew Mendelsohn, and Randy Besco. 2010. "Regionalism in Political Attitudes, 1993 to 2008." Presentation at the State of the Federation Conference, Toronto, ON, 19–20 November.

McLachlin, Beverley. 2013. "Defining Moments: The Canadian Constitution." *Remarks of the Right Honourable, P.C., Chief Justice of Canada.* 5 February. http://www.scc-csc.ca/court-cour/judges-juges/spedis/bm-2013-02-05-eng.aspx.

Mendelsohn, Matthew, Andrew Parkin, and Maurice Pinard. 2004. *A New Chapter or the Same Old Story? Quebec Public Opinion and the National Question from 1996–2003*. 18–21 January. https://library.carle ton.ca/sites/default/files/find/data/surveys/pdf_files/cric-poc-03-not1_000.pdf.

Mendelsohn, Matthew, and J. Scott Matthews. 2010. "The New Ontario: The Shifting Attitudes of Ontarians Toward the Federation." *Mowat Centre*, 23 February. http://mowatcentre.ca/research-topic-mowat.php?mowatResearchID=57.

Parkin, Andrew. 2004. "Patterns of Regional Discontent in Canada." *Centre for Research and Information on Canada* (CRIC). Presentation to PCO–Intergovernmental Affairs, Ottawa, ON, 19 May.

Perry, J. Harvey. 1951. *Taxation in Canada*. Toronto: University of Toronto Press.

"Politique provinciale et fédérale, sondage annuel de l'Idee federale." 2012. CROP. 17–22 October. http://www.ideefederale.ca/docu ments/idee_federale_sondage_oct_2012.pdf.

"Portraits of Canada 2002." 2002. CRIC Papers 8. http://www.library.carleton.ca/sites/default/files/find/data/surveys/pdf_files/cric-poc-02-not1_000.pdf.

"Portraits of Canada 2003." 2003. CRIC Papers 12. http://www.library.carleton.ca/sites/default/files/find/data/surveys/pdf_files/cric-poc-03-not1_000.pdf.

"Portraits of Canada 2004." 2004. CRIC Papers 16. http://www.library.carleton.ca/sites/default/files/find/data/surveys/pdf_files/cric-paper_16-2004.pdf.

"Portraits of Canada 2005." 2005. CRIC Papers 19. http://www.library.carleton.ca/sites/default/files/find/data/surveys/pdf_files/cric-paper_19-2005.pdf.

Report of the Royal Commission on the Economic Union and Economic Prospects for Canada. 1985 (3) Ottawa: Supply and Services.

Savoie, Donald J. 2000. "All Things Canadian Are Now Regional." *Journal of Canadian Studies* 35 (1): 203–17.

Smith, Jennifer. 1998. "The Meaning of Provincial Equality in Canadian Federalism." Working Paper 1, Intergovernmental Relations, Queen's University, Kingston, ON. http://www.queensu.ca/iigr/sites/webpublish.queensu.ca.iigrwww/files/files/WorkingPapers/Archive/1998/1998-1JenniferSmith.pdf.

Trudeau, Pierre Elliott. 1971. "Multiculturalism." Government Response to Volume 4 of the Report of the Royal Commission on Bilingualism and Biculturalism, Commissioners to the House of Commons, 8 October. http://www.canadahistory.com/sections/documents/Primeministers/trudeau/docs-onmulticulturalism.htm.

Tully, James. 2001. "Introduction." In *Multinational Democracies* by Gagnon and Tully, 1–33, Cambridge: Cambridge University Press.

Vipond, Robert C. 1993. "Seeing Canada Through the Referendum: Still a House Divided." *Publius: The Journal of Federalism* 23 (3): 39–56.

Watts, Ronald L. 1991. "Canadian Federalism in the 1990s: Once More in Question." *Publius: The Journal of Federalism* 21 (3): 169–90.

3

Checkmate to the Spanish Decentralization? The Decline of Public Support for Spain's Autonomous Communities

Mireia Grau Creus

Introduction

The autonomous communities had been considered for decades as one of the most important pillars of restoring and making democracy work in Spain (Subirats and Gallego 2002). In addition, public support for decentralization grew simultaneously with the expansion of self-government and the rise of dual identities (i.e., of people feeling as much from Spain as from their autonomous community). However, harmony between citizens and their decentralized institutions started to decline in the early 2000s and dramatically deteriorated with the blast of the post-2008 economic crisis. While support for decentralization has shrunk, support for centralization has increased, and recentralization has become a top political issue. This chapter describes the context and indicates the factors that could help to explain this change; it also assesses and aims at provoking some discussion on whether these changes might indicate that, after all, political decentralization values were ever really assimilated by citizens, given that they were not at all em-

Identities, Trust, and Cohesion in Federal Systems: Public Perceptions, edited by Jack Jedwab and John Kincaid. Montréal and Kingston: McGill-Queen's University Press, Queen's Policy Studies Series. © 2018 The School of Policy Studies, Queen's University at Kingston. All rights reserved.

braced by the central government's institutions.

Evolution of National Identities and Public Support for Territorial Decentralization

The return to democracy in Spain at the end of the 1970s was accompanied by a political determination to accommodate the cultural and political distinctiveness of Catalonia and the Basque Country, which had been repressed for thirty-six years under the hyper-centralized regime of Francisco Franco. The institutional solution for accommodation was enshrined in the Constitution of 1978, which projected a system of decentralization. Although the system mainly addressed the concerns of the Basques and the Catalans, it could be implemented throughout the whole country, as finally occurred with the establishment of seventeen autonomous communities.

The Evolution of Public Support for Decentralization (1980s–2015)

During the years following 1978, the decentralization process garnered long-term support from most citizens. Starting from scratch in the early 1980s, the expansion of regional self-government to the whole country and, consequently, the establishment of the seventeen autonomous communities regularly generated positive feelings, while support for centralism fell continuously. In this sense and according to the Centro de Investigaciones Sociológicas (CIS) opinion polls, between the early 1980s and the beginning of the 2000s, citizens' attachments to decentralization and self-government grew stronger, going from 30 percent of support in the late 1980s to 50 percent—and almost 60 percent by the late 1990s; meanwhile, support for centralism, starting from very similar figures (30 percent in 1990), decreased continuously and reached its lowest score in early 2000: 9 percent (see Figure 3.1).[1]

---

1. Centro de Investigaciones Sociológicas [Centre of Sociological Research], CIS, is an entity attached to the Ministry of Presidency of the government of Spain. Its main function is to conduct opinion polls. Over the last twenty years, the CIS has systematically carried out opinion polls regarding different aspects of the development of political decentralization. Among other issues, its surveys have attempted to provide evidence of citizens' support for the Spanish model of political decentralization as a whole, their perceptions of the impact of the different levels of government on their daily lives, and citizens' attachments to their respective autonomous governments. One of the questions refers to citizens' preferences regarding the model of territorial organization. This question has

Figure 3.1

Evolution of Preferences Regarding the Model of Territorial Organization (1984–2015) Spain-wide Figures (%)

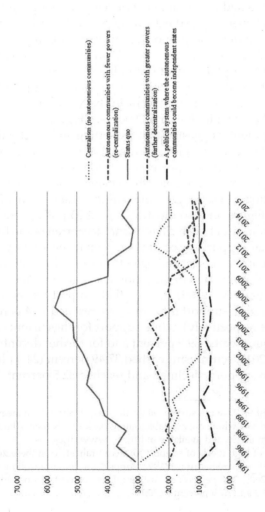

Source: Data for 1984 from survey #1441; 1986, #1558; 1988, #1764; 1989, #1773; 1994, #2123; 1996, #2211; 1998, #2286; 2002, #2455; 2003, #2535; 2005, #2610; 2007, #2736; 2008, #2757; 2009, #2799; 2011, #2920; 2012, #2966; 2013, #2987; 2014, #3029; 2015, #3101.

A plausible interpretation of data and trends shown in Figure 3.1 may suggest that the Spanish people progressively internalized the basic aspects of the decentralized system and were satisfied with it. The Catalan and Basque cases showed expectedly different pictures, with large parts of the populations of those communities aiming at further decentralization and even secession, but the relevant point is that, despite coming from a highly centralized political system and holding onto an exclusive Spanish identity as a result of the Francoist past, decentralization seemed to have reversed path-dependence moods in those territories where citizens had never aimed at developing self-government institutions.[2] Simultaneously to the growing positive attachments toward the institutional setting, the proportion of people defining themselves as being as much Spanish as from their own autonomous community (dual national identity) also rose from almost 40 percent in the early 1990s to more than 50 percent, while the percentage of people feeling exclusively Spanish, almost 20 percent in the early 1990s, declined to values under 10 percent in the early 2000s (see Figure 3.2).

These developments suggested that the setting and functioning of the institutionalized system of regional self-government had not only interacted positively with citizens' perceptions and attitudes about the territorial model of governance, but also that such interaction had legitimated decentralization and self-government as the best governance model.

However, as Figure 3.1 also illustrates, in 2005 polls started to indicate that the harmony between citizens and decentralization had begun to break down as support for centralism revitalized slightly and support for the decentralized system began to shrink. These initial signs of change became more evident in the following years. In 2009, an opinion poll by the CIS (survey #2799) showed that support for recentralizing powers together with support for centralism reached 27.4 percent (12.1 and 15.3 percent respectively), while support for the current decentralization (status quo) scored 39.9 percent and for further decentralization 19.2 percent; in 2012, centralism reached 37.49 percent (24.9 plus 13.40), while status quo supports declined and reached 32.5 percent.

---

appeared in most Spain-wide surveys since the early 1980s, which means that figures for Spain as a whole are available dating back to this time. Almost all surveys are open-access and available at http://www.cis.es.

2. Some examples of high levels of support for decentralization in these autonomous communities are: in Extremadura in 1992, support for decentralization scored 46 percent, and in 2005, 74.5 percent; in Castilla y León, percentages of support were 36 percent in 1992 and 67.5 percent in 2005.

Figure 3.2

Evolution of National Self-Defined Identity 1990–2015 (%)

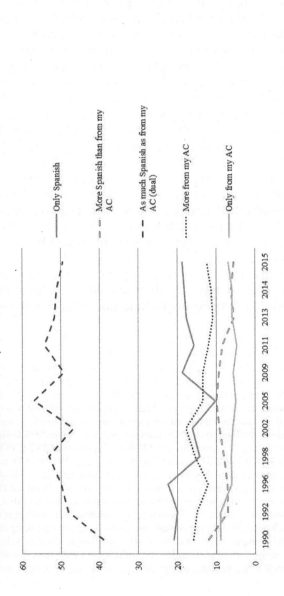

Source: data for 1990 and 1992 from Moreno (1997, 131). Data from 1996 to 2015, Centro de Investigaciones Sociológicas: 1996, survey #2228; 1998, survey #2286; 2002, survey #2455; 2005, survey #2610; 2007, survey #2667; 2010, survey #2829; 2011, survey #2920; 2013, #2990; 2014, #3029; 2015, #3101.

On the other side of the coin, support for a territorial model allowing secession has continued growing in Catalonia since 2005, showing the increasing dissatisfaction Catalans feel toward the current decentralization system (Guibernau 2013; Serrano 2013). According to CIS polls, in 2002 in Catalonia people's support for a political system that would allow secession from Spain reached 17.4 percent; in 2005, 20.7 percent; in 2011, 23 percent; and in 2012, 37.4 percent.[3] Other polls carried out by the Catalan government's opinion centre have given higher figures. In late 2009, 60.8 percent of Catalans thought that the level of self-government of Catalonia was insufficient, and 21.6 percent of Catalans supported the independence of Catalonia. In late 2013, these percentages rocketed to 70.4 percent and 48.5 percent respectively, although 2015 polls showed a reduction of the intensity of these trends; 63 percent thought that the level of self-government was insufficient, and 37.8 percent would support independence (Centre d'Estudis d'Opinió, 2009, 2013, 2015).

Thus, from these data and their trends, one could infer that, for very opposite reasons, the level of citizens' satisfaction with the decentralization model established in the early 1980s (status quo) dropped rather low, to levels similar to the 1980s (see Figure 3.1 above). For some people, decentralization and self-government should be limited and reduced; for others, enlarged and even transformed. In any case, data seem to show that the autonomous communities went from being perceived by citizens all across Spain (Catalonia included) as the best model of governance to being double-questioned for extreme opposite reasons.[4]

---

3. Source: CIS surveys #2610 (for 2005), #2920 (for 2011), and #2990 (for 2012).
4. The case of the Basque Country stands out as rather stable, showing little changes on the evolution of preferences on territorial models. In other words, in the Basque Country secessionism has not grown considerably in support. At least two reasons might explain this situation. First of all, levels of secessionism have been traditionally much higher in the Basque Country than in Catalonia. Yet, in 1992, Basque support for secession reached 19 percent (CIS #2040); 22.5 percent in 2002 (CIS #2455); 25.40 percent in 2007 (CIS #2734); and 25.7 percent in 2012 (CIS #2956). Data show an increase of support but neither as sudden nor as radical as in Catalonia. Also the other preferences remain rather stable. The second reason might lie on the fact that the Basque Country's self-government is based on a fiscal arrangement that provides it with almost full fiscal autonomy. The margin of economic and political manoeuvre is, therefore, independent from the central government's spending-power influence. Recentralization strategies have not so far affected the Basque Country's singular fiscal position. In the light of uncertainties brought about by the secessionist Catalan movement, people in the Basque Country have stuck to their traditional preferences,

At this point, what explanations might account for this change of trends? If one looks at the political arguments that have been stated, the possible answers could be connected with two successive events that may have undermined the positive image that decentralization and the self-government institutions had previously enjoyed among citizens. The first one is the highly controversial Catalan-led wave of self-government reforms initiated in 2004.[5] The second event is the vast and intense economic crisis that hit the country or, rather, the political argument that attributes the responsibility for the crisis to self-government institutions; that is, to the autonomous communities.

As for the wave of self-government reforms initiated in the early 2000s, although some of these reforms were aimed mainly at enlarging and updating the contents of powers, the crucial and most controversial issue was related to a novel objective established and introduced by Catalonia's reform, which was followed by other autonomous communities; namely, the establishment of legal mechanisms designed to improve the quality of self-government.[6] These mechanisms were basically designed to prevent the central government from intruding into the exclusive powers of the autonomous communities, establish the participation of Catalonia within statewide institutions, and provide a degree of financial sufficiency (Grau Creus 2011, 190).

The political and social turmoil aroused by these reforms, together with the political frustrations generated after the Constitutional Court of Spain ruled against major aspects of the Catalan reform in 2010, generated different arguments that had in common the questioning of the goodness of the decentralized system but that majorly differed in the reasons provided. For the leading actors of the reforms (in Catalonia basically), the frustrated reform was understood as the exhaustion of the current system of decentralization as a mechanism to accommodate their self-government claims; for other actors, mainly outside Catalo-

---

since the status quo provides a proven independence while secession, now a real and not any longer hypothetical debate, brings a scenario full of uncertainties.

5. The autonomous communities that proposed the reform of their self-government charters were the Basque Country in 2004 (never approved); Catalonia (passed in 2006 and modified by the 2010 ruling of the Constitutional Court), Valencian Community (2005), Andalusia, the Balearic Islands, Aragon, the Canary Islands, Castile and León (2006), Castilla La Mancha (2007), Extremadura (2008), and Navarre (2009). However, those proposed by the Canary Islands and Castilla-La Mancha were withdrawn by their respective autonomous parliaments.

6. Aragon, Andalusia, and Canary Islands.

nia, reforms were understood as totally unnecessary from an institutional point of view and even as a dangerous political instrument that could end up jeopardizing the unity of the country.

Political arguments emphasizing the negative effects that decentralization had on the Spanish economy came afterward. For this line of thought, recentralization, or even total centralization, was not a matter of ideology and identity but a matter of "economic rationalization" mainly understood as the need to reduce and simplify the size and extension of public administration and, as such, a necessary and imperative instrument to fight the crisis successfully. The existence of different levels of government was perceived as a waste of economic resources as many of the functions performed by these different levels were perceived to be simply duplicated.

Thus, without denying the importance of analyzing the constitutional and political issues associated with decentralization, I will turn to focus on contextualizing the extent to which 2011 opinion data, when macroeconomic data were showing the worst of the crisis, might suggest that citizens' shrinking support for decentralization and increasing support for centralization and recentralization might have something to do with the economic rationalization argument. It might have contributed to the change of people's minds or may have had a bleaching effect; that is, precisely because of its intentionally shaped neutral dimension, it might have contributed to bringing to the surface views that some years ago were understood as politically incorrect and, also, views that could not be grasped by the indicators that have been used traditionally to measure the satisfaction and "decentralization values" of citizens.

In order to do so, in a first step I will contextualize and describe the rise of the discourse that links the economic crisis with decentralization, featuring its bases and rationales. In a second step, I will show the extent to what citizens changed their attitudes and opinions toward decentralization and self-government between 2005 and 2015, paying special attention to changes in support for centralism and recentralization and their link to national identities.

Political Discourses on Self-Government and the Autonomous Communities: From Saints to Sinners

In April 2012, Esperanza Aguirre, then the first minister of Madrid (autonomous community) and one of the most powerful regional leaders of the party in office at the central government, the Partido Popular

(PP), declared that, in the light of the economic crisis and having in mind the weight of the devolved services in Spain's debt and deficit, one should consider recentralization; that is, bringing some powers devolved to the autonomous communities back to the central government. Her view reflected a perspective that had been quietly growing in Spain since the mid-2000s but rocketed, both politically and socially, with the economic crisis. This view holds that decentralized systems promote duplication, inefficiencies, and increased economic costs and that, more specifically, the autonomous communities, because of their spendthrift behaviour, are to be blamed for worsening (when not causing) Spain's economic crisis. Since 2012, this perspective has gained political support; within the PP, it has become a leading motto in both the governmental and party-politics dimensions. Other political parties also have embraced the idea that political decentralization has promoted economic inefficiencies and that these inefficiencies can be solved by re-devolving powers to the central government and/or "rationalizing" (meaning reducing and abolishing) the administrative structures of the autonomous communities. In this sense, the most notorious example is Ciudadanos, a relatively new political party that advocates for a firm revision of decentralization (Ciudadanos, 2015).[7]

The view that links decentralization to economic crisis and/or economic inefficiencies departed, thus, from the initial optimistic perspectives on devolution. From a historical perspective, large positive attachments to decentralization and the autonomous communities strongly relied on the fact that democratization came, hand-in-hand, with the process of decentralization; such companionship created a quite indissoluble tandem between the two. In addition, and probably most importantly for younger generations, decentralization also involved the building of the welfare state in Spain because its pillars (i.e., health, education, and social services) fall under the powers of the autonomous communities, something that citizens have learned to identify not without difficulties.[8]

---

7. Ciudadanos is a relatively new political party. It was forged in Catalonia in 2006 around the issue of language and equality in public services and electorally competing only in Catalan elections. In 2014–15, the party organized its structure on a Spain-wide basis. According to CIS (July 2015), its estimated share of votes in a general election would be 11 percent. More information: Vote Estimation Time Series at the CIS web page, http://www.cis.es/cis/export/sites/default/-Archivos/Indicadores/documentos_html/sB606050020.html

8. In this sense, a 2010 survey (CIS #2829) asked citizens about which order of

Meanwhile, negative views of decentralization and of the autonomous communities had been clustered for years in the core of minority and conservative pro-Spanish nationalist sectors, highly embedded, thus, in old-fashioned Spanish-identity ideology and reminiscences of the Francoist past. The citizens' growing support for the politically decentralized system and for the autonomous-community institutions reached levels close to 90 percent in autonomous communities that lacked any previous self-government aim. Also growing was the percentage of citizens that felt their national identity was a compound of their Spanish identity and their regional identity.

However, while harmony between citizens, politicians, and decentralization kept growing and seemed to be consolidating into stable patterns, legal experts early indicated that central government institutions did not behave according to decentralized manners. The constant encroachments of powers and interferences by central institutions on matters falling within the powers of the autonomous communities have been widely reported and depicted as covert recentralization actions disguised, most of the time, under the rubric of coordination (Viver 2010; Viver and Martin 2012). Thus, the practice of passing expansive Spanish legislation, coupled with the central government's spending power and an autonomous-community financing system almost lacking fiscal accountability instruments, contributed to undermining the political and legal margin of manoeuvre for self-government institutions. Thus, recentralization, under the label of coordination, existed well before the economic crisis, although it was an issue unperceived by public opinion but fully grasped by academic legal experts and autonomous-community legal practitioners.

In the first half of the 2000 decade, just before the crisis affected the global economy, in Catalonia the increasing institutional, political, and social dissatisfaction toward decreasing margins of self-government led Catalan political leaders to launch a reform of the Catalan self-government system. The impetus of the Catalan reform stimulated reforms

---

government was responsible for housing, policing, education, unemployment, public infrastructure, health, environment, and immigration. A large majority of citizens identified correctly the policy areas falling under the powers of the central government—unemployment (69.2 percent), infrastructure (49.6 percent), economy (76.5 percent), and immigration (74.4 percent)—but fewer than half of them attributed to the autonomous communities those policy areas falling under their power, such as education (43.3 percent), health (48.4 percent), and environment (35.1 percent).

in other autonomous communities, although not in all. The wave of reforms, most of them elite-generated and lacking social support, helped to fuel anti-decentralization discourses that based their criticisms of the reforms on the dangers the latter posed to Spain's unity. Enough was enough: the "decentralization" patience of some political and social sectors ran short, and these sectors, mainly led by the conservative Partido Popular, openly argued that decentralization should have explicit limits so as not to fracture the unity of the Spanish nation. However, as it has been reported elsewhere (Fundación Alternativas 2011, 70–1), revitalizing a negative message toward decentralization and self-government on the bases of preserving the Spanish identity and nation was probably not the best move for the PP, which was aiming at enlarging its electoral support in Catalonia and the Basque Country, "the two regions that were responsible for the socialist victory in the 2008 general elections, and where the PP was traditionally unpopular" (Fundación Alternativas 2011, 70–1). In this sense, from the end of 2010 and onward the PP re-elaborated its criticisms of decentralization, moving the issue from its exclusive Spanish identity and national dimensions to the economic efficiency and rationality dimensions. The apparent neutrality of these labels also wooed the electoral lust of the Socialist party, which in 2011 adopted the message almost entirely by linking it to the traditionally argued need for strengthening intergovernmental cooperation under the umbrella of the central government's impulse (PSOE 2011). However, the growing tension between Catalan political forces and the central government (PP) brought the Socialist party to partially redefine its message in 2013 with the launching of a federal proposal to reform the Spain's Constitution (PSOE 2013).

The deep strength with which the economic crisis hit Spain provided more arguments for restructuring decentralization, this time as a measure needed to fight the crisis. Conservative think tanks, mostly linked to the PP, have since produced a large variety of studies pointing at two main consequences of decentralization: institutional irrationality and economic inefficiencies. As for the first aspect, it has been argued that decentralization and its subsequent political and legal diversity have brought about a completely irrational system of multiple legislation, administrative duplication, and unnecessary institutions that also were highly politicized. As an example, "Ten proposals to rationalize the Spanish Autonomous-community system," a report issued by Fundación Ciudadanía y Valores (Avezuela et al. 2011) stated that the legal and political diversity derived from self-government generated a chaos that could only be solved by central government action (via coordination, once again). One of the measures the report's authors proposed was to downgrade the functions and structure of the autonomous-community legislatures, because, they argued, the autonomous-community legislatures had already passed all the important legislation and their only function since then had been that of introducing minor legislative changes. Such downgrading, the report followed, should also involve the election of part-time members who should have a job somewhere else so that "politics" and politicization had fewer chances to interfere in the system.

Arguments on the second aspect, the economic inefficiencies of decentralization, focused on the economic consequences derived from such an irrational institutional system, pointing at the autonomous communities as the main cause of Spain's enormous debt and deficit, the main obstacle to accomplishing the European Union's budget-deficit targets, and a burden to the full development of single-market principles (Salafranca Sánchez-Neyra 2012).[9] In this sense, re-centralization was argued to be the most suitable instrument to fight the crisis. Very illustrative examples of this vision can be found in the reports by the Committee to Reform the Public Administrations (attached to the Spanish Ministry of Treasury and Public Administrations), which, by emphasizing pure economic cost–benefit perspectives, indicated measures addressed to centralize the managing of some services falling under the powers of the autonomous communities (e.g., grants and expedition of driving licences) and suppress several autonomous-community agencies and institutions (some of them of a high political profile, such as agencies of data protection, statistics offices, international affairs agencies, and ombudsman institutions) understood as superfluous (Committee to Reform the Public Administrations 2013a, 2013b).

But not only the central government is recentralizing; some autonomous communities ruled by the PP strictly followed the suggestions made by the central government, as the latter were part of the PP political program, and implemented several measures addressed to reduce both the institutional dimension and the political significance of self-government. As an example, in Castilla La Mancha between 2011 and 2012, apart from suppressing several institutions (such as the Om-

9. As an example of how this perspective has been assumed by the international media, see, for instance, "Spain ready to intervene in Asturias," *Financial Times*, 13 May 2012.

budsman and as the Audit's Office), the government introduced new legislation abolishing salaries for the regional members of the parliament whose income is now based on allowances for their attendance at parliamentary sessions. In sum, recentralization, even self-recentralization, replaced the "coordination" label so much used in the past.

The first formal consequence of this argument at the Spain-wide level was the speedy constitutional reform of August 2011 that established limits and controls on public deficits of all orders of government and its consequent derived legislation that frames the capacity and instruments of the central government's intervention into the autonomous communities' finances (Lago Peñas 2012). This was followed by several other pieces of legislation that have interfered with autonomous-community powers under the justification of economic rationalization, such as labour market reform and measures addressed to stabilize the health system.[10]

From a societal point of view, by depriving recentralization and centralization of their political dimension and bringing them into the realm of imperative and efficient economic decisions, the issue clearly jumped from being the flag carried by some old-fashioned and minority pro-Spanish nationalist sectors to flags also carried by other societal sectors. One indicator of this was the perspective that citizens had about the consequences of decentralization: whether the latter brought about positive or negative benefits to the whole of Spain. As Table 3.1 shows, between 1998 and 2005 more than 65 percent of citizens thought that decentralization (and, thereby, the autonomous communities) had positive results for the whole of Spain. This percentage decreased to less than 40 percent in 2012, while obviously the percentage of people attributing negative consequences to decentralization rose notably; in 1996, it accounted for a bit less than 18 percent; in 2005 for just 15 percent; and in 2012 for more than one-third of the population (37.1 percent).

Since the economy seems to have been the substitute for identity in the political arguments aiming at justifying recentralization, the key goal is to understand and measure whether and how much this economic perspective has permeated public opinion; that is, whether and how much economic arguments explain the rise of citizens' support for

---

10. Royal decree-law 3/2012, on urgent measures to reform the labor market; Royal decree-law 16/2012, on urgent measures to warranty the National Health System and improve its services.

Table 3.1

Effects of Decentralization on Spain (in %)

	1996	1998	2002	2005	2010	2012
Rather positive effects	59.3	65.1	67.4	68.3	47.9	39.9
Rather negative effects	17.4	10.1	12.6	15.2	26.4	37.1
Neither positive nor negative	9.4	14.5	10.8	8.9	12.9	12.1
DK	13.4	9.8	8.5	6.9	12.1	10.2
NA	0.6	0.5	0.8	0.6	0.7	0.6
(N)	4,932	9,981	10,476	10,371	10,409	11,180

Source: CIS surveys (in chronological order): #2228, #2286, #2455, #2610, #2829, and #2956.

recentralization and centralization.

Identities, Supports for Models of Territorial Organization, and the Imperative Need to Rationalize: Is There Any Relation?

From a purely contextual perspective, the time series on the preferences for the territorial model of political organization (see Figure 3.1 earlier) illustrated that the rise of support for recentralization and centralization, together with the decrease of support for the status quo, might imply a change of rather stable trends and that such a change coincides with the start of the economic crisis. Simultaneously, and in the light of the traditionally established strong knot between centralism and exclusive Spanish national identity, Figure 3.2 (earlier), which illustrated the evolution of self-defined national identities between 1990 and 2015, shows that national identities have been stable, although some variations exist, especially from 2000 onwards. In this sense, Figure 3.3 (below) provides details of the global composition of national identities among citizens of Spain in 2005, 2011, 2013, and 2015 (June), showing that changes were very slight and confirming a well-established

Figure 3.3

National Self-defined Identity 2005, 2011, 2013, 2015 (%)

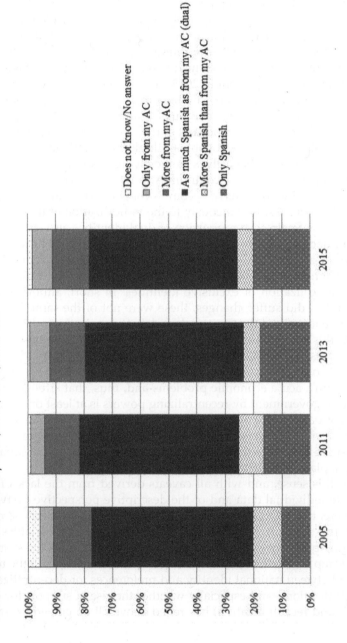

Source: CIS, survey #2610 for 2005; #2920 for 2011, #2990 for 2013, #3101 for 2015.

knowledge: national identities are less prone to change. Still, in spite of the stability of the image, Figure 3.3 illustrates that changes have been concentrated on exclusively Spanish national identities and on dual identities. The proportions of the former increased and those of the latter decreased. In 2005, around 10 percent of people defined their own national identity as Spanish only; in 2010, this percentage reached 15.8 percent, 16.9 percent in 2013, and 18.8 percent in 2015. In parallel, 10 percent of people in 2005 defined themselves as being more Spanish than from their own autonomous community; in 2011 the proportion slightly decreased to 8.5 percent and to around 5.5 percent in 2013 and 2015. Thus, it seems reasonable to think that "soft" Spanish identities, those who define themselves as mostly Spanish but who partially include their autonomous-community personal attachments in their national identity, could have become stronger and exclusive (only Spanish) from 2005, simultaneously to the radicalization of the secessionist tension in Spain. The proportion of dual identities also suffered a constant decrease, from 59.6 percent in 2005 to 54.2 percent in 2011, 51.6 percent in 2013, and 49.4 percent in 2015. "Regional" identities were kept almost untouched, although they showed a slight trend toward the radicalization of exclusive identities. In short, although national identities did suffer changes, these were not of the same intensity as preferences about the territorial model of organization.

In this context, therefore, it seems plausible to hypothesize that the recent rise of centralism and recentralization support could have been linked to an acceptance by citizens that self-government lies at the roots of Spain's acute economic problems and, thus, that strengthening the central government by recentralizing powers is at least one of the necessary paths to follow for economic recovery. However, even though the hypothesis seems plausible, the main problem is how to trace opinion-poll indicators that could give hints to establish that, apart from being plausible, the hypothesis is scientifically sound.

In this sense, and with all caveats derived from the lack of appropriate individual data and of the descriptive perspective I have taken in here, the path I have followed includes two steps. Because national identity seems to have been one of the most crucial variables in predicting preferences about the territorial organization of the system, the first step was to detect whether there have been changes in the relationship between national identity and preferences for decentralization or centralization—and especially whether the rise of support for centralism (and recentralization) has relied above all on citizens who define themselves as mostly Spaniards and exclusively Spaniards or on those in other categories. The second step was to try to detect in a 2011 poll (CIS #2920) whether the internalization of the economic rationalization arguments could have had something to do with changes of support for the territorial model of political organization. Hence, 2011 data have been confronted with 2015 data in order to update the information.

As for the first step, 2005 and 2011 surveys from the CIS provide clear and comparable indicators (CIS time-series questions on "preferences for territorial model" and "national identities"; see Figure 3.4 below). However, as for the second step, to choose indicators that could provide some evidence about the importance of the "economic reasons" to explain the rise of centralism was neither easy nor satisfactory. Lacking "good" indicators, the choice turned to questions asking about the economic prospects for the country; in other words, about whether people felt rather pessimistic or rather optimistic about the economic future. Two questions from CIS surveys were selected: one asking people's opinion on the economic perspective of Spain in general (very good, good, regular, bad, very bad) and a second asking about their own personal economic situation (very good, good, regular, bad, very bad).

The assumption underlying this choice was that these questions could provide some information about how radical the measures to be taken to fight the crisis might be perceived to be. Therefore, one would expect that a pessimist would be also more keen to think that a change of the model of territorial organization was necessary. This rationale also would account for people supporting the independence of their own autonomous community for purely economic reasons, assuming that independence would place them in a better-off situation. As a matter of fact, the relation between economic arguments (improving the economic situation) and the increasing support for independence in Catalonia was statistically tested by Muñoz and Tormos (2012). According to their analysis, the increase of support for independence is partially explained by pragmatism, leaving aside identity reasons. Independence, as it is perceived by many of its proponents, would improve the economic situation in Catalonia. Having this interesting point in mind, let us make the first step: to detect recent variations in the relationship between support for centralism and national identities at several moments in time: 2005, 2011, 2013, and 2015.

Figure 3.4 below represents the percent distribution of support for the different territorial models of organization within each of the national

Figure 3.4

Preferences for Territorial Organization & National Identities 2005, 2011, 2013, 2015 (%)

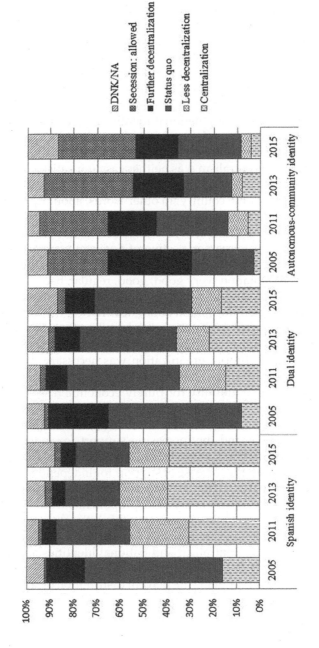

Source: CIS, survey #2610 for 2005; #2920, 2011, #2993, 2013, #3101, 2015.

identity categories in 2005, 2011, 2013, and 2015 (June).[11] These categories are (1) Spanish identity (including exclusively Spanish and mostly Spanish); (2) dual identity (people saying they feel as much from Spain as from their own autonomous community; and (3) autonomous-community identity (including people who declared that their identity is mostly and exclusively forged by their autonomous community). The figure thus shows comparatively whether within each national-identity category of people, there has been a relevant redistribution of support.

At first sight, Figure 3.4 confirms our previous idea. Support for centralization has grown within all categories, but above all such support has grown among people with Spanish identities. In 2005, only 17.6 percent of Spanish national identity people preferred centralism, while more than two-thirds (63.5 percent) supported the status quo. By 2011, this situation changed significantly; almost one-third of citizens self-defined Spanish citizens (32.5 percent) declared their support for centralism, while almost another one-third supported the status quo (32.2 percent) and a bit more than one-quarter (26.7 percent) supported the newly introduced fifth option (see footnote 11), a country where the autonomous communities would have fewer powers (recentralization). This trend was even more accented in the following years. In 2013, 43.2

---

11. Data come from two CIS surveys, survey #2610 (2005) and survey #2920 (both available online at http://www.cis.es). The sample of both surveys is autonomous-community representative, and both surveys include questions about national identity and about preferences on the model of territorial organization. In this sense, the surveys allow one to produce comparative cross-tables. However, while the question about national identity is identical in both questionnaires, the question about preferences on the model of territorial organization is not. In the 2005 survey, following the path established by the CIS since the 1980s, the questionnaire proposed four alternative models for organizing political power: (1) a centralist political system; (2) a political system with autonomous communities "as they are" (a status quo system from now onward); (3) a system in which the autonomous communities would have higher levels of power (a status quo-plus system, from now onward); and (4) a system where the autonomous communities would become independent states. In the 2011 survey, following a change in the questionnaire introduced in 2010, in addition to these four options a fifth was included: a decentralized political system based on autonomous communities but with fewer powers than at present (a status quo-minus, from now onward). Of course, this difference complicates the comparative analysis but, by itself, the introduction in 2010 of this new option after more than twenty years of implementing a questionnaire based on the four options is an indicator of both the change and the timing of the change of perceptions on the virtues and vices of the autonomous-community system.

percent of self-defined Spanish citizens preferred a centralist system, and in 2015 this percentage reached 44.3 percent. In 2013, around 22 percent preferred a regression on decentralization; in 2015, around 19 percent.

Altogether, then, in 2011, 59 percent of self-defined Spaniards supported total or partial recentralization, and in 2015 the percentage was five percentage points higher (64 percent). In other words, in ten years (2005–15), coinciding with the blast of the economic crisis, self-defined Spanish people went from mostly supporting the status quo to being supporters of self-government regression. In 2013 and 2015, polls showed that a large majority of the self-defined Spanish people preferred a centralizing change in the system of decentralization.

Although not reaching as high a percentage, self-government regression also reinforced support among dual-identity people. In 2005, less than 10 percent of them preferred centralism, but the percentage grew to 16 percent by 2011 and to 24.2 percent by 2013. Support declined in 2015 (19.5 percent). Thus, after 2005, centralist dual-identity people, together with dual-identity people who support re-centralization, accounted for more than two-thirds of them (37 percent in 2011, 39 percent in 2013, and 34 percent in 2015), still a very high percentage among people who, in principle, are not driven by strong national identity concerns. To what extent could one say, then, that the economic rationalization argument is behind this change of mind?

As said earlier, important methodological handicaps burden the detection and the measurement of the extent to which the economic rationalization argument has had an impact on the increase of support for centralization and recentralization. Being fully aware of these limitations and their consequent results and with the mere objective of providing a descriptive picture of data, the next two tables (Table 3.2 and Table 3.3 below) show the crossing of two variables: preferences on territorial model and economic perceptions (perceptions of Spain's economy in Table 3.2 and perceptions of personal economic perspectives in Table 3.3). As said, the objective is simply to detect hints on whether there is any possible link between perceptions about the economy and support for centralization. However, the fact is that both tables illustrate that perceptions about the economy do not provide any hints at all helping to discriminate reasons for supporting centralization.

Data in Table 3.2 suggest that people's support for centralization seems to have increased independently of their massively negative perceptions about the country's economy. Around 84 percent of the 2011

Table 3.2

Supports to the Territorial Model & Negative Perceptions on Spain's General Economic Prospective (2011 and 2015)

	Regular	Bad	Very bad
2011			
Centralism and recentralization	37%	35.9%	40.9%
Status quo	47.1%	43.3%	40.9%
Further decentralization & secession	15.9%	20.8%	18.2%
(N = 6082)			
2015			
Centralism and recentralization	40%	34.4%	35.1%
Status quo	40.9%	36.6%	37%
Further decentralization & secession	19%	29%	27.9%
(N=2484)			

Source: CIS surveys #2920 (2011, questions 19*8) and #3101 (2015, questions 22*1).

survey's sample (#2920) thought that the country's prospects were "bad" and "very bad" (it reached 93 percent when I added the "neither good nor bad" category), and only 0.3 percent thought the prospects were "good" and "very good." In 2015, the intensity of negative perceptions had diminished; negative views constituted 61 percent of the sample, and although positive views had increased these represented only 2.5 percent of citizens. In any case, the distribution of support for the territorial model among "indifferent," "pessimistic," and "very pessimistic" people does not differ significantly. Table 3.3 (preferences on the territorial model in relation to personal economic perspectives) also shows that any hypothesis indicating that pessimistic people would tend to be more keen to centralize seems not at all evident. Although opinion-poll data show that people tend to perceive their own economic prospects more optimistically than they perceive their country's prospects, both optimistic and pessimistic people show a rather similar

Table 3.3

Supports to the Territorial Model & Perceptions on Personal Economic Prospective (2011 and 2015)

	Good and very good	Neither good nor bad	Bad and very bad
2011			
Centralism	44.59%	34.91%	31.57%
Status quo	34.28%	41.01%	42.59%
Further decentralization	16.8%	17.79%	18.11%
(N = 6082)			
2015			
Centralism	37.4%	29.36%	28.3%
Status quo	29%	35.06%	31.6%
Further decentralization	22.9%	21.76%	21.88%
(N = 2484)			

Source: CIS surveys #2920 (2011, questions 19*63) and #3101 (2015, questions 22*30).

distribution of support for the territorial model in 2011 and in 2015. Differences between 2011 and 2015 refer to a minimal revitalization of the option for "further decentralization" which, in any case, affect similarly both pessimistic and optimistic people. Nothing is conclusive, then. From this view on Table 3.2's data, however, one cannot straightforwardly discard the notion that the discourse blaming decentralization for the economic situation has been deprived of consequences. Actually, another plausible hypothesis is that it might not be the economy that has contributed to changing perspectives on decentralization but, rather, the message that attributes a scapegoat role to decentralization and the autonomous communities—but we absolutely lack instruments to detect this empirically.

Conclusions and Attempted Prognosis

Spain's decentralization system had for years evidenced a capacity to establish roots in a society traditionally conflicted by the territorial issue, especially over the Basque Country and Catalonia. The creation of autonomous communities in areas originally lacking self-government expectations seemed to contribute to the development of rather strong institutional attachments with citizens. In this sense, it could be said that, at least from the political and institutional point of view, people accepted and approved the legitimacy of self-government institutions and, consequently, of decentralization.

Nevertheless, simultaneously with the wave of self-government reforms of the early 2000s, perceptions started to show signs of change across the country. Changes became more evident with the blast of the economic crisis. Decentralization and self-government became openly questioned. It seems rather reasonable to hypothesize that self-government reforms, especially the frustrated Catalan reform, could have brought awareness about the real values of decentralization, both in favour of and against it, and that the economic crisis helped to foster the process. In Catalonia, the clearest consequence of the frustrated reform has been broad extension of awareness about the high structural limitations of the Spanish decentralization model as an instrument to accommodate and fulfill the self-government expectations demanded since the return of democracy in 1978. In this sense, for large sectors of Catalan society, secession, not institutional reform, is the political solution. In the rest of Spain, the wave of reforms came along with processes of institutional detachment from decentralization simultaneously with rising support for centralization which, nevertheless, has not altered national identities in the same extension. Neither the growing support for recentralization and centralization nor the growing support for secession in Catalonia has come in parallel with similar growing rates of Spanish or Catalan exclusive identities. Thus, although some authors have shown that strong national identities are at the base of the exacerbation of governance preferences (Muñoz and Tormos 2012; Liñeira 2013), the change of preferences on governance does not seem to have much influenced changing national identities.[12]

---

12. At the moment of updating this chapter (2015), such an affirmation can be nuanced; empirical evidence for the Catalan case (Tormos, Muñoz, and Hierro 2015) suggests that the relationship between preferences for the territorial model of governance and national identities is not just unidirectional. The rise of strong Catalan identities in recent years and its link with the previous rise of secessionist preferences seems empirically sound.

Besides, another possible line of explanation for such striking changes in public opinion puts the blame on us, political scientists. It points
at whether we were using the appropriate indicators to measure the
political attachments and comprehension of citizens toward decentralization. For years, our most common indicators have been linked to
grasping citizens' preferences on rather abstract features of decentralization (e.g., institutional setting and powers) that have meant very
little to people's day-to-day reality and have been very much related
to public political discourses and, thus, to the political mood. These
indicators did not manage to reach perceptions and attitudes toward
the concrete effects of decentralization (e.g., implementation of services
and differences in public policies), thereby missing all chances to comprehend how people reacted to actual legal and policy diversity across
jurisdictions and how people understood and accepted, if that was the
case, the political and social values of decentralization.

Perhaps we should talk not just about changes of citizens' perceptions but also about not having been able to define, in the past, indicators that could have grasped other dimensions of people's perceptions
of decentralization less linked to the political mood and convenience,
such as indicators of people's perceptions of policy diversity and differences in public services across the autonomous communities, which
might not have shown the positive attitudes that the above-mentioned
indicators did and thus would have offered a more contrasted picture.
As an exception (and a hint) to this lack of contrasting indicators, in
2010 a CIS survey included a question about diversity of services and
decentralization that has never been asked again (survey #2829, question 18): "on which statement do you agree the most: (a) the autonomous communities should be able to offer distinctive public services;
(b) no differences should exist among the public services offered by the
autonomous communities." The results were that 67.3 percent thought
that differences in public services should not exist, and 24.8 percent
thought that differences should exist. In other words, according to the
results of this question, some political values of decentralization (policy
diversity) seemed to be far from being assimilated by the general public, a paradox that has been detected and analyzed in other works and
has been called "the devolution paradox" (Henderson, Jeffery, Wincott,
and Jones 2013). As they remark, such a paradox seems to point at an
apparent discordance among citizens between, on one hand, wishes for
strong(er) regional governments and, on the other hand, the policy consequences of this strengthening (i.e., policy diversity).

However, individual analyses suggested that, rather than a paradox, the discordance could be linked to sophisticated political preferences (i.e., citizens having clear perceptions of which level of government would more efficiently pursue their collective goals, switching preferences accordingly) and also to divided citizenship (i.e., competition between statist and regionalist preferences). In any case, the authors also suggested the difficulty of measuring them empirically, which brings the issue back to the methodological tools. In the Spanish case, although there is an unquestionable decline of citizens' support for decentralization, explanations cannot just be centred on factors of sudden change but also on what we, the analysts, missed in the past that was hiding such potential for change, such as the extent to which the "devolution paradox" existed all over Spain and the extent to which it was based either on competitive visions, on multi-leveled citizenship, or on insufficient instruments to capture the nuances.

In any case, the future of the Spain's decentralized system and, especially, of Spain itself is more than uncertain. Two opposite and increasingly strong forces are pulling the cord toward incompatible scenarios: secessionism from Catalonia, and recentralization and centralization from the PP government and Ciudadanos. In between stand the still general and controversial proposal of the Spanish and Catalan Socialist parties to re-found a federal Spain (PSOE 2013), and the not yet formalized proposal suggested by Podemos (the new political party founded in 2014 with an estimated 15.7 percent share of vote in July 2015), which seems mostly in favour of allowing a vote on secession but which lacks a clear position on a Spain-wide territorial model.

Dissatisfaction with decentralization is, thus, a broad opinion in Spain although the reasons for it and reactions to it are very different across the country. In Catalonia, such dissatisfaction has been largely translated into the rise of secessionist sentiment, which has influenced the commitment of the Catalan government to hold a vote on secession. So far, the reaction of the PP central government has been that of denying any possible political negotiation that could approach Catalonia's position and stating that the referendum cannot be held because it has no constitutional grounds.[13] Many view this attitude as extraordinary fuel to further exacerbate the territorial political tensions in Catalonia. Preventing a referendum on secession can be seen as a matter of pure legality, as the PP government states, or as a matter of lack of democ-

---

13. This attitude has been noted by several international media. As an example, see the *Financial Times* article.

racy, as the pro-independence parties and other voices state. The institutional crisis is crossing the very strict limits of the territorial issue by getting into the boundaries of questioning the legitimacy of politics and even democracy since it has come along with an intense societal distrust and discontent toward the political system all over Spain. In recent years, opinion polls have been showing the worst values ever on most indicators of institutional and political trust; there has been a spread of public marches protesting against both government policies and unilateral styles of policy-making; and corruption scandals have daily filled the journals and have even spilled over onto the monarchy (Sánchez Cuenca 2014). In this context, thus, the territorial issue not only sits on the classical nation-building dimensions but also on the consequences and spill-over effects of a broad institutional failure.

References

Avezuela, Jesús, Miguel Córdoba, et al., coord. 2011. *Diez propuestas para la racionalización del Estado Autonómico.* Madrid: Fundación Ciudadanía y Valores.

Centre d'Estudis d'Opinió. 2009. *Baròmetre d'Opinió Pública*, 4th edition. http://ceo.gencat.cat/ceop/AppJava/loadFile?fileId=11870&fileType=1.

Centre d'Estudis d'Opinió. 2011. *Baròmetre d'Opinió Pública*, 3rd edition. http://ceo.gencat.cat/ceop/AppJava/loadFile?fileId=19930&fileType=1.

Centre d'Estudis d'Opinió. 2013. *Baròmetre d'Opinió Política*, 3rd edition. http://ceo.gencat.cat/ceop/AppJava/loadFile?fileId=22212&fileType=1.

Ciudadanos. 2015. "La España autonómica." https://www.ciudadanos-cs.org.

Committee to Reform the Public Administrations [Comisión para la reforma de las Administraciones Públicas]. 2013a. *Medidas de la Subcomisión de Duplicidades Administrativas,* Madrid: Ministry of the Treasury and Public Administrations. http://www.mpt.gob.es/dms/es/areas/reforma_aapp/Subcomision-1-Fichas-de-Medidas-CORA-18-nov-2013-enviado-a-CPFF-CCAAs.pdf.

Committee to Reform the Public Administrations [Comisión para la reforma de las Administraciones Públicas]. 2013b. *Reform of the Public Administrations.* Madrid: Ministry of the Treasury and Public Administrations. http://www.sefp.minhafp.gob.es/dam/en/web/areas/

reforma_aapp/CORA-INGLES--web-.pdf.

Fundación Alternativas. 2011. *Report on Democracy in Spain*. Madrid: Fundación Alternativas. http://www.fundacionalternativas.org/public/storage/publicaciones_archivos/35550ee7ef5d9ddf3f8d0436 9d61d7b2.pdf.

Grau Creus, Mireia. 2011. "Self-Government Reforms and Public Support for Spain's Territorial Model (1992–2010)." *Revista d'Estudis Autonòmics i Federals* 13: 186–214. http://www.raco.cat/index.php/REAF/article/view/249079/333356.

Guibernau, Montserrat. 2013. "Secessionism in Catalonia: After Democracy." *Ethnopolitics* (Formerly *Global Review of Ethnopolitics*). 12 (4): 368–93.

Henderson, Ailsa, Charlie Jeffery, Daniel Wincott, and Richard Wyn Jones. 2013. "Reflections on the 'Devolution Paradox': A Comparative Examination of Multilevel Citizenship." *Regional and Federal Studies* 47 (3): 303–22.

Lago Peñas, Santiago. 2013. "The New Budgetary Stability in Spain: A Centralising Approach." *IEB's Report on Fiscal Federalism '12*. Barcelona: Institut d'Economia de Barcelona: 74–7.

Liñeira, Robert. 2013. *Catalunya davant de la consulta sobre la independencia. Participació, vot i motivacions*. Quaderns de l'ICPS, Barcelona: Institut de Ciències Polítiques i Socials.

Moreno, Luis. 1997. *La federalización de España. Poder político y territorio*. Madrid: Siglo, XXI.

Muñoz, Jordi and Raül Tormos. 2012. "Identitat o càlculs instrumentals? Anàlisi dels factors explicatius del suport a la independència." *Papers de treball*, Centre d'Estudis d'Opinió.

PSOE (Partido Socialista Obrero Español). 2011. "Lo que hay que hacer," *Manifiesto autonómico 2011*. Document approved by the Convención Autonómica, Zaragoza, 28–30 January: 20–21.

PSOE. 2013. *Hacia una estructura federal del Estado*. Document approved by the party's Territorial Council, Granada.

Salafranca Sánchez-Neyra, Pedro Mª. 2012. *La unidad de Mercado: un imperativo para recuperar la competitividad*. Papeles de la Fundación FAES.

Sánchez Cuenca, Ignacio. 2014. *La impotencia democrática: Sobre la crisis política en España*. Madrid: Los Libros de La Catarata.

Serrano, Ivan. 2013. "Just a Matter of Identity? Support for Independence in Catalonia." *Regional and Federal Studies* 23 (5): 523–45.

Subirats, Joan, and Raquel Gallego, eds. 2002. *Veinte años de autonomías en España: Leyes, políticas públicas, instituciones y opinión pública*. Madrid: Centro de Investigaciones Sociológicas.

Subirats, Joan. 2013. "Involución democrática." *El País*. https://elpais. com/ccaa/2013/12/21/catalunya/1387657206_181603.html.

Tormos, Raül, Jordi Muñoz, and Maria José Hierro. 2015. "Identificació nacional: causa o conseqüència? Els efectes del debat sobre la independència en la identitat dels Catalans." In *Papers de Treball*. Barcelona: Centre d'Estudis d'Opinió. http://ceo.gencat.cat/ceop/AppJava/export/sites/CEOPortal/estudis/workingPapers/contingut/idnacweb.pdf.

Viver, Carles, and Gerard Martín. 2012. "The Recentralisation Process of the State of Autonomies." *IEB's Report on Fiscal Federalism '12*. Barcelona, Institut d'Economia de Barcelona: 46–59. http://www.ieb.ub.edu/index.php?option=com_phocadownload&view=category&download=402&id=5&Itemid=131.

Viver Pi-Sunyer, C. 2010. "Centralization and Decentralization Trends in Spain: An Assessment of the Present Allocation of Competences between the State and the Autonomous Communities." In *Decentralizing and Re-centralizing Trends in the Distribution of Powers within Federal Countries*. Barcelona, Institut d'Estudis Autonòmics: 155–78. http://gencat.cat/drep/iea/pdfs/iacfs08_edpaper10.pdf.

4

Federalism and Solidarity in Belgium: Insights from Public Opinion

Peter Thijssen, Sarah Arras, and Dave Sinardet

Introduction

In 1981, Arend Lijphart wrote: "What is remarkable about Belgium is not that it is a culturally divided society—most of the countries in the contemporary world are divided into separate and distinct cultural, religious or ethnic communities—but that its cultural communities co-exist peacefully and democratically. The prospects for the Belgian con-sociational experiment must be regarded as highly favourable. Belgium can therefore serve as an extremely valuable and instructive example for other divided societies" (Lijphart, 1981, 1). This observation may have seemed valid in 1981; however, in 2011, international media an-nounced the imminent breakup of Belgium as the country reached the world's record for the longest time needed to form a government af-ter elections. The Belgian federal elections of 2010 were followed by a political deadlock and institutional crisis, culminating in 541 days of difficult negotiations, mostly on a sixth reform of the state, before a new federal government was installed.

Based on the rhetoric of politicians and media, one could conclude that the gap between Flemings and Walloons is bigger than ever. Bel-gium appears to be in a deadlock because most representatives of the two main language communities—Flemings and Walloons—do

Identities, Trust, and Cohesion in Federal Systems: Public Perceptions, edited by Jack Jedwab and John Kincaid. Montréal and Kingston: McGill-Queen's University Press, Queen's Policy Studies Series. © 2018 The School of Policy Studies, Queen's University at Kingston. All rights reserved.

not agree about where Belgium's fairly unique ethno-federal system should go (Roeder 2009). In the end, Belgium may also be a painful illustration of the paradox of federalism, stating that self-rule has a potential to both accommodate and exacerbate ethnic divisions (e.g., Erk & Anderson 2009). On one hand, granting more autonomy to different ethno-linguistic groups can be a way to manage ethno-linguistic conflicts peacefully. On the other hand, this recognition may strengthen and consolidate the identities of these groups and hamper intergroup interactions that may be necessary for the federal shared rule that coexists with the self-rule of the constituent groups. In the long run, federalism may also provide nationalist parties with tools to completely hollow out the constitutionally enshrined elements of shared rule (Riker 1964). To the extent that the federal shared rule encompasses interregional transfers that reduce income inequality, its hollowing out may endanger redistributive policies. In other words, there may be a trade-off between politics of ethnic recognition and interethnic redistribution (e.g., Banting and Kymlicka 2006).

Interestingly, on the level of solidarity, this last logic is diametrically opposed to the way Émile Durkheim and many of his modern cosmopolitan interpreters (Alexander 2006; Van Parijs 2011) expected solidarity to evolve in modern states. In *Division of Labour*, Durkheim foresaw an evolution from mechanical solidarity to organic solidarity. This is an evolution from solidarity based on the strength of in-group commonality to a solidarity based on the complementarity of exchanges among different individuals. After a cursory review of *Division*, it might seem that this solidarity process is solely a structural phenomenon anchored in an expanding division of labour. Organic solidarity in Western industrialized societies is a *fait social*, related to that other French term *fait accompli*. However this exclusively structuralist interpretation does not take into account the importance of emotive reactions and symbolic interpersonal exchange in the later work of Durkheim (e.g., Gane 1992; Thijssen 2012, 2016). Each of Durkheim's structurally imposed forms of solidarity can ultimately be linked to subjectively based emotions and cognitions. Moreover, the notion of division of labour does not only refer to distinctive roles and positions in the labour sphere but also to other spheres such as leisure or consumption. Hence, it still makes sense to use Durkheim's typology to differentiate solidarities in contemporary societies and to link them with distinctive forms of identity. After all, the problematization of identity is a relatively new phenomenon that may just be a correlate of more deep-seated solidarity emotions and behaviour (Stråth 2017). Identification with the *conscience collective* is instinctive and quasi-automatic, just like cogs in a machine; therefore, Durkheim called it mechanical solidarity. By contrast, the functional interdependence and intersubjective empathy involved in organic solidarity leads to a much more reflexive form of identification that is strengthened by a strong education system and a vigorous civil society. Hence, the so-called paradox of federalism could be translated in Durkheim's terms, in the sense that federalism could lead to a regression of the modern evolution of solidarity, from organic back to mechanical solidarity (Thijssen 2012). In other words, the paradox of federalism implies a reciprocal relationship between deepening institutional federalization (the transfer of ever-more-autonomous competences to the regional ethno-linguistic governments) and increasing "mechanical solidarity in ethnolinguistic substate entities" and decreasing "organic solidarity between ethnolinguistic substate entities."

The deepening institutional federalization seems to receive support among Belgium's elites. In this chapter, we evaluate whether such sentiments also are evident among members of Belgium's general public. Most of the research dealing with the problematic link between territorial models that guarantee a parity of esteem between different ethno-linguistic groups and public solidarity have looked rather one-sidedly at interregional exchanges (so-called "solidarity streams") at the macro level, particularly in terms of social security benefits. However, as Van Parijs (2011, 194) has noted, micro-level public emotions and behaviours underlying redistributive exchanges have been largely neglected. Although public opinion research has often found a strong congruence between the issue positions of elites and the public on the aggregate level, this may not necessarily be the case for so-called community-based issues (Page and Shapiro 1983). While elites in the consociational tradition used to be pacifiers of community differences (Lijphart 1981), in recent years they have more and more chosen a confrontational majoritarian stance on community-related issues despite the constitutionalization of consociational mechanisms (Sinardet 2010). In the former situation, elites might overestimate the public's ignorance; in the latter case, they might overestimate the public's militancy. In both situations, there is a fair chance of a significant incongruence between elites and the public.

Therefore, we study the reciprocal relationship between the continuing process of devolving competences to the ethno-linguistic subgroups in Belgium and the strengthening of ethno-linguistic identifications (substate mechanical solidarity) and decreasing intergroup encounters and communication (state organic solidarity). This is an innovative question. First, only limited attention has been given to the second organic factor because of the unavailability of suitable data. As far as we know, this study is the first to take into account the cognitive and affective dimensions of interregional encounters in Belgium. Second, to evaluate the contra-productive effects of federalism, existing research has focused on a very exigent dichotomous criterion; namely, that ethno-federalization may ultimately lead to complete disintegration. However, by looking at public opinion data in relatively young federations such as Belgium, one can gain insight into the early and intermediate consequences of the federalization process. We specifically will evaluate public support for further devolution of competences to the separate regional governments. This is an interesting continuous alternative for the dichotomous "secession criterion." Moreover, if we were to use the secession criterion, the Belgian case would be closed very quickly. In Belgium, there is no substantial proof for the secession-inducing effect of federalism at the level of public opinion because only about 10 percent of Belgians favour separatism. However, this does not exclude that Belgians might want further devolution. To answer our research questions, we will primarily use a unique data set assembled in 2007 by the two Belgian quality newspapers, the French-speaking *Le Soir* and the Dutch-speaking *De Standaard*, which could shed new light on the evolution of organic solidarity. If similar indicators are available in other public opinion studies (e.g., ISPO-PIOP and PartiRep), we will also use them to gain insight in evolutions over time. However, given that we do not have panel data at our disposal, our causal claims regarding the longitudinal effects of past federalization are a little speculative.

In what follows, we give an overview of the Belgian federalization process, specify our hypotheses, present our data and the indicators for our concepts of solidarity, and then present and discuss our results.

The Belgian Federation

Belgium became a full-fledged federal state in 1993. The first article of the Constitution, which had stated that Belgium was composed of nine provinces, was amended to say: 'Belgium is a federal state which consists of communities and regions' (Deschouwer 2009). Belgium's transformation from a unitary state into a federation was the result of a long incremental process that took several decades (De Winter 2014; Deschouwer 2013; Sinardet 2010; Delmartino 2010, Bursens 2009; Dumont 2006; Deschouwer 2005).

The Belgian federation is an example of federalization by disaggregation, as opposed to federal systems that emerge from the aggregation of existing states or territories, such as the Swiss and US federations (Swenden, Brans, and De Winter 2006). Authors also refer to these two forms as "holding together" versus "coming together" federalism (Stepan 1999; Deschouwer 2009). Granting autonomy in a number of substantial areas is supposed to mitigate the autonomy claims of nationalists by removing some of the perceived threats to their existence as a group. Self-government enables them to protect and promote their own culture and values (Martinez-Herrera 2010). However, what distinguishes Belgium from some other "holding together" federations, such as Spain and the United Kingdom, is that the sub-state units had no history of their own before the birth of the Belgian state. Unlike the Basque Country and Scotland, for example, Belgium's regions and communities did not exist before Belgium was created in 1830 (Deschouwer 2009).

The Belgian Federal System

Contemporary Belgium is also the only federation that has created different types of federated entities on the same territory: three territorially based regions (i.e., Flemish, Walloon, and Brussels) and three culturally based and language-based communities (i.e., Flemish, French-speaking, and German-speaking). This is the consequence of a historical compromise between the demand of the Flemish movement for cultural autonomy and that of the Walloon movement for more autonomy on economic matters. The communities are mostly competent for culture, media, education, health policy, assistance to individuals, use of language, and international cooperation (within the limits of their competences). The regions are mostly competent for regional development planning, housing, environment, rural development and nature conservation, agriculture, employment, economy, water policy, energy policy, public works and transport, subordinate authority, and international cooperation (within the limits of their competences).

The borders of the regions and communities have been based on those of the language areas, through which language use is officially regulated. There are four language areas (three unilingual and one bilingual): a Dutch-speaking area, which overlaps with the Flemish region; a French-speaking area, which overlaps with the Walloon region minus the German-speaking community; a German-speaking area, which overlaps with the German-speaking community; and a bilingual (French/Dutch) area, which overlaps with the Brussels region. In every language area, only the official language(s) can be used in administration, education, and justice. The borders of these language areas have been fixed since 1963 through the establishment of a linguistic borderline, mostly to protect the Dutch-speaking area from frenchification. The officially bilingual Brussels region is actually an overwhelmingly French-speaking city geographically located in Flanders.

The Belgian system is thus based on territorial unilingualism (except in Brussels). However, some exceptions exist within the three unilingual areas (Sinardet 2010). Sixteen communes (of which six border the Brussels region) with significant linguistic minorities enjoy "language facilities"; that is, inhabitants have the right to communicate with the authorities or have primary school organized in a language other than the official language (i.e., French in some Dutch-speaking communes, Dutch in some French-speaking communes, German in some French-speaking communes, and French in some German-speaking communes). The institutions of federal Belgium are both a product and a pacemaker of (political) identity construction: "they created permanent boundaries that gave additional subjective meaning to cultural markers and/or territory in addition to favoring identity politics" (Lecours 2001, 63).

Although Belgium consists of three regions, three communities, and four language areas, the dynamic in the federal arena is largely bipolar, based on the two main language communities of Dutch-speakers and French-speakers, which form respectively around 60 percent and 40 percent of the total population of 11 million Belgians. This bipolarity is externalized on different levels. In the federal parliament and government, a number of consociational devices, obliging power-sharing in institutional matters, were introduced in 1970. All MPs have to belong to either the Dutch or French language group, a number of "special majority laws" can only be passed by a majority in both language groups, an "alarm bell procedure" protects one language group from being dominated by the other, linguistic parity is guaranteed in the council of ministers (i.e., the federal government with the exception of secretaries of state), which also decides in consensus. In terms of the party system, Belgium is also a unique federation; there are no national parties of importance because the three traditional parties split along language lines between 1968 and 1978. For elections, two electoral colleges based on the language communities were created to elect members of the Senate and the European Parliament. For the Chamber of Representatives, most electoral districts do not cross the borders of the regions. This leads to federal elections being in fact "community elections." "Community" parties compete with parties of the same community for "community" voters through "community" campaigns in "community" media. After election day, however, two "community" election results have to be put together to form one federal government (Sinardet 2010).

Although the Belgian system and practice of consociational democracy and federalism were supposed to lead to political pacification between the communities, the bipolar institutional characteristics are, instead, incentives that foster political conflict. Due to the way the party and electoral systems are organized, parties only compete for votes within their own language community; therefore, they are not incited to take into account or be accountable to voters of the other language group. This stimulates taking polarized positions on community issues and consequently also the creation of homogenous fronts of Dutch-speaking and French-speaking politicians on these issues, which leads to still more issues being framed in a community dimension.

Institutional explanations can therefore largely account for community conflicts being much more salient among political elites than among the Belgian population. Indeed, public opinion research shows that community issues generally score among the lowest as vote-determining issues among Dutch-speaking as well as French-speaking voters (Deschouwer and Sinardet 2010). Also the number of separatists remains limited to about 10 percent in the Flemish region and 4 percent in the Walloon region (Billiet, Maddens, and Frognier 2006). Research on ethno-territorial identity feelings shows a majority of citizens still identifies with Belgium and does not at all consider Flemish or Walloon/Francophone identity on one hand and Belgian identity on the other to be mutually exclusive (Deschouwer and Sinardet 2010).

As well as being unique for the absence of national political parties, Belgium is unique in comparison to other federal—also multilingual—countries for the absence of a national public media structure. The bipolarity of Belgium's political system is also reflected in its media system. In most other federal—also multilingual—countries, at least some kind of overarching media structure exists, which unites broadcasters of the different communities or other federated entities. Also quite unique in an international context—and obviously linked to the previous—is that in the agreement between the regional governments and the broadcasters, enumerating the obligations of the latter, there are explicit references to stimulating the cultural identity of the concerned language community but no references to the federal context. In most other federal countries, broadcasters are instructed to also disseminate national culture and stimulate national cohesion. Together with the bipolarity of the Belgian political system, the media dynamic contributes to hindering the existence of a federal public sphere. Media tend to reinforce the political consensus in their own language community instead of being a platform for federal debate (Sinardet 2013).

However, the linguistic divide has also been instrumentalized by the political elite for other partisan or ideological goals (Sinardet 2012). Regionalism and federalism in Belgium have always been linked to the socio-economical, left–right divide and, to a lesser extent, to the philosophical divide between Catholics and liberals. As Huyse (1981, 124) explains, the gain of importance of the community issue from the 1960s onward can in part be explained by how pacification of the other two main divisions in Belgian political life, which had occurred in the years after the Second World War through consociational pact-making, was not as complete as it might have seemed. In both the North and the South, strong factions within both majority groups (Catholics in Flanders and socialists in Wallonia) opposed the status quo that had taken form in pacts. Instead, they found in regional and cultural ideas "new, more compelling instruments for the diffusion of their clerical/anti-clerical or socioeconomic blueprints," leading Huyse (1981, 124) to conclude that "the federalist idea became more attractive to more people in the 1970s not strictly for linguistic or cultural or ethnic reasons, but because it bears the promise of the ultimate achievement of socialism in Wallonia and of a sort of Catholic model of societal harmony in Flanders." In this sense, one can historically read the federalization of Belgium as a division of power between the dominant Christian-Democratic party in the North and the dominant Socialist party in the South. Together with substate nationalist parties, these two parties were the main driving forces behind the process of federalization through which they strongly reinforced their dominant position.

Belgium's federalization is also a clear example of the dynamic described in the federal paradox. The creation of communities and regions in 1970 was seen by some political actors as a way to pacify community relations, while others considered it a first step toward greater regional autonomy. Clearly autonomy has prevailed over pacification. There has been pacification, but not for the long term. This can be illustrated by the period of political crisis between 2007 and 2011. Although Belgium had already broken its own record of government formation length after the federal election of June 2007, four years later Belgium broke the world's record when a federal government was formed 541 days after the 2010 federal election. Consequently, the media speculated about a possible split of the country. The francophone press pointed to Flemish nationalism and separatism as the cause of the crisis; the Flemish press blamed francophone politicians for their stubborn refusal to talk about further institutional reforms.

Belgium, Federal Paradox, and Solidarity

The purpose of this research is to discover how different forms of solidarity and identity in Flanders and Wallonia affect citizens' preferences about the future degree of autonomy for the substate entities after the completion of a long federalization process. Our point of departure is the paradox of federalism, which assumes that granting autonomy to ethno-linguistic groups may strengthen the identities of these groups and hamper intergroup interactions. This could especially be the case in the Flemish region, which used to be poor and discriminated against but is now the most prosperous region. Hence, Flemish nationalist parties renounce the so-called excessive "solidarity streams" flowing toward the Walloon region. However, according to the Durkheimian cosmopolitans, higher education might be an effective restraint on the subnational tendency of self-absorption because it can enlighten citizens' self-interest. Alternatively, we expect lower levels of education to correlate with stronger support for granting further autonomy to subnational entities.

> H0a: Flemings are more supportive of devolving additional competences to the regional governments than are Walloons.

> H0b: Higher-educated Flemings and Walloons are less supportive of devolving additional competences to the regional governments than are lower-educated Flemings and Walloons.

Furthermore, it is interesting to link the literature on federalism, which neglects the importance of processes of reciprocal recognition and public opinion, to the rich sociological tradition of solidarity research. Measuring solidarity at the micro-level is a challenge, however, especially if one is interested in the attitudinal basis of both the mechanical and the organic component. As mentioned above, Belgian research has focused rather exclusively on national and subnational group identification, which is an important component of mechanical solidarity. This story of territorial identities in Belgium is quite complex because many people combine national and subnational identities. The Belgian identity coexists with a strong Flemish identity in the North and with a weaker Walloon identity in the South. This situation is further complicated by the existence of a Brussels identity in the Brussels Capital Region and a German-speaking identity in the German-speaking area (Lecours 2001). Yet, due to the progressive federalization process spread out over the last forty years, maybe this multi-dimensional identity has been tilting more and more toward the sub-regional pole. In this respect, it is probably better to look at the evolution of the institutional level one identifies the most with in order to assess the paradox of federalism in Belgian public opinion.

> H1a: Identification with the substate regional community has
> become stronger over time.

> H1b: Belgians who first and foremost identify with a substate
> community want more competences to be devolved to the
> regional governments.

However, if one wants to understand the shift in identifications, it makes sense to link them with the status of organic solidarity; notably, intergroup contact and encounter seem to be crucial because interaction is usually a fruitful breeding ground for mutual recognition and empathy (Thijssen 2012). Many commentators have stated that Flanders and Wallonia are drifting farther apart and increasingly turning into two separate societies (Billiet et al. 2006), but usually this observation is based solely on differences in elite and mass-media discourse. In this respect, it is very interesting to look at the state of organic solidarity in Belgium. Of course, as many commentators on Durkheim's work have concluded, it is more difficult to measure organic solidarity, independently from mechanical solidarity. Nevertheless, the work of the socio-psychologists Allport and Pettigrew provide the missing link. The "intergroup contact theory," introduced by Allport in *The Nature of Prejudice* in 1954, states that intergroup contact typically diminishes intergroup prejudice (Pettigrew 1998). The idea is that intergroup contact facilitates learning about each other. If this new knowledge corrects negative views of the other group, this should in turn reduce prejudice. In Belgium, Flemings are typically portrayed as intolerant and racist, while Walloons are depicted as lazy and unwilling, or even unable, to learn Dutch. Increased contact between Flemings and Walloons could reduce these prejudices and foster organic solidarity. Physical contact and information acts as a mediator between intergroup contact and diminishing prejudice. The mutual empathy arising from this process is the very foundation of organic solidarity between groups (Pettigrew 1998; Pettigrew and Tropp 2008). We will investigate the state of organic solidarity in Belgium by assessing both an affective and a cognitive component of intergroup contact.

First, we will investigate the role of intergroup communication and mass media as providers of information about the other community. This is a cognitive component enabling indirect intergroup contact. Of course, sufficient mastery of each other's language is an important factor in this respect, as linguistic diversity between Flemings and Walloons is expected to negatively affect solidarity by making communication more laborious (Van Parijs 2011). But perhaps the recognition of subnational communities involved in federalization has a similar effect. The fact that the Belgian media are completely segregated along linguistic lines is crucial in this respect. The three communities each have their own newspapers, television broadcasts, and radio stations. Virtually no francophone newspapers are read in Flanders, and no one there watches francophone Belgian television channels anymore. *Mutatis mutandis,* very few Walloons or francophone Brussels residents follow the Flemish media (Billiet et al. 2006).

> H2a: The knowledge of each other's language and media supply (cognitive organic solidarity) has decreased over time.

> H2b: Those Belgians who have knowledge of the other community's language and media supply want less devolution of further competences to the regional governments.

Second, the affective component highlights the empathic element in intergroup relations and encounters. Intergroup relations may facilitate understanding of the other group's perspective and foster empathy with each other's concerns. These insights can strengthen the public support for federal shared rule and slow down the urge for increasing self-rule of the constituent groups, as they correct mutual negative prejudices (Pettigrew and Tropp 2008). Applied to Belgium, friendship between Flemings and Walloons could reveal that differences between both groups are less impressive than some politicians tend to claim, which might positively affect support for living together in one state. Moreover, we will not only look at intergroup relations but also at the behavioural consequences of these relations. How often do Flemings and Walloons actually encounter each other?

> H3a: The number of intercommunity relations and encounters (affective organic solidarity) has decreased over time.

> H3b: Those Belgians who have relations or regular encounters with members of the other ethno-linguistic group want less devolution of further competences to the regional governments.

Research

Research Design

To test our hypotheses, we mainly use data from a representative survey conducted by TNS Dimarso during 5–26 February 2007. This data set was collected for a joint project on the Belgian community issues by the high-quality newspapers *De Standaard* (Dutch-speaking) and *Le Soir* (French-speaking). Altogether, 1,809 Belgians aged sixteen or older were interviewed by CATI methodology; of these, 1,165 respondents were from the Flemish region and 644 from the Walloon region. This data set is unique because, as far as we know, it is the only one that contains reliable information on intercommunity encounters. Moreover, it is the first time that these data were made available for academic use. As far as possible, we will compare the TNS data of 2007 with the Belgian election studies (ISPO-PIOP and Partirep) that are usually used for these purposes.

Variables

Dependent Variable. The dependent variable is the desired degree of policy autonomy for Flanders, Wallonia, and Brussels. We computed this variable by taking the sum of seven dichotomous variables, based on the following questions:

> Should Flanders, Wallonia, and Brussels decide autonomously about (1) pensions, (2) reimbursement of medicine expenses, (3) the military, (4) employment, (5) crime, (6) prisons, and (7) traffic.

The dependent variable ranges from 0 (no autonomy in any of the policy areas) to 7 (autonomy in all the policy areas). The issue areas listed above are some important competences of the federal authorities. Pensions and the reimbursement of medicines are part of the social security system, often seen as the institutional expression of solidarity (Béland and Lecours 2008). Their complete regionalization would put an end to solidarity between Flemings and Walloons in its most material form. The competences covering crime, prisons, and the military represent the oldest and most basic function of a nation-state; namely, the protection of its citizens. The regionalization of these core functions would undermine the very nature of Belgium as a state. Considering this, our dependent variable seems an acceptable indicator for more or less presence of secessionist aspirations.

A simple comparison of the means for both groups shows some surprising results. The mean desired degree of policy autonomy is 2.60 for Flemings and 2.96 for Walloons. Keeping in mind that the range of the dependent variable is between 0 (no autonomy in any of the policy areas) and 7 (autonomy in all the policy areas), both means are quite low. The difference is small but nevertheless significant. Contrary to hypothesis 0a, and completely contrary to the dominant political perception in the Belgian political debate and to the positions of the main political parties, these numbers indicate that Walloons want more policy autonomy than Flemings.

Table 4.1 shows the proportion of Flemings and Walloons for each category of the dependent variable. In general, the distributions for both groups follow a similar pattern. When taking a closer look, smaller differences between Flanders and Wallonia become clear. Some 37.5 percent of the Flemings do not want to give supplementary autonomy to Flanders, Wallonia, and Brussels on any of the seven policy issues mentioned in the questionnaire, which is more than the 33 percent for Wallonia. At the same time, more Walloons than Flemings seem to favour complete autonomy for the substate levels. About 19.9 percent of the Walloons want policy autonomy in all areas mentioned in the questionnaire, which is the case for only 15.1 percent in Flanders.

Table 4.1

Desired Degree of Policy Autonomy for Flanders and Wallonia (%)

Degree of policy autonomy	Flanders	Wallonia	Belgium
0 – No autonomy	37.5%	33.0%	35.9%
1	8.3%	10.7%	9.2%
2	10.0%	8.9%	9.6%
3	8.7%	6.5%	7.9%
4	7.7%	6.5%	7.3%
5	6.4%	3.9%	5.5%
6	6.3%	10.6%	7.8%
7 – Complete autonomy	15.1%	19.9%	16.8%
	100.0%	100.0%	100.0%

Source: TNS Dimarso (2007).

Since we constructed the dependent variable by taking the sum of seven questions about different policy areas, the value indicates about how many of the policy areas the respondents want Flanders, Wallonia, and Brussels to decide autonomously, not about which areas. Table 4.2 compares the proportions of Flemings and Walloons wanting policy autonomy for each area. The results indicate that the preferences of Flemings and Walloons are not as incompatible as often thought. The last column in the table shows whether the difference in proportion between Flemings and Walloons is statistically significant. In three of the seven policy areas, Flemings and Walloons have significantly different preferences. More specifically, more Walloons than Flemings want the subnational levels to decide autonomously about the military, crime, and traffic issues. The biggest difference is observed concerning traffic issues. Whereas 50.5 percent of the Walloons want policy autonomy in this area, only 36.1 percent of the Flemings favour autonomy. Compared to the other four policy areas, the regionalization of these three

Table 4.2

Proportion of Flemings and Walloons Wanting Autonomy in Seven Different Policy Areas

	Flanders	Wallonia	Significant difference (p <0.05)
Pensions	41.2%	38.7%	No
Reimbursement of medicines	38.8%	39.3%	No
The military	23.9%	31.9%	Yes
Employment	50.4%	48.7%	No
Crime	34.5%	46.8%	Yes
Prisons	35.9%	40.2%	No
Traffic issues	36.1%	50.5%	Yes

Source: TNS Dimarso (2007).

domains will probably have less redistributive effects. It remains to be seen, however, if this commonality really explains the choice pattern.

Independent Variables: Symmetrical Analyses

Mechanical Solidarity. Respondents were asked which identity is the most important for them: the subnational (Flemish or Walloon), Belgian, or European identity. The group of primary affiliation can be interpreted as an indicator of the extent to which mechanical solidarity prevails within Belgium; Flanders or Wallonia; or Europe.

Table 4.3 shows significant differences between the proportions of Flemings and Walloons in each category. The biggest difference is observed with respect to the subnational identity. Fully 34.7 percent of the Flemings feel Flemish in the first place, while only 9.7 percent of the Walloons have a strong Walloon identity. However, the Belgian identity scores best in both groups, although significantly more Walloons than Flemings feel Belgian in the first place. Finally, the European identity

Table 4.3

Percentage of Respondents Feeling Flemish/Walloon, Belgian, or European in the First Place

First choice	Flanders	Wallonia	Belgium
Flemish/Walloon	34.7%	9.7%	25.8%
Belgian	44.1%	58.7%	49.3%
European	21.2%	31.7%	24.9%
N	1,160	641	1,801

Source: TNS Dimarso (2007).

is the most important for 21.2 percent in Flanders and for 31.7 percent in Wallonia.

These results are consistent with previous research on multiple identities in Belgium. Deschouwer and Sinardet (2010) found that Belgians have been answering the identity question in more or less the same way since 1991. Figure 4.1 shows the evolution of the answers for Flemings and Walloons between 1991 and 2009. We have to take into account that the addition of the category "Europe" in 2009 means a decrease of the proportions in all other categories. The same logic applies to our own results. Our variable has three categories, while in the figure below more (only in 2009) possibilities are given.

In both Flanders and Wallonia, the Belgian identity has scored highest over the past two decades. Despite what media and politicians proclaim, most Belgians feel Belgian in the first place. Although in general we see similar results for Flemings and Walloons, there are some important differences. The proportion of Walloons feeling Belgian in the first place has always been higher than the proportion of Flemings, which is the case for our results as well. The same goes for the European identity; more Walloons than Flemings indicate Europe as their primary group affiliation. Finally, the difference between Flemings and

Figure 4.1

Evolution of Belgians' Primary Identification between 1991 and 2009

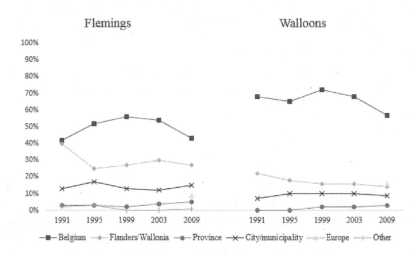

Source: Deschouwer and Sinardet (2009).

Walloons is the largest in their regional identification. Historical explanations can account for the stronger Flemish versus the weaker
Walloon identity. While the Flemish identity has its roots in the Flemish
movement as a means to gain linguistic and cultural freedom, Walloons
still seem to struggle with the recognition and promotion of a distinct
Walloon identity. Regional identity is also a more complex matter in
the South of Belgium than in the North. While the Flemish region and
community have been merged, leading to the political promotion of
one Flemish identity, a Walloon regional identity gets competition from
a francophone alternative, uniting Walloons and French-speakers in
Brussels within the French-speaking community.

Organic Solidarity. The indicators for organic solidarity deal with intergroup contact and the cognitive resources that enable these encounters. Unfortunately, no longitudinal data are available in this respect.
However, by comparing different indicators in different age groups, we

Table 4.4

Cognitive Component of Organic Solidarity in Flanders and Wallonia

	Age	15–24	25–34	35–44	45–54	55–64	65+
Language mastery (% respondents)	Flanders	82.5	76.4	75.5	74.8	79.2	74.6
	Wallonia	42.4	31.7	37.9	23.2	32.9	28.5
Media usage (mean sum score)	Flanders	10.5	9.4	8.7	8.5	8.4	9.4
	Wallonia	7.4	7.8	7.1	6.9	6.8	6.4

Source: TNS Dimarso (2007).

can get some rudimentary insight into the evolution. Because most of the people below forty-five years of age have always known a territorial regime that guarantees substantial regional autonomy, according to the logic described in the literature on the federal paradox we may expect them to have fewer intergroup contacts and fewer cognitive resources that support those contacts.

We will first focus on the cognitive component of organic solidarity by determining the active mastery of the other community's language and usage of its media outlets (see Table 4.4), measured by respondents' self-assessment. With respect to mastery of the other community's language, Flemish respondents definitely score much better than Walloons in every age group. This can be explained by differences in education, which is one of the primary competences of the communities. In the Flemish education system, French is taught as a second language after Dutch, both in primary and secondary school. In the francophone education system, however, offering Dutch in primary school is not mandatory. In secondary school, pupils have to choose a second language next to French, but Dutch is again not compulsory. Pupils can choose between Dutch, English, or German as their second language. Interestingly, the three groups aged below forty-five score no worse than the older age groups. On the contrary, in both Flanders and Wallonia, the share of respondents claiming a good knowledge of the other community's language is larger in the youngest age groups. In other words, hypothesis 2a is not confirmed because knowledge of the other community's language has not declined during federalization. In fact, there is a slight tendency among Flemings and a marked tendency among Walloons for younger people to claim more knowledge of the other community's language than older people.

In order to evaluate attention to the other community's media, we constructed a summated scale using five questions ($\alpha = 0.78$). Respondents were asked how often they:

- watch Belgian francophone/Flemish television?
- listen to a Belgian francophone/Flemish radio station?
- read Belgian francophone/Flemish newspapers?
- read Belgian francophone/Flemish magazines?
- surf Belgian francophone/Flemish websites?

Francophone respondents were asked about their use of Flemish media, and vice versa. The response categories for each of the four questions range between 1 (less than annually or never) and 5 (daily or almost daily). This implies that the global range of the new variable is between 5 and 25. Overall, Flanders' mean sum score of 9.1 is significantly higher than Wallonia's 7.1, but, given the range of the variable, both values are low. Again, we find no confirmation for hypothesis 2a because the groups aged below forty-five also score better in terms of mutual media attention than the older age groups in both Flanders and Wallonia.

The affective component taps the intensity of personal relations between Flemings and Walloons. Respondents were asked, therefore, whether they have friends from the other community and also how often they visit people and places in the other community. Table 4.5 shows the results. Some 44.1 percent of the Flemings have francophone friends, while no less than 63.8 percent of the Walloons say they have Flemish friends. This difference is statistically significant. However, both proportions are higher than we had expected. Hence, it is possible that social desirability may be at play here. Nowadays, having an extensive social network is a desirable attribute because social capital is a scarce resource (Putnam 2000). However, there is no reason to expect that this bias—declaring more friends than one actually has—is stronger in Wallonia than in Flanders. Furthermore, we again do not see a systematic pattern of fewer friendships in the groups under age forty-five.

Similar results pop up with respect to the number of times the other

Table 4.5

Affective Component of Organic Solidarity in Flanders and Wallonia

	Age	15–24	25–34	35–44	45–54	55–64	65+
Having friends (% respondents)	Flanders	48.4	31.9	45.6	39.6	43.2	52.8
	Wallonia	55.6	68.3	62.1	67.9	61.2	66.4
Visit frequency (mean sum score)	Flanders	3.9	4.1	4.2	4.1	4.1	4.0
	Wallonia	4.4	4.7	4.5	4.5	4.4	4.1

Source: TNS Dimarso (2007).

community is visited. Again, this behavioural measure of affective organic solidarity is calculated by a summated scale based on three items ($\alpha = 0.64$):

> How often do you visit Flanders/Wallonia to (a) spend your holidays or pass your spare time, (b) visit family, friends or acquaintances, and/or (c) go shopping?

Flemish respondents were asked how often they visit Wallonia, and vice versa. The answers range between 1 (less than annually or never) and 4 (one or several times a week). Consequently, the summary scores range from 3 to 12. A comparison of the means for both communities shows that Walloons visit Flanders more frequently than vice versa. Flanders scores 4.1 while Wallonia scores 4.4. The difference is small but statistically significant ($p < 0.001$). However, we also find that, overall, the younger age groups do not score lower than those aged forty-five or older. Consequently, hypothesis 3a is not confirmed either; that is, the number of intercommunity relations and encounters (affective organic solidarity) has not substantially decreased during the genesis of Belgian federalism.

Asymmetric Analyses: Negative Binomial Regression

Because our dependent variable contains "over-dispersed" count data, we use a negative binomial regression (with log link) to predict its

Table 4.6

Negative Binomial Regression: Effects on the Extent to which Belgians Want Additional Policy Autonomy for the Regional Governments

	Model 1 B	Model 2 B	Model 3 B	Model 4 B	Model 5 B
Sex (ref. female)	-0.05	-0.03	-0.03	-0.04	-0.05
Age (ref. 15–34 years)	0.09	0.08	0.10	0.12	0.12
Education (ref. lower)	-0.07	-0.47***	-0.47***	-0.45***	-0.43***
Region (ref. Wallonia)	-0.13*	-0.31***	-0.44***	-0.39***	-0.45***
Education * Region		0.59***	0.58***	0.57***	0.57***
Subnational identity			0.43***	0.43***	0.41***
Mutual language knowledge				0.05	-0.00
Mutual media attention				0.01	0.01
Inter-communal friends					-0.18**
Inter-communal visit frequency					0.04
Constant	1.09***	1.20***	1.15***	0.93***	0.91**
Log-likelihood ratio χ^2	10.75	34.77***	79.65***	80.92***	91.21***
Deviance/df	1.24	1.23	1.20	1.20	1.19
AIC	8136	8114	8032	7931	7829

Level of significance: * $p < 0.05$ ** $p < 0.01$ *** $p < 0.001$

Source: TNS Dimarso (2007).

values. Table 4.6 shows the results of the regression analyses. The dependent variable equals 0 when a respondent wants no further autonomy for the regional governments on all seven policy domains, while it equals 7 if a respondent wants subnational autonomy on all seven policy domains. We add the independent variables in four cumulative steps. The first model shows the effects of the socio-demographic variables, inclusive region. In a second step, we add the variable interaction of higher education and region. The third model includes subnational identification, which we use as the indicator for mechanical solidarity. Finally, in the fourth and fifth step, we complete our models with the indicators for organic solidarity, by adding cognitive and affective factors respectively. The test for multicollinearity showed no highly correlated variables.

Model 1: Socio-Demographic Variables. To make the model easier to interpret, we dichotomized the variables age and education, which did not appear to have an influence on the findings. The variables sex, age, and level of education all have non-significant effects on the dependent variable whatever the categorization format. Interestingly, the effect of region is significant and negative. This means that Walloons are more in favour of granting additional autonomy to the subnational communities than are Flemings. These results again reject hypothesis 1 that we derived from the paradox of federalism literature. Considering the media discourse and the popularity of the Flemish nationalist party, the Nieuw-Vlaamse Alliantie (N-VA), one could expect Flemings to favour regional autonomy more than Walloons. However, it appears to be just the opposite. In this regard, there is a clear discrepancy between citizens and politicians. Walloons who favour more regional autonomy can be considered as an "unserved audience," given that no francophone political parties explicitly campaigned for such autonomy in 2007 (Deschouwer and Sinardet 2010), while Flemings who support more autonomy can be regarded as an "overserved audience."

Model 2: Education and Enlightened Self-Interest. The findings of our second model point out that education has a distinct effect in both Belgian regions. This time the sign of the effect runs in the hypothesized direction (0b). Higher educated Belgians are less in favour of transferring additional competences to the subnational governments ($B = -0.47^{**}$). Nevertheless, the conditional effect of higher education is not significant in Flanders ($B = -0.47+0.59 = 0.12$), while it is remarkably strong in Wallonia ($B = 0.13-0.59 = -0.46^{**}$). Figure 4.2 shows the predicted degree of policy autonomy by region and level of education. The difference between lower- and higher-educated Flemings is indeed very small, while the effect of education is considerable for Walloons. In other words, the finding that Walloons are more in favour of regional autonomy is mainly caused by the lower-educated residents of this region.

Figure 4.2

Predicted Count of Policy Autonomy by Region and Level of Education

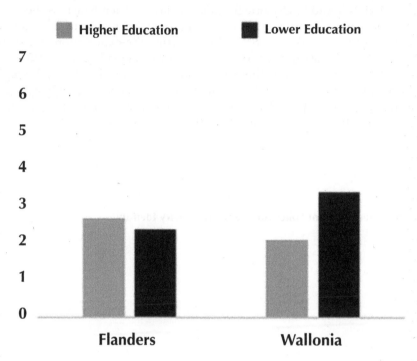

Source: TNS Dimarso (2007).

Model 3: Mechanical Solidarity. Those whose most important identity is Flemish or Walloon differ significantly from those with a Belgian or European identification. A strong subnational identity leads to a stronger wish for additional subnational autonomy, as shown in Figure 4.3. Here, we do find proof for a hypothesis that is directly linked to the paradox of federalism. Importantly, this positive relation between a strong subnational identity and the desire for further devolution of competences does not necessarily imply a vicious circle toward ever more federalization. This is only possible if indeed ever more Belgians would consider their subnational identity to be the most important. However, according to our data and previous research on identities, regional identification has not substantially increased throughout Belgium's federalization.

Models 4 and 5: Organic Solidarity. Having friends across the language border appears to diminish the demand for more devolution of competences ($B = -0.18**$). This confirms the expectation stated in hypothesis 3b. More affective relations between Flemings and Walloons decrease the wish for further subnational autonomy. However, the cognitive component of organic solidarity—more specifically, language knowledge and media attention—does not seem to have a significant effect on the wish for more autonomy.

Figure 4.3

Predicted Count of Policy Autonomy by Primary Identity

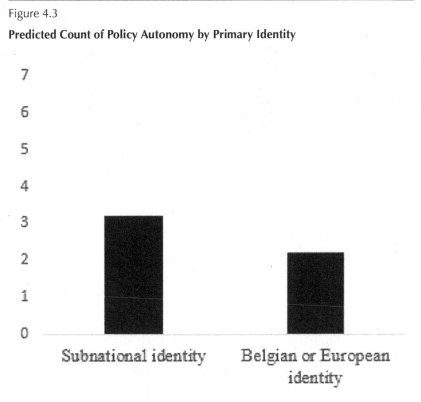

Source: TNS Dimarso (2007).

Conclusion

Recently, attention has been given to a paradoxical side effect of federalism; namely, that it could lead to a devolutionary spiral in which recognition of territorial singularity tends to strengthen intra-communal solidarity and weaken inter-communal solidarity. Hence, ethnolinguistic groups become increasingly assertive, and, as a result, ever more competences will be transferred to the subnational communities, thereby ultimately hollowing out the *raison d'être* of the overarching federation. We have argued that this so-called paradox of federalism could be framed in a much broader discussion about the tension between the politics of recognition and the politics of redistribution, which ultimately boils down to the classical binary pointed to by Durkheim; namely, pre-modern mechanical solidarity versus modern organic solidarity.

Empirically, this paradox is supported by the fact that federalism provides elites with necessary tools for completely hollowing out the constitutionally enshrined elements of shared rule. Hence, most research has studied this phenomenon only by looking at institutional settings, the position of nationalist parties, or elite discourse. However, because we believe that the paradox of federalism is also inextricably bound up with the consolidation of distinctive ethno-linguistic public spheres, it makes sense to look at this process at the level of public opinion as well. It is very plausible that, in this respect, elite discourse is not congruent with public opinion. After all, this incongruence is often considered to be a crucial ingredient of traditional consociational politics in the sense that "overarching cooperation at the elite level can be a substitute for cross-cutting affiliations at the mass level" (Lijphart 1968, 200). However, it is possible that we should turn around Lijphart's initial observation. Perhaps fierce inter-communal political competition at elite level is sometimes a threat to initial cross-cutting affiliations at the mass level.

Belgium is an interesting case because it was in a deadlock between 2007 and 2011 due to the disagreement of elite representatives of the two main language communities about where the federal system should go. The agreement on a sixth state reform in October 2011 permitted the country to have a government again, but it is unclear how long this pacification can last, given among other factors the continued success of the Flemish-nationalist and separatist party N-VA.

Nevertheless, and quite in contrast to the assumptions in mainstream political and media discourse, our research points out that the dead-lock among elites was not at all reflected in the public. Based on a unique data set from 2007, the year when the political crisis started, we learned that Walloons are actually stronger adherents of additional devolution than Flemings, a mirror image of the situation among elites. While intra-communal identification indeed has positive effects on the wish for further devolution, and inter-communal encounters have the expected negative effect, we do not find that each of these factors has substantially changed during the federalization process. Obviously, things could have changed in recent years. In this respect, some indications already are present in the Partirep survey following the 2009 regional elections, where Flemish respondents were slightly more in favour of autonomy than their Walloon counterparts (Deschouwer and Sinardet 2010). This might be attributed to the fact that the question was asked in a different way, but it could also point to an evolution in attitudes on this matter. However, also in 2009, the most striking remains the incongruence between public opinion and elite discourse. Still almost half of Flemish voters do not favour more regional autonomy, in contrast to four out of ten Walloon voters who do support this. In both cases, 40 percent to 50 percent of the voters did not see their opinions reflected by their political elites.

One possible explanation for this incongruence is the split of the political parties and the consociational way the federal system was organized, which strengthened the significance of the linguistic cleavage for the elites. Also, political elites are, more than the public, confronted on a daily basis with the functioning of political institutions they might find unsatisfactory. Calls for institutional reform, therefore, originate mostly from the elite level. A call for more autonomy can also be linked to other ideological and party interests and, in a partitocracy such as Belgium, to an increase in political and administrative mandates, with certainly the dominant parties in each region having much to gain by creating and reinforcing a political level at which they can maximize their power and/or reinforce their ideological (left or right) position.

The question is then why nationalist and even separatist parties, such as the N-VA, have done so well in recent elections. Concerning separatism, the N-VA knows this is a minority position among Flemish voters, which is the main reason why it has been advocating the less radical and more vague "confederalism," which in Belgian political discourse has come to mean a form of more strongly defederalized Belgium.

More generally, the N-VA has understood the lack of interest among large parts of the electorate for autonomy in its pure form and has been able to link autonomy to socio-economic and immigration discourse, focusing on the fact that Flemish voting results are more right-wing than those in Wallonia, resulting in policies that are (too) left-wing at the federal level. The N-VA went so far in presenting autonomy not as a goal in itself but as a means to conduct other policies (such as lowering taxes) that, in the 2014 election campaign, it even left open the possibility to participate in a federal (right-wing) government without further state reform in the short term.

Combined with the fact that the position of Brussels—institutionalized as the third region next to Flanders and Wallonia but at the same time also as a meeting point between both large language communities—makes an actual split very difficult, the disappearance of Belgium is not likely in the near future. However, given the way the federal and party systems are organized and the continued success of nationalist parties, one can expect tensions and conflicts to reappear regularly even though they are not always a reflection of concerns among public opinion. An analogy could be made with Belgium's budget situation. Belgium is a state with extensive public debt; nevertheless, it is usually regarded as a rather stable economic member of the European Union. One reason for this is that much of the debt is domestic, in the sense that the public deficit is easily counterbalanced by the accumulated private savings of the Belgians. In the same way, one could say that on the exterior, as it shows from elite and media discourse, Belgium may appear to be completely divided; however, Belgian society generally does not reflect such a division.

References

Alexander, Jeffrey C. 2006. *The Civil Sphere*. Oxford: Oxford University Press.

Banting, Keith, and Will Kymlicka, eds. 2006. *Multiculturalism and the Welfare State: Recognition and Redistribution in Contemporary Democracies*. Oxford: Oxford University Press.

Billiet, Jaak, Bart Maddens, and André-Paul Frognier. 2006. "Does Belgium (Still) Exist? Differences in Political Culture between Flemings and Walloons." *West European Politics* 29 (5): 912–32.

Bursens, Peter, and Françoise Massart-Piérard. 2009. "Kingdom of Belgium." In *Foreign Relations in Federal Countries*, edited by Hans J. Michelmann, 91–113. Montreal and Kingston: McGill-Queen's University Press.

De Winter, Lieven, and Caroline Van Wynsberghe. 2015. "Kingdom of Belgium: Paritocracy, Corporatists Society, and Dissociative Federalism." In *Political Parties and Civil Society in Federal Systems*, edited by Klaus Detterbeck, Wolfgang Renzsch, and John Kincaid, 40–69. Don Mills: Oxford University Press.

Delmartino, Frank, Hugues Dumont, and Sébastien Van Drooghenbroeck. 2010. "Kingdom of Belgium." In *Diversity and Unity in Federal Countries*, edited by Luis Moreno and Cesar Colino, 48–74. Montreal and Kingston: McGill-Queen's University Press.

Deschouwer, Kris. 2005. "Kingdom of Belgium." In *Constitutional Origins, Structure, and Change in Federal Countries*, edited by John Kincaid and G. Alan Tarr, 46–75. Montreal and Kingston: McGill-Queen's University Press.

———. 2009. *The Politics of Belgium: Governing a Divided Society*. Basingstoke and New York: Palgrave Macmillan.

———. 2013. "The Belgian Federation: A Labyrinth State." In *Routledge Handbook of Regionalism and Federalism*, edited by John Loughlin, John Kincaid, and Wilfred Swenden, 211–22. Oxon: Routledge.

Deschouwer, Kris, and Dave Sinardet. 2010. "Identiteiten: communautaire standpunten en stemgedrag." In *De stemmen van het volk: een analyse van het kiesgedrag in Vlaanderen en Wallonië op 7 juni 2009*, edited by Kris Deschouwer, Pascal Delwit, Marc Hooghe, and Stefaan Walgrave, 75–98. Brussel: VUB Press.

Dumont, Hugues, Nicolas Lagasse, Marc Van Der Hulst, and Sébastien Van Drooghenbroeck. 2006. "Kingdom of Belgium." In *Distribution of Powers and Responsibilities in Federal Countries*, edited by Akhtar Majeed, Ronald L. Watts, and Douglas M. Brown, 34–65. Montreal and Kingston: McGill-Queen's University Press.

Erk, Jan. 2008. *Explaining Federalism: State, Society and Congruence in Austria, Belgium, Canada, Germany and Switzerland*. London and New York: Routledge.

Erk, Jan, and Lawrence Anderson. 2009. "The Paradox of Federalism: Does Self-Rule Accommodate or Exacerbate Ethnic Divisions?" *Regional and Federal Studies* 19 (2): 191–202.

Gane, Mike. 1992. *The Radical Sociology of Durkheim and Mauss*. New York: Routledge.

Huyse, Luc. 1981. "Political Conflict in Bicultural Belgium." In *Conflict and Coexistence in Belgium: The Dynamics of a Culturally Divided Society*, edited by Arend Lijphart, 107–26. Berkeley: Institute of International Studies, University of California.

Lecours, André. 2001. "Political Institutions, Elites, and Territorial Identity Formation in Belgium." *National Identities* 3 (1): 51–68.

Lijphart, Arend. 1981. *Conflict and Coexistence in Belgium: The Dynamics of a Culturally Divided Society*. Berkeley: Institute of International Studies, University of California.

———. 1999. *Patterns of Democracy: Government Forms and Performance in Thirty-Six Countries*. New Haven: Yale University Press.

Martinez-Herrera, Enric. 2010. "Federalism and Ethnic Conflict Management: Rival Hypotheses, the Attitudinal Missing Link and Comparative Evidence." In *New Directions in Federalism Studies*, edited by Jan Erk and Wilfred Swenden, 145–56. London: Routledge/ECPR.

Page, Benjamin I., and Robert Y. Shapiro. 1992. *The Rational Public: Fifty Years of Trends in Americans' Policy Preferences*. Chicago: University of Chicago Press.

Pettigrew, Thomas F. 1998. "Intergroup Contact Theory." *Annual Review of Psychology* 49: 65–85.

Pettigrew, Thomas F., and Linda R. Tropp. 2008. "How Does Intergroup Contact Reduce Prejudice? Meta-analytic Tests of Three Mediators." *European Journal of Social Psychology* 38 (6): 922–34.

Putnam, Robert. 2000. *Bowling Alone: The Collapse and Revival of American Community*. New York: Simon & Schuster.

Riker, William H. 1964. *Federalism: Origin, Operation, Significance*. Boston: Little, Brown and Co.

Roeder, Philip G. 2009. "Ethnofederalism and the Mismanagement of Conflicting Nationalisms." *Regional and Federal Studies* 19 (2): 203–19.

Sinardet, Dave. 2010. "From Consociational Consciousness to Majoritarian Myth: Consociational Democracy, Multi-level Politics and the Belgian Case of Brussels-Halle-Vilvoorde." *Acta Politica* 45 (3): 346–69.

———. 2012. "Federal Reform and Party Politics: The Case of the Fifth Belgian State Reform." In *Changing Federal Constitutions: Lessons from International Comparison*, edited by Arthur Benz and Felix Knuepling, 135–60. Farmington Hills, MI: Barbara Budrich Publishers.

———. 2013. "How Linguistically Divided Media Represent Linguistically Divisive Issues: Belgian Political TV-Debates on Brussels-Halle-Vilvoorde." *Regional and Federal Studies* 23 (3): 311–30.

Stepan, Alfred C. 1999. "Federalism and Democracy: Beyond the U.S. Model." *Journal of Democracy* 10 (4): 19–34.

Stråth, Bo. 2017. "Identity and Social Solidarity: An Ignored Connection." *Nations and Nationalism* 23 (3): 227–47.

Swenden, Wilfred, Marleen Brans, and Lieven De Winter. 2006. "The Politics of Belgium: Institutions and Policy under Bipolar and Centrifugal Federalism." *West European Politics* 29 (5): 863–73.

Thijssen, Peter. 2012. "From Mechanical to Organic Solidarity, and Back: With Honneth beyond Durkheim." *European Journal of Social Theory* 15 (4): 454–70.

———. 2016. "Intergenerational Solidarity: The Paradox of Reciprocity Imbalance in Ageing Welfare States." *British Journal of Sociology* 67 (4): 592–612.

Van Parijs, Philippe. 2011. *Linguistic Justice for Europe and for the World.* Oxford: Oxford University Press.

5

Political Trust in Switzerland: Again a Special Case?

Paul C. Bauer, Markus Freitag, and Pascal Sciarini

Introduction

In the present study, we investigate political trust in Switzerland. Political trust can be defined as a judgment made by an individual A regarding a political actor or institution B, for example governments, parties, and administrations (Bauer and Freitag 2017; Levi and Stoker 2000). Trust judgments generally reflect beliefs about the trustworthiness of a political actor or a political institution. Trustworthiness can be equated with a trustee's commitment to act in the truster's perceived interest (Bauer 2017; Levi and Stoker 2000, 476; Hardin 2000). Political trust then can be generally understood as an individual's expectation that a political actor will act trustworthily; that is, in a way preferred by the truster.[1]

Taking a comparative perspective, we investigate how political trust among Swiss citizens varies both with regard to the institutions of the different orders of government (i.e., federal, cantonal, and local) as well

---

1. Various scholars argue that trust should be conceived of as a three-part relationship (Bauer 2017). In this study, however, we depart from an understanding that can be described as "A trusts B" and refrain from specifying a specific behaviour expected of the trustee.

Identities, Trust, and Cohesion in Federal Systems: Public Perceptions, edited by Jack Jedwab and John Kincaid. Montréal and Kingston: McGill-Queen's University Press, Queen's Policy Studies Series. © 2018 The School of Policy Studies, Queen's University at Kingston. All rights reserved.

as with respect to its development over time.[2] Switzerland is a highly decentralized country in which subnational political entities, in particular the cantons, possess far-reaching political competences. At the same time, Switzerland is a culturally diverse federal state (Fleiner and Hertig 2010). Stein Rokkan once called Switzerland a microcosm of Europe because of its cultural, linguistic, religious, and regional diversity (Linder 1994, xii).[3] Switzerland has further been described as composed of three cultural groups that "stand with their backs to each other" (Steiner 2001, 145). Studies have shown that the three Swiss cultural-linguistic regions have more in common with their neighbouring countries than with each other regarding specific aspects of civil society and cultural life (Freitag and Stadelmann-Steffen 2008; Kriesi et al. 1996). "The French-Swiss stand facing towards France; the Italian-Swiss facing towards Italy; and the German-Swiss facing towards Germany, each focused on their own internal cultural life and the culture of the neighboring country whose language they share" (Kymlicka 2003, 155).

In general, both theory and empirical studies suggest that political trust is a vital resource for the functioning of democratic political systems and an important element of the citizen–state relationship. For instance, the post-communist experience in East European countries has shown that individuals withhold commitments from public institutions, try to outwit authorities, and evade rules as a consequence of low political trust (Sztompka 1999, 156, 164). A recent study revealed that low political trust is connected to legal permissiveness (Marien and Hooghe 2011). Moreover, it is argued that political trust provides political leaders with room to govern effectively and institutions with a store of support that is independent from an incumbent's performance (Hetherington 1998, 803). Conversely, low trust can hamper the success of domestic policymaking (Chanley and Rahn 2000; Hetherington and Husser 2012; Hetherington 2005; Hetherington and Globetti 2002; Rudolph and Evans 2005).

---

2. To date, only a few studies have investigated the development and societal distribution of political trust in Switzerland (Brunner and Sgier 1997; Freitag 2001, Scheidegger and Staerklé 2011; Widmer and de Carlo 2010). While Brunner and Sgier (1997) and Freitag (2001) show that trust in federal institutions has declined between 1989 and 1996, Widmer and de Carlo (2010) find that trust in government has risen between 1996 and 2007. Our investigation extends these analyses by covering a longer period and by adding subnational institutions to the analysis.

3. This statement has to be taken with a grain of salt: clearly, Europe is much more diverse than Switzerland.

Given that federal states also have relevant subnational political institutions, trust judgments about these subnational institutions are of specific relevance, too. This holds presumably even more in a country like Switzerland, where cantons pre-existed the federal state; the Swiss federal state has historically been a bottom-up construction, with cantons delegating competences step by step to the confederation. In this respect, trust judgments of subnational political institutions are important in their relative relationship to trust judgments for national institutions (Hetherington and Nugent 2001; Roeder 1994; Schneider and Jacoby 2003; Schneider et al. 2010). If citizens' trust in national political institutions is very low, and trust in subnational institutions (e.g., cantonal institutions) is very high, citizens may start to question the legitimacy of the national institutions and, possibly, demand a shift of power and competences to the institutions of the order of government they trust the most.[4] Obviously, this could be accompanied by consequences regarding the cohesiveness of the federal state.

Conversely, if citizens ask for power transfers to the central government because of their comparably low trust in subnational political institutions, this could lead to a loss of regional identity. In general, empirical evidence for the United States indicates that trust in state and local government institutions is higher in comparison to trust in national government institutions (Hetherington and Nugent 2001, 137; Cole and Kincaid 2006; Conland 1993; Wolak 2010), with exceptions (Kincaid and Cole 2011). Surveys show that Canadians also have less trust in their federal government starting in 2002 compared to provincial and local governments, a finding that is reflected in survey data collected in Mexico for the year 2004 but not for the year 2009 (Kincaid and Cole 2011). In sum, a general pattern seems to emerge, although there are exceptions to this pattern.

Against this background, the development of political trust across time and space in Switzerland seems pivotal, and the following questions guide our contribution: Do trust judgments vary for different institutions on different federal levels? Has political trust changed over time? Are trust attitudes toward national and subnational institutions opposed to each other?

---

4. Scholars have investigated this phenomenon under the label of "support for devolution" (Hetherington and Nugent 2001). In this context devolution is understood as the shifting of responsibilities from the national level government to subnational institutions (Jennings 1998).

Switzerland: A Prototype of Decentralization and Cultural Diversity

During the world exhibition in 1992, visitors were greeted by Ben Vautier's famous motto "la Suisse n'existe pas" (Switzerland does not exist) at the official Suisse pavilion. Though a provocative assertion, this sentence conveys an element of truth because Switzerland is an extremely diverse country. Until the middle of the nineteenth century, Switzerland was neither a unified society nor a nation-state. It was composed of small societies with different ethnic backgrounds, languages, and religions that had become too limited to survive independently (Linder 1994, 36). Today, Switzerland is one of the most decentralized political systems in the world, in which the political institutions of the twenty-six cantons (and even municipalities) possess far-reaching competences (Lijphart 1999, 38). In almost no other country do the individual states dispose of such far-reaching competences and rights of self-determination as the twenty-six cantons in the Swiss federation. Cantonal autonomy in the framework of the Federal Constitution and the equal rights of the cantons, as well as their participation in federal decision-making and the duty to cooperate with the Federation and with each other, are regarded as the most important centrepieces of the Swiss political system. Switzerland is thus both a prime and an extreme example of a federal state (Fleiner 2006; Schmitt 2005; Vatter 2002).

Even though cantons have transferred many of their competences to the federal state during the last 150 years, they keep important powers in several policy domains, especially in the fields of health, education, and internal security (police and justice). In addition, and partly as a compensation for their loss of decision-making competences, they were granted increased competences with respect to the implementation of federal laws because of the Swiss "executive federalism" (Sciarini 2005).

It should also be mentioned that the Swiss federalism is truly symmetric in the sense that all cantons are granted the same rights and competences, irrespective of their size. Each canton is equally represented in the Council of States (*Ständerat*), the higher chamber of the Swiss parliament, with two seats for each canton (one for half-cantons). This institutional setting was deliberately meant to over-represent small cantons in decision-making and, therefore, protect minorities (Kriesi and Trechsel 2008). Similarly, any change in the distribution of competences between the federal state and the cantons must be approved by the double majority of people and cantons in a popular vote. This institutional setting considerably helped to win the support of political elites from small, Catholic cantons to the newly created federal state in the second half of the nineteenth century.

Therefore, it is not by coincidence that the late Karl Deutsch (1976) considered Switzerland as "a paradigmatic case of political integration" (see also Hug and Sciarini 1995). Successful political integration and the related development of consociationalism among political parties (Sciarini and Hug 1999) extended to the Swiss public. According to a widespread view, federalism—together with direct democracy and neutrality—has greatly contributed to the creation of a common sense of belonging among Swiss citizens, if not to a common national identity (Kriesi 1999; Sciarini et al. 2000).

Federalism allowed for the combination of two antagonistic principles; namely, unity and diversity. This feature has often been considered as the most typical element of the Swiss political system and political culture (Deutsch 1976; Linder 1994). Through the principle of subsidiarity, federalism left sufficient policy areas under the control of the cantonal authorities. This helped to defuse the potential for conflict between cultural subgroups (Sciarini and Hug 1999). Since this institutional arrangement allowed sufficient leeway for the different cultural entities to manage their internal affairs, it became a positive factor of integration and identity formation.

Although there are great similarities between the basic features of the federation's and the cantons' political decision-making structures and processes, and although the typical characteristics of Swiss politics, such as direct democracy and concordance, are particularly developed in the member states, there are also significant institutional differences between the federation and cantonal government systems (Vatter 2002, 2007). The cantons represent powerful entities not only politically but also in the minds of citizens. Thus, besides their national identity as "Swiss people," citizens have a strong feeling of belonging to their canton (Vatter 2002).

When asked with which level (commune, canton, linguistic region, country, Europe) they identify most, Swiss citizens first respond "the country" and second "the canton" (e.g., Kriesi et al. 1996, 55–6). This rank ordering holds for citizens from all three linguistic regions.

The most important institutional difference between the federation and the cantons is the procedure by which the government is elected. While the Federal Assembly (*Bundesversammlung*) elects the Federal Council (*Bundesrat*) for a legislative period of four years, the cantonal executives are elected directly by the people (Lutz and Strohmann

1998). Unlike the Federal Assembly, which consists of the National Council (*Nationalrat*) and Council of States (*Ständerat*), there is only one parliamentary chamber in the cantons. There is no second chamber to represent the interests of the lower sub-units (e.g., municipalities or districts), although communes—the third level of Swiss federalism—also play an important role in Swiss politics (Ladner 2009).

Popular rights (initiative and referendum) first originated in the cantons and have prevailed, particularly in German-speaking Switzerland, over the model of parliamentary democracy. Moreover, direct democracy is more strongly developed in the cantons than at the federal level. Compared to the federal Parliament, the cantonal parliaments occupy a relatively weak position *vis-à-vis* other political actors. In contrast to the governments, the cantonal parliaments continue to be only weakly professionalized (Bochsler et al. 2004, 29). When the cantonal legislatures are being appointed, the principle of proportional representation is the dominant electoral system (Lutz and Strohmann 1998). In most cantons, proportional representation applies to constituencies with more than one seat, which should, in principle, guarantee a distribution of seats that corresponds to the parties' electoral strength based on the number of listed votes. Today, Appenzell Innerrhoden and Graubünden are the only cantons that continue to elect popular representatives exclusively by majority election, although multiple-seat constituencies also exist in these cantons.

Besides being a strongly federalized country, Switzerland is culturally diverse. It is one of the few "old democracies," similarly to Belgium and Canada, that can be called a multilingual society (Stojanovic 2009, 10). However, the difference does not only lie in language but also in culture as the "Romansch-, Italian- and French-speaking minorities live within their own culture inside the boundaries of 'their' cantons" and the "notions about language can be extended to culture life in general" (Linder 1994, 22). Cultural differences are also reflected in differences in political behaviour between these regions (Linder 1994, 24).[5] In a nutshell, Switzerland's population may be divided along two relevant dimensions: institutional and cultural-linguistic (Hug and Sciarini 2002; Sciarini and Hug 1999). Accordingly, it is reasonable to scrutinize whether these subpopulations have differing views regarding both

---

5. Compared with the three bigger groups (German-speaking, French-speaking, Italian-speaking), the Romansch are considerably lower in numbers, and data for them is scarce. For this reason alone they are omitted from our empirical analyses.

national and subnational government institutions reflecting divergent economic, cultural, or political developments.

Data and Methods

For our analyses, we rely mostly on data from the Swiss Electoral Studies (SELECTS).[6] The survey contains trust questions for five different institutions (the Federal Council, the Parliament, political parties, cantonal authorities, and local authorities) over longer time periods and was administered every four years starting in 1995. The last wave was administered in 2011 (see Supplement 5.1 at end of chapter). In addition, to establish a comparative perspective, data from the European Social Survey (ESS) are used.

First, to compare levels of trust, we compute means for all individuals in Switzerland. Subsequently, we divide the sample and calculate averages for individuals belonging to cantonal as well as cultural-linguistic subgroups. To get a general idea of the level of political trust in Switzerland, we compare Swiss averages on different trust scales with other countries relying on the newest round of the European Social Survey. Second, to investigate time trends of trust for cantonal and cultural-linguistic subpopulations, we estimate multilevel models with time as sole predictor.[7] Here, we get a parameter describing the time trend for each subpopulation (cantonal as well as cultural-linguistic). Third, to investigate the relationship between trust judgments (trust scales) on the national and subnational orders of government, we simply compute correlations between these scales (again for different Swiss subpopulations). A positive correlation indicates that individuals having higher values on one trust scale also have higher values on another trust scale.

---

6. Swiss national election studies, cumulated data set 1971–2007 and data set for 2011. Distributed by FORS, Lausanne, http://www.selects.ch. SELECTS is the only study in Switzerland that provides data on trust in political institutions belonging to different federal levels over time.

7. In these models, trust in the respective institutions is the outcome variable, whereas time is the explanatory variable. The time trend is the coefficient for time on trust. Unfortunately, we have few data points for each canton/region (precisely four per canton, with the exception for trust in parties, where we have only data for three years per canton). Hence, estimating trends using the data of the single cantons would result in very imprecise estimations. Using a multilevel model allows for using the whole data (for all cantons and regions respectively) in the estimation of the trend coefficients. The statistical model is given by (Gelman and Hill 2007, 237), a linear model in which both intercept and slope vary by group.

Empirical Analyses

Figure 5.1 displays the evolution of trust averages across all individuals in the Swiss sample since 1995. Several things are notable. First, citizens clearly differentiate in their trust judgments regarding different institutions.[8] Second, local and cantonal institutions in the federal system (especially on local institutions) seem to elicit more positive trust judgments. However, while trust in local authorities is highest for the whole period, we find that trust in cantonal authorities also drops below trust in the Federal Council at some point. Third, trust in subnational institutions seems to have been lower in 1995 and 1999. This could be potentially explained by the economic crisis in Switzerland between 1992 and 1998 (Freitag 2000). Fourth, between 1995 and 2011 there was an increase in trust in local and cantonal authorities as well as in the national Parliament. During the same period, trust in the Federal Council decreased for most of the time but then increased again in 2011. Furthermore, trust in parties has been generally lower than trust in other institutions, a finding that seems to be universal across countries and may be explained by the fact that parties, in comparison with other institutions, are perceived to pursue their own interests (Freitag 2014). Nevertheless, from a general point of view, considering the scales (Figure 5.1 only depicts a part of the scale from 0 to 10), the changes in trust seem to be rather small.

From a comparative perspective, Switzerland shows relatively high values of political trust (see Figure 5.2). Within Europe, only respondents from Scandinavia and the Netherlands reveal trust judgments of similar height regarding the national parliament, the legal system, the police, politicians, and parties. Compared to their neighbours—the French, Italians, and Germans—the Swiss trust their political institutions to a higher degree.

Obviously, these averages across the complete Swiss sample may obscure differences between individuals belonging to different cantons and linguistic-cultural regions. Accordingly, in a next step, we take a closer look at the levels and development of trust for individuals belonging to different cantons as well as language regions. This also allows us to assess whether levels and trends of trust in these Swiss subpopulations strongly deviate from the aggregated means and trends above.

---

8. Hibbing and Theiss-Morse (1995) have strongly argued for this point before.

Figure 5.1

Swiss Means of Political Trust Across Time

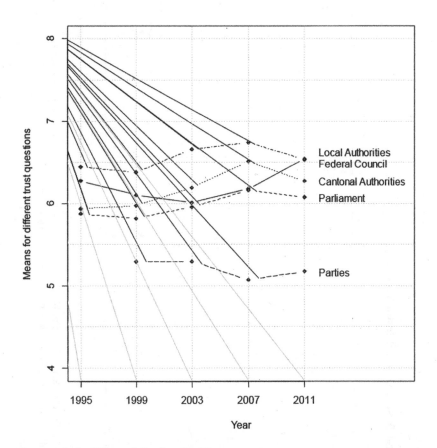

Source: Swiss Electoral Studies (2007).

In the first instance, we focus on the average trust levels of individuals belonging to the different cantons for the year 2011. Figure 5.3 demonstrates several important aspects. First, in 2011, cantonal means of individual-level trust for subnational institutions are, on average, of

Figure 5.2

Country Averages of Political Trust in Different Institutions (2010)

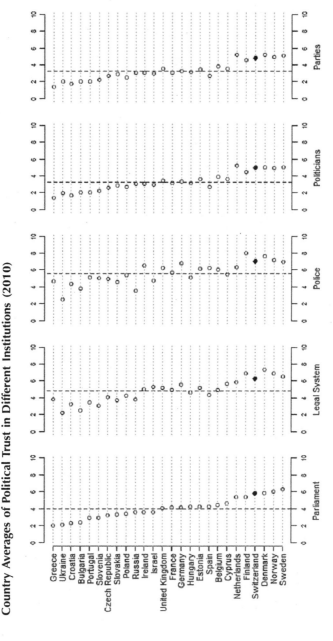

Note: Data = European Social Survey, Round 5; points = country averages; dashed line = average across country means; due to their small size (smaller than circle) confidence intervals are omitted.

Source: Authors' compilation.

Figure 5.3

Cantonal Averages of Political Trust in Different Institutions in 2011

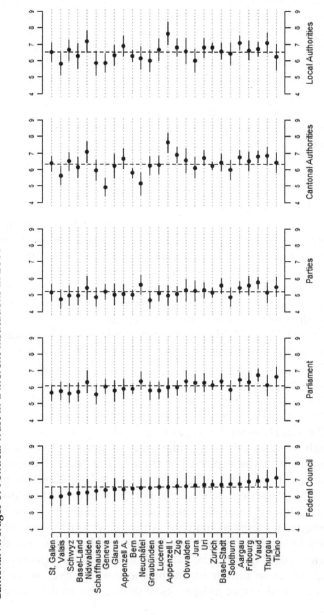

Note: Data = SELECTS 2011; points = means; black bars = 95% confidence intervals (see footnote 7); dashed line = average across cantonal means.

Source: Authors' compilation.

similar height as for the Federal Council; however, they are higher than the means for trust in Parliament and parties. Hence, in 2011, the Federal Council seems to be endowed with as much trust as its subnational counterparts, although this is a recent development. Analyses for 2007 (not shown here) show that this was not the case before. As might be concluded from Figure 5.1, trust in subnational institutions was higher than trust in national institutions in 2007. Second, it is apparent that the variation regarding trust in cantonal and local institutions is much higher than the variation of trust in the Federal Council, as well as in Parliament and in parties. This result is less of a surprise, considering that in the case of the national institutions, respondents all evaluate the "same" political object. Third, referring to local and cantonal authorities, the results indicate that in some cantons, citizens judge their respective cantonal and local authorities as less trustworthy than do citizens of other cantons. For instance, whereas Appenzell Innerhoden has a very high average, several cantons have much lower scores. One possible explanation lies in the varying strength of direct democratic institutions across cantons (Bauer & Fatke 2014). Appenzell Innerhoden is an exemplary case of strong direct democratic institutions, and, in general, direct democracy is stronger in German-speaking cantons.

However, by and large, cantons lie relatively close to each other ranging between the scores of 5 and 8. Internationally comparative data show that already values of 5 are relatively high.

In a next step, Figure 5.4 displays estimated trends of trust for populations of single cantons between 1995 and 2007. As one might expect, the trends vary more strongly for cantonal and local institutions than for national institutions. Although the average trend (dashed lines) in trust is rising for subnational institutions, there is considerable heterogeneity regarding overall levels (we have seen that already in Figure 5.3 for 2011) as well as regarding the development of trust.

Although we are primarily interested in general tendencies, we marked outliers in these plots. For trust in the Federal Council and the Parliament (Figure 5.4, Plot 1 and 2), trends seem stable and no cantonal subgroups deviate strongly. For trust in cantonal authorities (Figure 5.4, Plot 3), Neuchâtel and Geneva deviate from the overall trend. Here, trust seems to stagnate. Although characterized by different starting levels for most of the other cantonal populations, there is a slight increase in trust in the cantonal authorities. Appenzell Innerhoden represents an outlier regarding the starting level as well as its positive trend in the trust judgments of its citizens. In the case of trust

Figure 5.4

Trends of Trust in Single Cantons

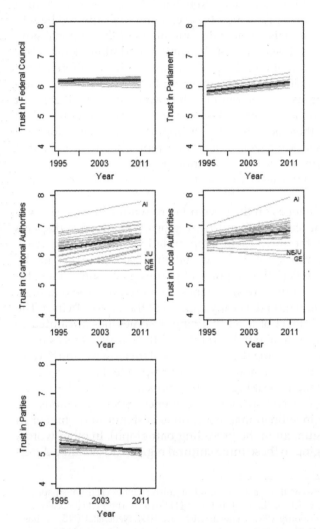

Note: Estimated trends for data points from 1995 to 2011 (1999 to 2011 for parties); black line is the average trend; grey lines are estimated trends for single cantons.

Source: Authors' compilation.

in local institutions (Figure 5.4, Plot 4), there are even cantons where we can observe slightly negative trends, such as Neuchâtel and Geneva. An explanation for the comparatively substandard performance of the French-speaking cantons (especially Neuchâtel, Jura, and Geneva) may lie in the fact that, during the 2000s, these cantons were affected by several "affairs" or "scandals" concerning members of the cantonal government or senior civil servants of the cantonal administration. This, together with the fact that French-speaking cantons have suffered more from economic recession, unemployment, and public deficits than German speaking-cantons, may account for the lower level of political trust toward cantonal and local authorities over the years (see Figure 5.4). In general, however, there is a positive development, and again, for local political authorities, Appenzell Innerhoden represents an outlier that strongly deviates in the positive direction. Finally, there is a decreasing trend for trust in parties, which seems to be relatively homogenous across cantons.

In a next step, we focus on the development within and across Switzerland's different cultural-linguistic regions.[9] Figure 5.5 displays trust averages for the three main subpopulations for 2007 (i.e., German-speaking, French-speaking, and Italian-speaking). Trust in the Federal Council, the Parliament, political parties, and cantonal institutions (but not in local authorities) is highest for individuals belonging to the Italian-speaking region (basically citizens of the canton Ticino). The comparatively high level of trust in Ticino is sometimes attributed to the fact that the Ticinesi take Italy and its political institutions as reference categories when judging the institutions of their own country (Freitag 2001, 105). Due to the small number of respondents, however, the estimates for the Italian-speaking region come with considerable uncertainty. Comparing German-speaking and French-speaking regions, we observe that trust in subnational institutions is significantly higher in the former (see argument in the preceding paragraph). In other words, individuals belonging to these three cultural regions do evaluate differ-

---

9. We differentiate between three main cultural-linguistic regions. The Italian-speaking region solely consists of the canton Tessin (TI/Ticino). The French-speaking region consists of Fribourg (FR), Geneva (GE), Jura (JU), Neuchâtel (NE), Valais (VS), and Vaud (VD). The German-speaking region consists of Aargau (AG), Appenzell Ausserrhoden (AR), Appenzell Innerrhoden (AI), Basel-Land (BL), Basel-Stadt (BS), Bern (BE), Glarus (GL), Graubünden (GR), Lucerne (LU), Nidwalden (NW), Obwalden (OW), Schaffhausen (SH), Schwyz (SZ), Solothurn (SO), St. Gallen (SG), Thurgau (TG), Uri (UR), Zug (ZG), and Zurich (ZH).

ent institutions differently on average. Nevertheless, the differences in the averages are rather small, certainly smaller than in the case of cantonal populations. Just as for cantons, these differences could be due to institutional differences (Freitag 2000, 191). German-speaking regions have very extensive direct-democracy procedures, whereas French- and Italian-speaking cantons are more strongly oriented toward the ideal type of a pure representative democracy with a restricted access to direct democratic instruments (Stadelmann-Steffen and Freitag 2011, 534–5).

Figure 5.6 reveals the trends of political trust for the populations of these cultural-linguistic regions. Again, the overall aggregate trend for the Swiss population partly obscures deviant regional developments in political trust. Although the trends seem relatively stable for trust in the Federal Council (and the Parliament), with respect to trust in cantonal institutions the citizens of the German- and Italian-speaking regions display positive trends whereas members of the French-speaking region do not (Figure 5.6). The same is true of trust in local institutions in which there seems to be a rise of trust mainly among individuals belonging to the German-speaking region. For parties, we do note a clear decrease for the Italian-speaking region and a less strong decrease for the German-speaking region.

As argued before, political trust should be of importance for the stability of federal states when there are converse attitudes toward the institutions of the federal system's different orders of government. As mentioned, negative correlations between the respective attitudinal scales indicate that negative views regarding national institutions (low trust) correspond to positive views regarding subnational institutions (high trust) or vice versa. In general, we would assume that trust in national political institutions should be low if citizens (or groups of citizens) perceive that those institutions are performing badly or are acting against the public (or the respective citizen's) interest (Mishler and Rose 2001). Thus, we would expect large differences in trust judgments of national and subnational institutions if citizens or groups of citizens perceive that subnational institutions perform very well and are taking care of their interests in contrast to national institutions or vice versa.

We examine correlations between all trust scales for each survey year, for the whole Swiss sample as well as subsamples of individuals belonging to different cultural-linguistic regions as well as individuals belonging to the single cantons. For the Swiss sample, we do not find any negative correlations (not reported here). However, it may well be

Figure 5.5

Averages of Political Trust in Different Institutions Across Cultural-Linguistic Regions in 2011

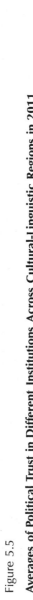
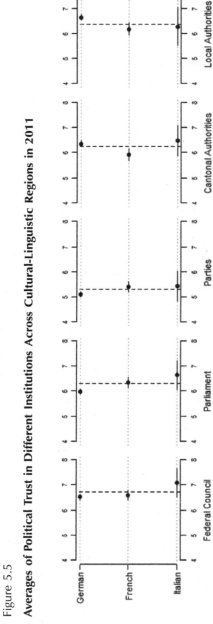

Note: Data = SELECTS 2007, trust scales from 0 to 10 where 0 = and 10 = points = means; bars = 95% confidence intervals (see footnote 7); dashed line = mean of regional means.

Source: Authors' compilation.

Figure 5.6

Trends of Trust in Single Regions

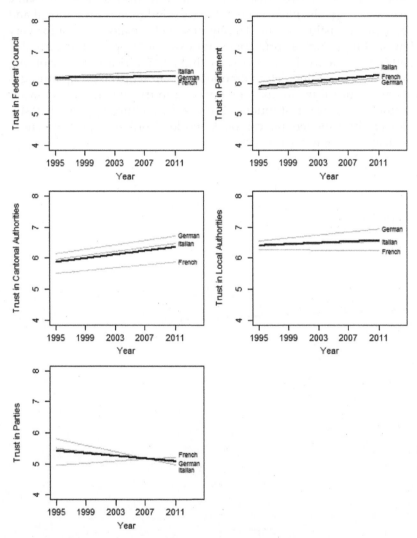

Note: Estimated trends for data from 1995 to 2011 (1999 to 2011 for parties); black line is the average trend; grey lines are estimated trends for single regions.

Source: Authors' compilation.

that only the populations of certain federal entities display such converse trust judgments. Figure 5.7 and Figure 5.8 show correlations for the different subgroups of the Swiss population. Each point represents the correlation of two trust scales that were measured in the same year. These graphs illustrate that the trust judgments for national and subnational institutions are largely positively related, except for very few slightly negative correlations, for example Appenzell Innerhoden and Glarus. Hence, in summary, we find no empirical evidence of cantonal or cultural-linguistic subpopulations in which trusting attitudes toward national institutions are opposed to trusting attitudes toward cantonal and local institutions. The overall picture suggests that attitudes toward the federal, cantonal, and local orders of government in Switzerland are not in conflict.

Figure 5.7

Correlations between Trust Scales for Different Years in Cantonal Subpopulations

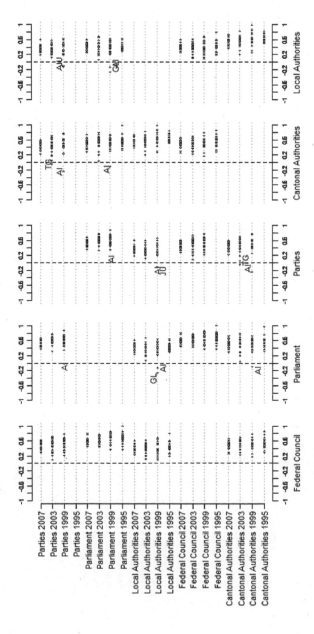

Note: Each point = correlation for a specific year (indicated on the y-axis) between the scale indicated on the x-axis and the scale indicated on the y-axis. One point for each cantonal subpopulation; dashed line = 0 line.

Data: SELECTS 1995–2011.

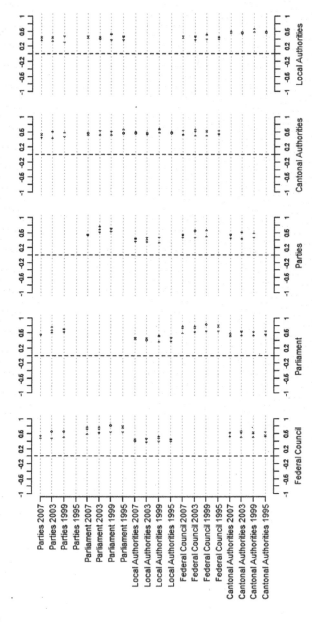

Figure 5.8

Correlations between Trust Scales for Different Years in Cultural-Linguistic Subpopulations

Note: Each point = correlation for a specific year (indicated on the y-axis) between the scale indicated on the x-axis and the scale indicated on the y-axis. One point for each regional subpopulation; dashed line = 0 line.

Data: SELECTS 1995–2011.

Summary and Conclusions

Several conclusions can be drawn from our analysis of the development of political trust in Switzerland. First, compared to other European countries, trust in political institutions is generally high in Switzerland. Similarly, cantonal and cultural-linguistic subpopulations trust their different national and subnational institutions. Moreover, aside from a few exceptions, trust averages were relatively stable between 1995 and 2011, for national political institutions but also for subnational institutions. In other words, Swiss federal, cantonal, and local political institutions seem to be relatively successful in maintaining citizens' trust. To put it differently, Switzerland seems to be a country that is relatively successful in satisfying the demands of citizens belonging to its different federal and cultural-linguistic subnational entities. What are possible explanations for this result?

Institutional theories hold that political trust is endogenous and a consequence of the political and economic performance of governments (Mishler and Rose 2001). Following this rationale, the relatively positive trust judgments in Switzerland would simply reflect the public's perceptions that the political institutions investigated are perceived to perform relatively well. As already mentioned, federalism has substantially contributed to Switzerland's peaceful and successful integration process, by helping to achieve both "unity and diversity" and, therefore, helping to increase citizens' trust in, and identification with, the overall institutional architecture (Sciarini et al. 2000; Fleiner and Hertig 2010). The successful reform of Swiss federalism, which was accepted by an overwhelming majority of the Swiss people and nearly all cantons in a popular vote in 2004 (Braun 2009; Cappelletti et al. 2013), can only strengthen federalism as an institutional cornerstone of the Swiss democracy and further reinforce the strength of citizens' attachment to federalism.[10] Moreover, Swiss subnational entities are characterized by a relatively homogenous economic performance and correspondingly a relatively low need for significant inter-regional transfers. This could further explain Swiss citizens' high esteem of federal-level institutions and the fact that attitudinal variance across cantonal authorities is not all that high. Relatedly, there were no dra-

---

10. This far-reaching reform resulted in the adoption of a fully new fiscal equalization scheme and in a new tasks distribution between the federal state and the cantons, as well as in a strengthening of cooperative federalism between cantons.

matic changes in economic performance between the years 1995 and 2011, which potentially explains the relatively stable trends.

Another decisive factor that is linked to institutional performance could be the strength of direct democracy in Switzerland. Stojanovic (2009) argues along the following lines. First, direct democracy enables minorities to place their concerns on the political agenda at various levels of the political system. Popular rights may operate as a "voice" that reduces the danger of mistrust (i.e., lack of confidence in political institutions). Second, direct democracy facilitates the creation of a common *demos* because referenda and the ensuing affirmations of politicians ("the Swiss people has decided") increase the feeling of belonging to a unified Swiss nation (see also Kriesi 1999; Sciarini et al. 2000). Third, direct democracy fosters horizontal integration by reinforcing cross-linguistic dialogues as well as the flow of political views and opinions from one language region to the other. Strong popular rights are supposed to counter developments that might endanger a federation, particularly the disregard of the demands of certain parts of the population that would lead to lower trust in national political institutions. There also is some empirical evidence that the variation we find across cantons and regions can be explained by the prevalence of direct democracy in these entities (Bauer and Fatke 2014).

Second, with exceptions, there seems to be a pattern that trust in subnational (especially local) institutions is higher than trust in national institutions. One reason could be that cantonal or local institutions are perceived to perform better than their national counterparts. Also, respondents may display more trust because they perceive that these institutions are closer to them and their daily lives.[11] Finally, Jennings (1998, 239–40) argues that trust in the national government is related to evaluations of performance, whereas trust judgments concerning subnational governments are based on perceptions of access, accountability, and responsiveness.

Third, we found that trust attitudes for the regional subpopulations are not converse; that is, low (or high) trust in national institutions is not countered by opposing attitudes for subnational institutions. Such

---

11. Nevertheless, referring to the questions one must note that they are not strictly comparable between the different levels. For subnational institutions, respondents were asked if they trust the "cantonal/local authorities." Potentially, respondents think of the cantonal/local administrations in this case, institutions that they might have more faith in them than in political institutions such as the government.

opposing attitudes that might lead to calls for devolution and challenges to the legitimacy of national institutions and the federation seem rare in Switzerland. However, it should be noted that our approach in this study was descriptive and exploratory. To understand the dynamics of political trust in federal political systems, we need more empirical research that explores political trust in national and subnational institutions across cultural contexts.

Supplement 5.1

Trust Questions in the SELECTS Data Set Over Survey Years

1995   I will now read some important public authorities of Switzerland to you. Please indicate each time how much trust you have in the respective institutions, if 0 means "no trust" and 10 "complete trust."
Swiss Federal Council
Parliament (National Council, Council of States)
Political authorities of your canton
Political authorities of your commune

Ich lese Ihnen jetzt einige wichtige Instanzen in der Schweiz vor. Bitte sagen Sie mir jedesmal, wie stark Sie der Institution vertrauen, wenn 0 "kein Vertrauen" und 10 "volles Vertrauen" heisst.
Bundesrat
Parlament (Nationalrat, Staenderat)
Behörden von Ihrem Kanton
Behörden von Ihrer Wohngemeinde

1999   I will now read some important public authorities of Switzerland to you. Please indicate each time how much trust you have in the respective institutions, if 0 means "no trust" and 10 "complete trust."
Swiss Federal Council
Parliament (National Council, Council of States)
Political parties on the national level
Political authorities of your canton
Political authorities of your commune

Ich lese Ihnen jetzt einige wichtige Institutionen in der Schweiz vor. Bitte sagen Sie mir jedesmal, wie stark Sie der Institution vertrauen, wenn 0 "kein Vertrauen" und 10 "volles Vertrauen" heisst.
Bundesrat
Parlament (Nationalrat, Ständerat)
Die politischen Parteien auf nationaler Ebene
Behörden von Ihrem Kanton
Behörden von Ihrer Wohngemeinde

Supplement 5.1, continued

Trust Questions in the SELECTS Data Set Over Survey Years

2003   I will now read some important public authorities of Switzerland
        to you. Please indicate each time how much trust you have in the
        respective institutions, if 0 means "no trust" and 10 "complete
        trust."
        Swiss Federal Council
        Parliament (National Council, Council of States)
        Political parties on the national level
        Political authorities of your canton
        Political authorities of your commune

        Ich lese Ihnen jetzt einige wichtige Institutionen in der Schweiz
        vor. Bitte sagen Sie mir jedesmal, wie stark Sie der Institution ver-
        trauen, wenn 0 "kein Vertrauen" und 10 "volles Vertrauen" heisst.
        Bundesrat
        Parlament (Nationalrat, Ständerat)
        Die politischen Parteien auf nationaler Ebene
        Behörden von Ihrem Kanton
        Behörden von Ihrer Wohngemeinde

2007   I will now read some important public authorities of Switzerland
        to you. Please indicate each time how much trust you have in the
        respective institutions, if 0 means "no trust" and 10 "complete
        trust."
        Swiss Federal Council
        Parliament (National Council, Council of States)
        Political parties on the national level
        Political authorities of your canton
        Political authorities of your commune

        Ich lese Ihnen jetzt einige wichtige Institutionen in der Schweiz
        vor. Bitte sagen Sie mir jedesmal, wie stark Sie der Institution ver-
        trauen, wenn 0 "kein Vertrauen" und 10 "volles Vertrauen" heisst.
        Bundesrat
        Parlament (Nationalrat, Ständerat)
        Die politischen Parteien auf nationaler Ebene
        Behörden von Ihrem Kanton
        Behörden von Ihrer Wohngemeinde

Supplement 5.1, continued

Trust Questions in the SELECTS Data Set Over Survey Years

2011   Please state how much trust on a scale from 0 to 10 you have in
          the following institutions or organizations.
          Swiss Federal Council
          Parliament (National Council, Council of States)
          Political parties on the national level
          Political authorities of your canton
          Political authorities of your commune

          Bitte sagen Sie wie stark Sie den folgenden Institutionen und Orga-
          nisationen auf einer Skala von 0-10 vertrauen.
          Bundesrat
          Parlament (Nationalrat, Ständerat)
          Die politischen Parteien auf nationaler Ebene
          Behörden von Ihrem Kanton
          Behörden von Ihrer Wohngemeinde

Note: Data source is the Swiss national election studies, cumulated file 1971–
2007 [data set], distributed by FORS, Lausanne, 2010. http://www.selects.ch.

References

Bauer, Paul C. 2017. "Conceptualizing Trust and Trustworthiness." *Working Paper*. 9 February. http://dx.doi.org/10.2139/ssrn.2325989.

Bauer, Paul C., and Markus Freitag. 2017. "Measuring Trust." In *Handbook of Social and Political Trust*, edited by Eric M. Uslaner. Oxford: Oxford University Press.

Bauer, Paul C., and Matthias Fatke. 2014. "Direct Democracy and Political Trust: Enhancing Trust, Initiating Distrust—Or Both?" *Swiss Political Science Review* 20 (1): 49–69.

Braun, Dietmar. 2009. "Constitutional Change in Switzerland." *Publius: The Journal of Federalism* 39 (2): 314–40.

Bochsler, Daniel, Christophe Koller, Pascal Sciarini, Sylvie Traimond, and Ivar Trippolini. 2004. *Die Schweizer Kantone unter der Lupe: Behörden, Personal, Finanzen*. Bern: Paul Haupt.

Brunner, Matthias, and Lea Sgier. 1997. "Crise de confiance dans les institutions politiques suisses? Quelques résultats d'une enquête d'opinion." *Swiss Political Science Review* 3 (1): 1–9.

Cappelletti, Fabio, M. Fischer, and Pascal Sciarini. 2009. "'Let's Talk Cash': Cantons' Interests and the Reform of Swiss Federalism." *Regional and Federal Studies* 24 (1): 1–20.

Chanley, Virginia A., Thomas J. Rudolph, and Wendy M. Rahn. 2000. "The Origins and Consequences of Public Trust in Government: A Time Series Analysis." *Public Opinion Quarterly* 64 (3): 239–56.

Cole, Richard L., and John Kincaid. 2006. "Public Opinion on U.S. Federal and Intergovernmental Issues in 2006: Continuity and Change." *Publius: The Journal of Federalism* 36 (3): 443–59.

Deutsch, Karl W. 1976. Die Schweiz als ein paradigmatischer Fall politischer Integration, Bern: Haupt Verlag.

Fleiner, Thomas. 2006. "Swiss Confederation." In *Distribution of Powers and Responsibilities in Federal Countries*, edited by Akhtar Majeed, Ronald L. Watts, and Douglas M. Brown, 265–94. Montreal & Kingston: McGill-Queen's University Press.

Fleiner, Thomas, and Maya Hertig. 2010. "Swiss Confederation." In *Diversity and Unity in Federal Countries*, edited by Luis Moreno and César Colino, 320–48. Montreal & Kingston: McGill-Queen's University Press.

———. 2000. "Soziales Kapital und Arbeitslosigkeit: Eine empirische Analyse zu den Schweizer Kantonen." *Zeitschrift für Soziologie* 29 (3): 186–201.

————. 2011. "Das soziale Kapital der Schweiz: Vergleichende Einschätzungen zu Aspekten des Vertrauens und der sozialen Einbindung." Swiss Political Science Review 7 (4): 87–117.

————. 2014. "Politische Kultur." In Handbuch der Schweizer Politik 5, edited by Peter Knoepfel, Pascal Sciarini, Yannis Papadopoulos, Adrian Vatter, and Silja Häusermann, 71–94. Zürich: NZZ Verlag.

Freitag, Markus, and Isabelle Stadelmann-Steffen. 2008. "Schweizer Welten der Freiwilligkeit: Das freiwillige Engagement der Schweiz im sprachregionalen Kontext." In Sozialbericht, edited by Christian Suter, Silvia Perrenoud, René Levy, Ursina Kuhn, Dominique Joye, and Pascale Gazareth, 170–90. Zürich: Seismo.

Hardin, Russell. 2002. Trust and Trustworthiness. New York: Russell Sage.

Hetherington, Marc J. 1998. "The Political Relevance of Political Trust." American Political Science Review 92 (4): 791–80.

————. 2005. Why Trust Matters: Declining Political Trust and the Demise of American Liberalism. Princeton, NJ: Princeton University Press.

Hetherington, Marc J., and Jason A. Husser. 2012. "How Trust Matters: The Changing Political Relevance of Political Trust." American Journal of Political Science 56 (2): 312–32.

Hetherington, Marc J., and Suzanne Globetti. 2002. "Political Trust and Racial Policy Preferences." American Journal of Political Science 46 (2): 253–75.

Hetherington, Marc J., and John D. Nugent. 2001. "Explaining Public Support for Devolution: The Role of Political Trust." In What is it About Government that Americans Dislike? edited by John R. Hibbing and Elizabeth Theiss-Morse, 134–51. New York: Cambridge University Press.

Hibbing, John R., and Elizabeth Theiss-Morse. 1995. Congress as Public Enemy: Public Attitudes toward American Political Institutions. Cambridge: Cambridge University Press.

Hug, Simon, and Pascal Sciarini. 1995. "Switzerland—Still a Paradigmatic Case?" In Towards a New Europe: Stops and Starts in Regional Integration, edited by Gerald Schneider, Patricia Weitsman, and Thomas Bernauer, 55–74. New York: Praeger/Greenwood.

————. 2002. Changements de valeurs et nouveaux clivages politiques en Suisse. Paris: L'Harmattan.

Jennings, M. Kent. 1998. "Political Trust and the Roots of Devolution." In Trust and Governance, edited by Valerie Braithwaite and Margaret Levi, 218–44. New York: Russell Sage Foundation.

Kincaid, John, and Richard L. Cole. 2010. "Citizen Attitudes Toward

Issues of Federalism in Canada, Mexico, and the United States." *Publius: The Journal of Federalism* 4 (1): 53–75.

Kriesi, Hanspeter. 1999. "Introduction: State Formation and Nation Building in the Swiss Case." In *Nation and National Identity: The European Experience in Perspective*, edited by Hanspeter Kriesi, Klaus Armingeon, Hannes Siegrist, and Andreas Wimmer, 13–28. Chur: Rüegger.

Kriesi, Hanspeter, and Alexander H. Trechsel. 2008. *The Politics of Switzerland: Continuity and Change in a Consensus Democracy*. Cambridge: Cambridge University Press.

Kriesi, Hanspeter, Borsi Wernli, Pascal Sciarini, and Matteo Gianni. 1996. *Le clivage linguistique. Problèmes de compréhension entre les communautés linguistiques en Suisse*. Bern: Bundesamt für Statistik.

Kriesi, Hanspeter, Peter Selb, Romain Lachat, Simon Bornschier, and Marc Helbling. 2005. *Der Aufstieg der SVP. Acht Kantone im Vergleich*. Zürich: NZZ-Verlag.

Kymlicka, Will. 2003. "Multicultural States and Intercultural Citizens." *Theory and Research in Education* 1 (2): 147–69.

Lachat, Roman, and Peter Selb. 2010. "Strategic Overshooting in National Council Elections." *Swiss Political Science Review* 16 (3): 481–98.

Ladner, Andreas. 2009. "Swiss Confederation." In *Local Government and Metroploitan Governance in Federal Systems*, edited by Nico Steytler, 329–62. Montreal and Kingston: McGill-Queen's University Press.

Levi, Margaret, and Laura Stoker. 2000. "Political Trust and Trustworthiness." *Annual Review of Political Science* 3 (1): 475–507.

Linder, Wolf. 1994. *Swiss Democracy: Possible Solutions to Conflict in Multicultural Societies*. Houndsmill: Macmillan.

Lutz, Georg, and Dirk Strohmann. 1998. *Wahl- und Abstimmungsrecht in den Kantonen*. Bern: Paul Haupt.

Marien, Sofie, and Marc Hooghe. 2011. "Does Political Trust Matter? An Empirical Investigation into the Relation between Political rust and Support for Law Compliance." *European Journal of Political Research* 50 (2): 267–91.

Mishler, William, and Richard Rose. 2001. "What Are the Origins of Political Trust? Testing Institutional and Cultural Theories in Post-communist Societies." *Comparative Political Studies* 34 (1): 30–62.

Roeder, Phillip W. 1994. *Public Opinion and Policy Leadership in the American States*. Tuscaloosa: University of Alabama Press.

Rudolph, Thomas J., and Jillian Evans. "Political Trust, Ideology, and Public Support for Government Spending." *American Journal of Polit-*

ical Science 49 (3): 660–71.

Scheidegger, Régis, and Christian Staerklé. "Political Trust and Distrust in Switzerland: A Normative Analysis." *Swiss Political Science Review* 17 (2): 164–87.

Schmitt, Nicholas. 2005. "Swiss Confederation." In *Constitutional Origins, Structure, and Change in Federal Countries,* edited by John Kincaid and G. Alan Tarr, 347–80. Montreal and Kingston: McGill-Queen's University Press.

Schneider, Saundra K., and William G. Jacoby. 2003. "Public Attitudes toward the Policy Responsibilities of the National and State Governments: Evidence from South Carolina." *State Politics and Policy Quarterly* 3 (3): 246–69.

Schneider, Saundra K., William G. Jacoby, and Daniel C. Lewis. 2010. "Public Opinion toward Intergovernmental Policy Responsibilities." *Publius: The Journal of Federalism* 41 (1): 1–30.

Sciarini, Pascal. 2005. "Le centralisme et les pouvoirs cantonaux: quelles évolutions?" In *Fédéralisme et centralisation: L'expérience suisse et les nouveaux défis européens,* edited by Oscar Mazzoleni, 101–25. Lugano: Casagrande.

Sciarini, Pascal, and Simon Hug. 1999. "The Odd Fellow: Consociationalism and Parties in Switzerland." In *Party Elites in Divided Societies: Political Elites in Consociational Democracy,* edited by Kurt R. Luther and Kris Deschouwer, 134–62. London: Routledge.

Sciarini, Pascal, Simon Hug, and Cedric Dupont. 2000. "Example, Exception or Both? Swiss National Identity in Perspective." In *Constructing Europe's Identity: The External Dimension,* edited by Lars-Erik Cedermann, 57–88. Boulder, CO: Lynne Rienner.

Stadelmann-Steffen, Isabelle, and Markus Freitag. 2011. "Making Civil Society Work: Models of Democracy and Their Impact on Civic Engagement." *Nonprofit and Voluntary Sector Quarterly* 40 (3): 526–51.

Steiner, Jürg. 2001. "Switzerland and the European Union: A Puzzle." In *Minority Nationalism and the Changing International Order,* edited by Michael Keating and John McGarry, 137–54. Oxford: Oxford University Press.

Stojanović, Nenad. 2009. "Is Democracy Possible in a Multilingual Country? The Swiss Experience and the Paradox of Direct Democracy." In *Public Opinion in a Multilingual Society. Institutional Design and Federal Loyalty,* edited by Dave Sinardet and Marc Hooghe, 9–22. Brussels: Rethinking Belgium.

Sztompka, Piotr. *Trust: A Sociological Theory.* Cambridge: Cambridge

University Press, 1999.

Vatter, Adrian. 2002. *Kantonale Demokratien im Vergleich: Entstehungs-gründe, Interaktionen und Wirkungen politischer Institutionen in den Schweizer Kantonen.* Opladen: Leske und Budrich.

———. 2007. "The Cantons." In *Handbook of Swiss Politics,* edited by Ulrich Klöti, Peter Knoepfel, Hans-Peter Kriesi, Wolf Linder, Yannis Papadopoulos, and Pascal Sciarini, 197–224. Zuerich: NZZ-Verlag.

Widmer, Eric, and Ivan de Carlo. 2010. "Why Do the Swiss Trust Their Government Less and Other People More Than They Used To? The Impact of Cohorts and Periods on Political Confidence and Interpersonal Trust in Switzerland." In *Value Change in Switzerland,* edited by Simon Hug and Hanspeter Kriesi, 171–90. Lanham: Lexington Books.

6

Attachments to Multiple Communities, Trust in Governments, Political Polarization, and Public Attitudes Toward Immigration in the United States

John Kincaid and Richard L. Cole

The United States is experiencing considerable political turmoil and polarization, as well as historically low public trust in the federal government—all of which preceded the 2016 election of Donald Trump to the presidency. This turmoil was displayed in the 2016 presidential contests that brought nativist, populist forces to the fore and highlighted race as a divisive issue. Polarization in particular has had several impacts on the federal system, including the displacement of Congress by presidents and the Supreme Court in shaping federalism and a weakening of the leverage of the states because of partisan polarization between states.

Yet, at the same time, Americans express high levels of trust in their local and state governments and high levels of attachment to, first, the English language, then to their country, their state, their city, their ethnic and ancestral group, the world, their neighbourhood, and their religious group, in that order. Americans express more ambivalent attitudes about immigrants, although survey responses are coloured by long-standing controversies about illegal immigration. Even so, majorities of Americans support immigration and are receptive to immigrant

Identities, Trust, and Cohesion in Federal Systems: Public Perceptions, edited by Jack Jedwab and John Kincaid. Montréal and Kingston: McGill-Queen's University Press, Queen's Policy Studies Series. © 2018 The School of Policy Studies, Queen's University at Kingston. All rights reserved.

contributions to American society.

The following analysis relies in part on 2010 data collected by the Association for Canadian Studies of a representative sample of the US population, as well as populations in Canada, Germany, and Spain. These data are supplemented by more recent surveys and social science analyses examining the subject matters of this chapter.

Attachments to Country, State, and Locality

Americans report high levels of "attachment" to the United States, their home state or region, and their city or town (see Table 6.1). However, their attachments to these political communities are the opposite of their evaluations of the governments of these communities. Even though Americans trust the federal government least, local governments the most, and state governments substantially more than the federal government (see below), 91 percent of respondents in the 2010 survey reported being very or somewhat attached to the United States (see Table 6.1), while just about 80 percent were so attached to their state and nearly 74 percent so attached to their city or town. Two-thirds reported being very or somewhat attached to their neighbourhood.

At the same time, 44 percent of Americans consider themselves as being from their country only, 26 percent from their country but also their state, and 18 percent equally from their country and state. Only 53 percent believe "it is a problem for American unity when people have a state identity that is stronger than their national identity" (results not shown in tables).

These patterns are not surprising. Americans have long distinguished country from government. Attachment to country (and also the US Constitution) remains extraordinarily high even when most Americans believe the government in power is ruining the country. At least since 1742, when the prominent preacher Jonathan Edwards called for "an agreement of all God's people in America" and for a union based on "love of the brethren" (Niebuhr and Heimert 1963: 16–17), political leaders have emphasized affection for country (not "nation" or "state") and the Constitution as the creedal foundations of an American identity forged in a melting pot (Zangwill 1909). Despite the considerable ethnic, religious, and linguistic diversity that existed in revolutionary America, the Declaration of Independence of 1776 spoke of "one people" dissolving "the political bands which have connected them with another"; the preamble to the US Constitution speaks of "We the People

Table 6.1

Level of Attachment to Various Communities

Attachment to:	Very	Somewhat	Not very	Not at all	No response
English language	74.6	19.3	3.9	1.0	1.0
Country	66.9	24.5	5.2	1.7	1.6
State/region	39.7	40.1	13.5	5.0	1.8
City/town	32.9	40.8	18.9	5.8	1.5
Ethnic/ancestral	34.2	34.9	19.9	8.2	2.8
The world	26.5	41.1	23.5	5.9	3.0
Neighbourhood	27.5	38.5	24.0	9.5	1.6
Religious group	31.8	23.7	18.4	19.5	6.7

Note: Responses ranked by degree of "very" or "somewhat" attached, so that highest level of attachment is shown to be the "English language," lowest is shown to be "religious group."

Source: Association for Canadian Studies (2010).

of the United States," not we the peoples of different states; and in *Federalist* 2, for example, John Jay, echoing Edwards, referred to Americans as a "band of brethren, united to each other by the strongest ties" who for "all general purposes ... have uniformly been one people—each individual citizen everywhere enjoying the same national rights, privileges, and protection." Although contemporary multiculturalists have tried to replace the melting-pot metaphor with more of a salad-bowl metaphor, most Americans construe their union as a covenant embracing a single people, not separate peoples, for national purposes. Given that nationalist-minded leaders since the Federalists have inveighed against the evils of sectionalism, states' rights, and local parochialism, it is surprising that Americans are not less attached to their states and localities.

These orientations help explain why Americans are less attached to their state and locality than are citizens of many other federal countries. US states and localities are congeries of individuals who choose to live there and create community through social, economic, and political interactions. The United States is a territorial, not multicultural or multinational, democracy (Kirk 1974). Some observers argue there is still some life left in state identities (Young 2015), and various states make efforts to project a particular image (e.g., Levitz 2015), but, for the most part, Americans do not have strong state attachments.

Except for Indian country, regions and localities are not sites of primordial attachment, transcendent identity, or ethnic, religious, or linguistic self-government. Ethnic groups do not attach "national" significance to their regional or local places of residence. Except, again, for some Indians, communal groups have not claimed to be "nations" (Kincaid 2016). During the 1930s, the Communist Party of the USA promoted the idea of black Americans as a nation and urged creation of a black state, but blacks spurned the proposals, appealing instead to the Declaration of Independence's idea of every American being an equal member of one people. The American identity, therefore, is ultimately rooted in the US Constitution, which is the product of the people of every constituent state having joined the federal union voluntarily. Consequently, unlike Canada, where Quebec has not ratified the Constitution Act, 1982, and Switzerland, where six of its twenty-six cantons have never accepted any of modern Switzerland's three constitutions (Kincaid 2005, 416), the United States has no non-ratifying jurisdictions (except for Indian tribes, which remain separate sovereigns).

Historically, moreover, Americans have been highly mobile geographically. In 1948, for example, 20.2 percent of Americans reported moving in the previous year, with 13.6 percent remaining in the same county, 3.3 percent moving elsewhere within their state, and 3.1 percent moving to a different state. The moving rate has declined since 1983 such that, in 2013, 11.7 percent of Americans had moved in the previous year, with 7.5 percent staying in the same county, 2.3 percent relocating elsewhere within the same state, and 1.6 percent moving to a different state (United States Census Bureau 2007, 2015; Brooks 2016). The Great Recession (2007–9) reduced this mobility, although an aging population combined with a weak labour market have perhaps depressed mobility permanently. Depressed mobility also might affect neighbourhood attachment when individuals cannot leave their neighbourhood for a more desired location.

Another possibility is that social media is hollowing out intermediate relationships. People devote attention to personal relationships with family and friends and to electronic relationships with far-off social media contacts and fellow partisans more than to relationships with neighbours. One study found 47 percent of Americans saying they know none or only a few of their neighbours by name (Dunkelman 2014).

Statistical analyses of the 2010 data (not shown in tables) revealed that higher proportions of older Americans reported higher levels of attachment to the United States but not to states or localities. Higher levels of education also are related to attachment to the United States but not to the other arenas. So too is birthplace. Respondents born in the United States reported higher levels of attachment to the country than did those born elsewhere. The only other statistically significant relationship is that a higher level of attachment to city or town was reported by those not born in the United States. Perhaps this is a function of locality as the experiential locus of assimilation into American society because immigrants from particular places abroad ordinarily settle in particular places in the United States.

However, despite multicultural criticisms of the United States and the role of race as an enduring cleavage, race is not a statistically significant differentiator of attachment to country, state, or locality. By contrast, blacks are more trustful of the federal government than are whites, perhaps because of the historic association of states' rights with racism (Kincaid and Cole 2008). Moreover, Americans' conceptions of their identity are not overly ethnocentric (Schildkraut 2010).

The 2010 survey also found 68 percent of Americans being very or somewhat attached to the world. Absent in-depth and longitudinal data, it is impossible to assess this result, although the fact that the United States is home to people from all over the world and is also the only federation that is a superpower might be relevant.

At the same time, 54 percent of Americans report being extremely proud to be an American, 27 percent claim to be "very proud," 14 percent "moderately proud," 4 percent "only a little proud," and 1 percent "not at all proud." The "extremely proud" proportion, though, is the lowest since Gallup first asked this question in 2001 (Swift 2015).

Along with their high level of attachment to the United States, 94 percent of Americans also feel very or somewhat attached to their language. More than 82 percent of US residents speak only English at home. The next most spoken language, at 10.7 percent, is Spanish—although most Spanish-speaking parents urge their children to learn English (Stritikus and Garcia 2005). For Americans, English, which is technically a foreign language because there is no "American" language, is a tool, not an identity (Kincaid 2010), although in 1923 the Illinois legislature declared "American," not English, to be the state's official language. The law, strongly supported by Irish and Jewish legislators from Chicago who opposed British policies in Ireland and Palestine, was repealed in 1969.

More surprising is that 69 percent of Americans said they were very or somewhat attached to their ethnic or ancestral group—more so than respondents in Canada, Germany, and Spain. These attachments, however, are not strident, even among groups often portrayed as being at the forefront of contemporary identity politics. For example, despite the prevalence of the labels "African American," "Latino," and "Native American" in academe and the media, only 17 percent of blacks prefer to be called African American, and only 10 percent of Hispanics prefer Latino, while 19 percent prefer Hispanic. Fully 65 percent of blacks and 70 percent of Hispanics say these labels do not matter to them (Jones 2013; Hugo 2013). Most "Native Americans" prefer to be called Indian, as in the National Museum of the American Indian, which opened in 2004. Further, despite concerted efforts by numerous Indian, civil rights, and media personalities to force a major-league football team to drop the name Washington Redskins, 90 percent of Indian respondents in a 2016 poll said they were not offended by the team's name—the same result as a 2004 poll (Cox, Clement, and Vargas 2016). For most whites, ethnic identity is weak and shallow, and their most common ethnic experience is eating special foods (Alba 1992).

Perhaps the absence of significant nationalistic, linguistic, and religious struggles between peoples in the United States has enabled Americans to be comfortable retaining ethnic identities. Given that such identities have no governmental expression (except on Indian reservations) as they do in many federations, they pose little threat to the federal polity. Furthermore, as the United States has historically sought to meld immigrants into a single people, ethnic identities remain largely harmless markers of differentiation. Additionally, the United States is a product of revolution based on ideas as expressed in the 1776 Declaration of Independence; hence, Americans identify with their country and their homeland, not with a fatherland, motherland, or "nation" in terms of blood lineage. This allows Americans to be attached to ancestral identities while still being attached to their country and feeling patriotic. There appears to be public support for a mild multiculturalism that combines recognition of ethnic identities with strong attachment to America (Citrin and Sears 2014).

Attachment to ancestral identities seems likely to decline over time, however. Since 1980, the Census Bureau has asked an open-ended question about national ancestry. Growing numbers of Americans pick "American." This decline could be due to two developments: more Americans are now four or more generations removed from their immigrant forebears; and more are products of mixed ancestral heritage, with no one ancestry dominant. Marriage rates across religious and ethnic lines are high and have been so for more than a century (Kennedy 1944). Racially, in 1968, only 56 percent of blacks approved of black–white marriages. By 2013, 84 percent of whites and 96 percent of blacks endorsed black–white marriages (Newport 2013). However, in 2012, only 54 percent of blacks actually favoured a close relative marrying a white person, while 26 percent of whites favoured a close relative marrying a black person (Djamba and Kimuna 2014). In 2015, 24 percent of recently married black men and 12 percent of black women had a spouse of a different race or ethnicity. Nearly half (46 percent) of US-born Asian newlyweds had a spouse of a different race or ethnicity, as did 39 percent of US-born Hispanic newlyweds (Pew 2017a). Hence, the number of Americans identifying as multiracial is rising and being layered atop traditional racial and ethnic identities (Hochschild and Weaver 2010). The United States Census Bureau is debating how to classify race and ethnicity in its 2020 census (Vega 2014). Even among Hispanics, often portrayed in the media as highly ethnically conscious, length of residence reduces ethnic feelings and increases attachment to American society (Citrin and Sears 2014). Only black Americans evidence heightened racial identification and weaker feelings of patriotism (Citrin and Sears 2014).

The lowest level of attachment reported by Americans is to "religious group," although more than half (56 percent) said they were very or somewhat attached to their religion—more than Canadians, Germans, or Spaniards. Most international surveys show the United States to be one of the world's most religious countries. A 2015 survey found 54 percent of Americans saying religion is very important in their lives, compared to 24 percent in Canada, 22 percent in Spain, 21 percent in Australia, and 21 percent in Germany (Gao 2015). Even though increasing numbers of Americans report no affiliation with any organized religion, most are nonetheless spiritual and hold personalized religious-like beliefs (Manseau 2015).

A number of factors probably contribute to this vitality. For one, competition among religious groups in an environment of freedom has facilitated their vigour. Second, in many European countries and elsewhere, modern revolutionaries viewed religion as a major legitimizer of an oppressive *ancien régime*. By contrast, most American religious groups supported revolution and federal democracy. Furthermore, religious leaders have often championed social change (e.g., the Rev. Dr. Martin Luther King Jr.). Third, Americans have tended to have a messianic view of themselves, thus melding God and country into a potent symbol of unity (Kincaid 1971). Fourth, there was a civil religious revival during the 1950s that emphasized the reconciliation of Protestants, Catholics, and Jews for the sake of a common civil religion in response to what were perceived by many Americans to be godless policies of the New Deal of the 1930s and atheist threats from communism. The words "under God" were added to the pledge of allegiance in 1954, and a federal statute was enacted in 1956 mandating that "In God We Trust" appear on US currency (Kruse 2015). Fifth, religious vitality is heavily embedded in the South. Except for Utah, the twelve most religious states (measured in terms of worship attendance) are in the South, which has high Protestant and black populations.

In summary, attachments to America and the English language are comparatively high among Americans, as are also attachments to ethnic ancestry and religion, while attachments to states, cities and towns, and neighbourhoods are comparatively lower. Most likely, it is the detachment of language, ethnicity, and religion from constituent places in the federal union that allows these identities to flourish without detracting from attachment to the United States.

Trust in the Federal, State, and Local Governments

Despite Americans' attachment to their country, public trust and confidence in the federal government declined markedly during the late 1960s and early 1970s, from an 80 percent range to less than 50 percent. By 2015, trust in the federal government reached a new nadir. Only 19 percent of adult Americans said they trusted the government in Washington, DC, to do what is right "just about always" (3 percent) or "most of the time" (16 percent; Pew 2015a). This percentage increased to 20 percent in 2017, though with the now-usual partisan division by which members of the party that controls the presidency express more trust than members of the opposition party. Thus, in 2017, 28 percent of Republicans and Republican-leaning independents trusted the federal government, compared to only 15 percent of Democrats and Democrat-leaning independents. The proportion of all Americans saying they trust the federal government has not exceeded 30 percent since 2007 (Pew 2017b). By contrast, local governments attracted "a great deal" or "fair amount" of trust from 71 percent of Americans in 2016, while state governments attracted trust from 62 percent (McCarthy 2016).

Another survey found 80 percent of whites, 70 percent of Hispanics, and 56 percent of blacks believing they get excellent or good value from local government for their local taxes (Capps 2014). On questions such as "which order of government gives you the most for your money," "which order needs more power," and "which order do you trust most to deliver programs and services important to you," Americans regularly rate local governments the best, followed by state governments, then the federal government as the worst (Kincaid and Cole 2008, 2011). In 2014, 80 percent of whites, 70 percent of Hispanics, and 56 percent of blacks believed they get excellent or good value from local government for their local taxes. Some 48 percent of whites, 34 percent of blacks, and 32 percent of Hispanics said that the quality of public services where they live is determined mostly by local government, while 38 percent of whites, 47 percent of blacks, and 38 percent of Hispanics said the quality of services was determined by state government. By contrast, 7 percent of whites, 10 percent of blacks, and 17 percent of Hispanics believed the federal government determines the quality of services (Capps 2014).

Trust in local and state governments has not varied much over the past 45 years, but the gap in trust between the federal government and state governments grew from 36 to 43 percentage points from 1975 to 2014 and from 29 to 53 percentage points between the federal government and local governments (Research Center 2015a; McCarthy 2014; Cole and Kincaid 2000). Consequently, the seemingly pervasive mistrust of government often highlighted by the mass media is directed mainly at the federal government.

There are partisan differences in trust among these governments. Trust in local and state governments has been increasing among Republicans. They have usually expressed the most trust in these governments in the past, but there is a growing gap between Democrats and Republicans that could have governance implications. Also, 35 percent of Republicans and 34 percent of independents (i.e., individuals who do indicate a party preference) see the federal government as an enemy, while 50 percent of Democrats see it as a friend—although these partisan differences arise partly from Democrat Barack Obama's occupancy of the White House. Republicans reported more positive views of the federal government after Trump's inauguration in January 2017. Yet even the public's approval rating of the United States Supreme Court, historically seen as the most trustworthy branch of the federal government, dropped from 65 percent in 2000 to 42 percent in 2016 (Jones 2016), partly because many citizens regard judges as activist "tyrants" who strike down laws enacted and supported by the people. Citizens increasingly recognize that judges' partisan affiliations affect their rulings (Keck 2014).

Some observers contend that distrust of the federal government has been manufactured by relentless attacks on the federal government by big business, wealthy elites, and conservative Republicans. Americans have been led by this propaganda to forget the federal government's great historical accomplishments and to believe instead, as President Ronald Reagan said in his 1981 inaugural address, that government is the problem, not the solution, to what ails America (Hacker and Pierson 2016). This explanation seems unlikely, however, because public trust in the federal government plummeted continuously from 77 percent in 1964 to 27 percent in 1980 under both Democratic and Republican presidents—although Democrats were the majority party in Congress during 1964–80. Trust levels have fluctuated since 1980, reaching a post-1980 high of 49 percent shortly after the terrorist attacks of 11 September 2001. A more plausible explanation is that divisive federal politics and policies during the late 1960s and the 1970s produced enduring cleavages and mistrust. Casting further doubt on the elite-manipulation thesis is that even though trust has not rebounded, Americans frequently report higher levels of trust in their governments than do citizens in their neighbouring federations (Kincaid and Cole 2011; Cole, Kincaid, and Rodriguez 2004).

The very low level of trust in the federal government appears also related partly to public anxiety about the state of the country. In a 2016 poll, 46 percent of Americans agreed with the statement "Compared with 50 years ago, life for people like you in America is worse." Belief that life is worse was highest among whites, less educated people, those aged fifty and older, and Republicans. By contrast, 58 percent of blacks and 41 percent of Hispanics reported that life is better for them than it was fifty years ago. During the Republican presidential primaries, 75 percent of Donald Trump's supporters and 63 percent of Ted Cruz's supporters reported that life for people like them had gotten worse, compared to 34 percent of Bernie Sanders' supporters and 22 percent of Hillary Clinton's Democratic supporters. However, 91 percent of Sanders' supporters and 73 percent of Clinton's supporters said the US economic system unfairly favours powerful interests, compared to 61 percent of Trump's supporters (Pew 2016a).

If Americans trust their state and local governments the most, then why is that trust not translated into significant demands for shifting powers from the federal government to states and localities? Public officials are somewhat willing to alter the intergovernmental distribution of functions in response to public attitudes (Arceneaux 2005).

The answer is that the federal government has become involved in all domestic policy fields since the 1960s, thus raising public expectations about federal roles. The public wants some federal involvement in most policy areas (Thompson and Elling 1999), and in some policy fields, such as environmental protection, the public wants the federal government to play the leading role while allowing state and local governments to manage local environmental matters (Konisky 2011). Americans see a need for the federal government to play a major role in other fields. Furthermore, despite their generalized distrust of the federal government, when asked about the federal government's performance in specific fields, majorities believe the federal government is doing a good job in most fields, except for reducing poverty and managing immigration. Partisan differences are found here, too. Only 36 percent of Republicans see a major role for the federal government in helping people to escape poverty, and only 34 percent see a federal role in ensuring access to health care, compared to 72 percent and 83 percent of Democrats respectively. Another disadvantage for states and localities is that they are less visible policy actors. The mass media rarely conveys substantive policy news about them, as opposed to bad news about crime and corruption, and media news coverage has declined, especially with the decline of newspapers. State houses since 2003 have lost more than one-third of the newspaper reporters who report full time on legislative affairs (Haughney 2014).

In summary, there has thus far been a substantial decline of public trust in the federal government since the early 1960s and a growing gap between mistrust of the federal government and trust in state and local governments. However, there is no public clamour to shift powers from the federal government to the states.

Political Polarization

Another obstacle to devolution is severe political polarization, which has increased steadily since the late 1960s (Poole and Rosenthal 1984; Abramowitz 2010). "Republicans and Democrats are more divided along ideological lines—and partisan antipathy is deeper and more extensive—than at any point in the last two decades" (Pew 2014, 1) and possibly in US history. Polarization also varies by education level and generation. On average, the youngest generation is the most liberal, while successive older generations are progressively more conservative, and distance has grown between the liberal (i.e., left-oriented) views of highly educated adults and the more conservative (i.e., right-oriented) views of less-educated Americans across a range of political values (Pew 2016b). This class chasm will likely be aggravated over time, because educated Americans ordinarily marry each other, rear their children together, and otherwise distance themselves from the lower classes. Further, there is a growing gap between the lifespans of upper- and lower-income Americans (Tavernise 2016).

Polarization has contributed to feelings of diminished social trust and civility (Putnam 2000). "Americans seem to be resorting more and more to preying, with methodical duplicity, on other Americans," wrote one journalist (Trippett 1980, 106). There also is evidence that Americans may be sorting themselves out geographically along ideological lines (Bishop 2009). "Two thirds of consistent conservatives and half of consistent liberals say most of their friends share their political views. And liberals say they prefer to live in cities while conservatives" prefer small towns and rural areas (Taylor 2016, 2). Polarization has contributed to gridlock in the federal government and to divisions among the states, both of which inhibit devolution and aggravate mistrust of the federal government. Polarization has been most evident along party lines. Party identification has become almost tribalistic as party allegiance has increasingly become an anchor of personal identity. Democrats and Republicans dislike each other more than they did fifty years ago, and they attribute negative characteristics to supporters of the other party. Also, even though, as noted above, marriage across racial and ethnic lines has become more common, growing numbers of people do not want to marry a member of the opposite party or have their children do so (Iyengar, Sood, and Lelkes 2012). Many are willing to discriminate against members of the opposite party, and party-based bias now appears to be more significant than biases based on race, religion, and gender (Iyengar and Westwood 2015). These developments make it more difficult to forge the kinds of political friendships that Aristotle, Hannah Arendt, and many others have believed essential for democracy (Allen 2004). However, even though conservatives and liberals, and Republicans and Democrats, view each other as being more extreme and polarized than they really are, people can moderate their views when they learn that their views of the other camp are based on misperceptions (Ahler 2014). It is possible that polarization is driven more "by incorrect beliefs than distaste for others" (Hernandez and Minor 2015, 34).

Elite polarization has led voters to sort themselves out ideologically between the two parties without necessarily polarizing ideologically themselves (Levendusky 2009), although voters, too, are polarizing, as evidenced in the 2016 elections. Some observers argue there is a disconnect between polarized elites and a public that is mostly moderate and pragmatic (Fiorina and Abrams 2010); others argue there is no disconnect because, while the disengaged public remains middle-of-the-road, politically active citizens are polarized (Abramowitz 2010). Politically engaged Democrats and Republicans are farther apart than less-politically-engaged citizens (Pew 2015b). The issue positions held by voters are not as polarized as party identification, but party identification has become a part of social polarization. "The strength of a person's identification with his or her party affects how biased, active, and angry that person is, even if that person's issue positions are moderate" (Mason 2015, 141). In an experimental study, Republicans did not express less trust in Democratic partners than in Republican partners, but Democrats trusted partners of their own party more than they trusted Republicans (Hernandez and Minor 2015).

There is some evidence that "sharp differences" (Jacoby 2014, 767) are developing in Americans' feelings about such fundamental values as freedom, equality, economic security, social order, morality, individualism, and patriotism. But other observers argue that Americans are not abandoning traditional moral values and are not divided so sharply (Baker 2005; Fiorina and Abrams 2010). "America has retained its traditional values while virtually all of its peers are losing their traditional values" (Baker 2005, 36; Wolfe 1998), and Americans have not become less religious, more violent, less compassionate, or more alienated from their work (Fischer 2010). These results generally accord with the findings on attachments reported above.

Members of Congress have responded to the public's sorting-out, especially because of the influence of party activists on primary elections. "From 1994 to 2008, voters became less willing to tolerate representatives who were out of step with their ideological preferences, and lawmakers responded by voting more in sync with their districts" (Friel 2010, 32). This trend continued in 2016 as members of Congress sought to calibrate their ideological positions with election outcomes (Ladewig 2010), though, on average, Republican voters are slightly more cohesively partisan than are Democrats. US senators appear to respond to the preferences of the contributors to their campaigns and are thus more ideologically extreme than their state's fellow partisans and even more distant from the preferences of their state's average voter (Barber 2016).

Polarization in Congress has advanced as well because of generational replacement, perhaps more than incumbent conversions, and much of the polarization has occurred outside of the South, which has become substantially Republican. As the parties have become more ideologically cohesive, they have elected more polarizing representatives willing to employ procedural tactics, such as filibusters in the Senate and prohibiting floor amendments to bills, that force members to vote along party lines (Theriault 2008). Such legislative behaviour reinforces feelings of loss on both sides, such that 79 percent of Republicans and 52 percent of Democrats in the country believe their party loses more than it wins on issues that matter to them, thus further aggravating public mistrust of the federal government. Voters also are more likely to believe their side's losses are due to corruption and system-rigging. During the 2016 primary elections, for example, candidates Donald Trump and Bernie Sanders and their supporters, when facing losses, claimed they were robbed of victory by a rigged and corrupt party system, thus aggravating public mistrust of the national political system.

At the same time, Americans have considerable dislike for the two political parties, and they perceive both parties to be too polarized and ideological. They believe the parties do not adequately represent their views and that the United States needs a third party. Yet they do not believe a third party would improve the quality of American democracy, and they show no eagerness to support third-party candidates (Gold 2015).

Polarization has seeped into most state governments and into some local governments. Polarization has become evident in state legislatures, with one study finding that more two-party competitive states have more polarized legislatures (Hinchliffe and Lee 2016). Polarization exists between states as well. In early 2017, Republicans controlled the legislature and governorship in twenty-five states while Democrats controlled six states. The remaining nineteen states had divided legislatures and/or divided state governments in which the party of the governor differed from the party controlling one or both houses of the legislature. It is possible, though not yet certain, that growing polarization has contributed to the slight decline of public trust in state governments that has occurred since 1998 (62 percent in 2016), whereas public trust in far less polarized local government (71 percent in 2016) has been fairly stable since 1998 (McCarthy 2016).

There also is a religious dimension to polarization. A 2013 study found 56 percent of Republicans being religious conservatives, 33 percent religious moderates, 5 percent religious progressives, and 6 percent nonreligious. By contrast, 13 percent of Democrats were religious conservatives, 42 percent religious moderates, 28 percent religious progressives, and 17 percent nonreligious. Among people aged sixty-eight and older, 47 percent were religious conservatives and 10 percent nonreligious compared to only 17 percent of Americans aged thirty-three and under being religious conservatives and 22 percent being nonreligious (Dionne 2013).

The salience and tenacity of religion for conservatives makes religion a potent element of polarization. Generally, religious conservatives have gravitated toward the Republican Party; secular liberals have joined the Democratic Party. Both groups, however, feel strongly about their views, with religious conservatives being strongly opposed to abortion and same-sex marriage, for example, and secular liberals being strongly supportive. While the Republican Party manifests an overt religiosity, the Democratic Party exhibits an "ethos of moral high-mindedness" that mirrors the teachings of the United Methodist Church (Woodward 2016, 372).

In turn, authoritarianism appears to have become more prominent in people's basic attitudes. Authoritarians "have (1) a greater need for order and, conversely, less tolerance for confusion or ambiguity, and (2) a propensity to rely on established authorities to provide that order" (Hetherington and Weiler 2009, 34). Authoritarians are less liberal and more resistant to immigration. Authoritarianism helps explain differences between Democrats (less authoritarian) and Republicans (more authoritarian) and also between members of the same party. During the 2008 presidential primaries, Americans scoring low on authoritarianism tended to support Barack Obama; those scoring high on authoritarianism supported Hillary Clinton (Hetherington and Weiler 2009).

Other research points to race as being an important contributor to polarization. White citizens having negative views of black Americans and other minorities and feeling more threatened by minority advances gravitate toward the Republican Party. Others, including many minorities, align with the Democratic Party. The Democratic Party's base consists mostly of the caucuses recognized by the Democratic National Committee in 1982: Asians, blacks, Hispanics, women, gays and lesbians, and liberal business and professional people. Because contemporary norms make negative discussions of race socially unacceptable, Democrats and Republicans attack each other instead. Partisanship, unlike race, is a choice; hence, partisans can legitimately criticize each other's choices. "While Americans are inclined to 'hedge' expressions of overt animosity toward racial minorities, immigrants, gays, or other marginalized groups, they enthusiastically voice hostility for the opposing party and its supporters" (Iyengar and Westwood 2015, 705). This facet of polarization makes party identification more affective and primal than instrumental or ideological. Partisans have little accurate knowledge of their party's specific policy positions, and most partisans hold centrist political views, but yet they lambaste the opposite party.

Plausible explanations for the rise of polarization are in short supply. Explanatory factors include the rise of income inequality in recent decades, which accentuates class-based differences. For example, rising income inequality exacerbates polarization by nudging state Democratic parties to the left while also moving many state legislatures to the right because moderate Democrats tend to get replaced by Republicans (Voorhees, McCarty, and Shor 2015). Other factors are said to be the proliferation of primary elections after 1968, increased gerrymandering (i.e., partisan manipulation) of election-district boundaries for the US House and state legislatures that reduce competitive districts, the professionalization of campaigns (Hall 2015), growing reliance on television advertising, the increased importance of big-money campaign contributors, media diversification, including the spread of the internet, that fragments the public into media niches, and changes in procedures in Congress. Another factor could be the rise of identity groups in politics. Being rooted in self-identity and peoplehood, the political objectives of such groups are less amenable to compromise than are those of instrumentally oriented interest groups (Gutmann 2003). Some observers even see polarization roots in family psychology: "Conservatives celebrate the 'strict father,' who enforces relatively fixed and hierarchical values … . Liberals prefer the 'nurturing mother' who makes context-based decisions designed to promote individual well-being" (Cahn and Carbone 2010, 32).

These explanations are less than plausible because polarization began in the late 1960s as reflected especially in the riotous divisions that rocked the Democratic Party at its 1968 presidential nominating convention and by Richard M. Nixon's "southern strategy" to lure southern whites into the Republican camp in order to win the White House in 1968. Furthermore, some of the explanatory developments have occurred in other countries that have not experienced such political polarization. The explanatory factors put forth may have helped facilitate and sometimes aggravate polarization, but some are the products of polarization while others are independent developments that came to play a role in the politics of polarization.

A more plausible explanation is that changes in the American federal system induced by social movements and generational change nationalized political cultural issues historically under the purview of state governments, thereby polarizing voters nationwide. The American federal system was highly non-centralized until the mid-twentieth century. The lion's share of domestic governance was reserved to the states and their local governments. So long as salient sociocultural issues remained the province of the states, conflict was diffused across the states and not concentrated in the white heat of national politics.

By the 1960s, however, issues previously decided by state and local governments were increasingly decided in the national political arena and then imposed uniformly on state and local communities. The US Supreme Court's school desegregation decision, *Brown v. Board of Education* (1954–5), was the initial trigger for polarization. Further polarizing nationalization flowed from, for example, the Civil Rights Act of 1964, the Voting Rights Act of 1965, and US Supreme Court rulings outlawing prayer and Bible reading in public schools in 1962 and 1963, mandating extensive school desegregation nationwide in several rulings in 1968, 1969, and 1971, and striking down state-law prohibitions on abortion in all fifty states in 1973. As a prominent conservative put it: "*Brown v. Board of Education* [1954] had taken the issue of school desegregation away from the states and Congress, and imposed Warren Court ideology on America, leading to decades of racial conflict … . In the same way, *Roe* [legalizing abortion nationwide] drove a religious wedge through America and ignited a culture war that is with us yet" (Buchanan 2017, 112).

In the past, state and local electorates pursued divergent prefer-ences on almost all domestic policies, but the nationalization of state and local decision-making produced numerous state and local losers and winners, each of which engaged in increasingly nationalized po-litical mobilization and moved farther apart as they battled over ever more nationalized issues. In 2016, for example, the United States was wracked by nationwide conflict over the rights of transgender persons to use public restrooms and school locker rooms associated with their gender identity. The Obama administration notified all state and lo-cal governments that failure to accommodate such transgender rights would violate federal civil rights laws and trigger huge losses of federal funding. Removing this issue from state and local decision-making fur-ther polarized the electorate.

Given that polarization appears to have a significant racial founda-tion, the roots of polarization can be traced at least to President Harry Truman's executive order desegregating the armed forces in 1948. The golden era of bipartisanship existed from about the late 1920s to the late 1960s, during which time issues of race and other cultural issues such as abortion were kept off the national political agenda. These were state and local matters. Truman's support for black civil rights violated that practice and triggered a revolt by many southern whites who spurned the Democratic Party and supported the presidential candidate of the States Rights Democratic Party in 1948. After the US Supreme Court ordered states to desegregate their public schools (*Brown* 1954), south-ern whites especially mounted massive resistance to the federal gov-ernment's policies and began to abandon the Democratic Party where they had lived since the end of the Civil War in 1865. Nixon's appeal to these sentiments helped him capture the presidency in 1968. In 1980, Republican Ronald Reagan began his successful presidential campaign in Mississippi where he praised states' rights. In 1973, the US Supreme Court struck down the laws in thirty states that prohibited abortion and the laws in twenty states that limited abortion. This judicial de-cision sparked a firestorm of opposition and was a major factor in the national mobilization of the previously quiescent Christian right and the shift of many Roman Catholic voters out of the Democratic Party. Likewise, proponents of such rights mobilize nationally to protect and extend them. Furthermore, many of the issues triggering polarization are rights issues that have zero-sum characteristics not amenable to compromises.

Three Culture Wars

Consequently, Americans are engaged in three culture wars. These conflicts further exacerbate conflict by generating different views of representation. Liberals usually prefer politicians who serve as delegates representing voters' views; conservatives support trustee representatives who will stick to their principles. These divergent views of representation reduce the political will to compromise (Barker and Carman 2012).

One culture war is the long-standing battle between religious believers in permanent, transcendent, and sacred truths and secularist believers in subjectivist and rational formulations of values that evolve through enlightenment. The traditionalists believe the United States is a Christian nation (Hunter 1991). "The vote differential between those with a consistently traditional moral orientation (rejecting homosexuality and holding a traditional vision of the future) and those with a consistently progressive moral orientation (accepting homosexuality and holding a fluid vision of the future) is dramatic" (Bowman 2010, 72).

The second war centres on values and fairness arising from growing inequality that rewards a few, especially people in the financial world, while devaluing those who labour for wages and salaries. Voters in places most adversely affected by international trade developments, especially since China's entry into the World Trade Organization in 2001, have more often swung toward the far right or far left politically. Trade-exposed districts initially held by Republicans more often elected more conservative Republicans; trade-exposed districts initially controlled by Democrats more often elected liberal Democrats or conservative Republicans. Race also plays a role in this polarization. Trade-exposed districts having a majority white population disproportionately replaced moderate representatives with conservative Republicans; places with a majority non-white population more often replaced moderates with more liberal Democrats (Autor et al. 2016).

The third war revolves around national identity, especially whether that identity is fixed and rooted in a single cultural tradition or is fluid and multicultural. Samuel P. Huntington especially advanced an influential and controversial thesis that America's historic national identity is waning. That identity, he argued, was based on a political creed expressed in the Declaration of Independence and rooted in an Anglo-Protestant culture that includes the "Christian religion, Protestant values and moralism, a work ethic, the English language, British traditions of law, justice, and the limits of government power, and a legacy of European art, literature, philosophy, and music" (Huntington 2004, 40). Huntington saw Hispanics as the main threat to America's Anglo-Protestant culture. He also pointed to Canada and Belgium as exemplars of the destabilizing consequences of multiculturalism. Although this thesis has been subject to some blistering critiques (e.g., Symposium on Immigration 2006), it nonetheless evokes the anxieties of many white Americans, including those who were attracted to Donald Trump's "Make America Great Again" slogan and his promise to build an impenetrable wall along the US–Mexico border. The white share of the US population dropped from 84 percent in 1965 to 62 percent in 2015, and non-white minorities are projected to outnumber whites by 2042 (United States Census Bureau 2008).

Attitudes Toward Immigration and Immigrants

Although the United States has been termed "a nation of immigrants" (Kennedy 1964), Americans have often been ambivalent about immigrants, and immigration is one of the flashpoints of contemporary polarization. More than 20 million immigrants arrived between 1880 and 1920. These included many Canadians, such that 785,958 English Canadians and 395,297 French Canadians resided in the United States in 1900 (Wickett 1906, 192), equalling 22 percent of Canada's population (Kelly 2013). Federal legislation in 1921 and 1924 sharply curtailed immigration, but the Immigration Act of 1965 reopened immigration and abolished discriminatory regional quotas. Consequently, about 41.3 million immigrants now live in the United States, accounting for 13.1 percent of the US. population, which is close to the 15 percent high of the early twentieth century. The US-born children of immigrants constitute another 37.1 million people, or 12 percent of the population. Thus, together, the first and second generations make up about one-quarter of the US population. In turn, more than 300 languages are spoken in the United States.

However, illegal immigration has emerged as the major, polarizing controversy, and those opposed to assimilating illegal immigrants more often distrust the federal government for its failure to control the country's borders. Some 11.3 million illegal aliens reside in the country, accounting for about 3.5 percent of the US population. About 49 percent of them came from Mexico. Approximately 60 percent of unauthorized immigrants live in California, Texas, Florida, New York, New

Jersey, and Illinois. Arguing that the federal government has done too little to enforce its own immigration laws, Arizona enacted an omnibus immigration-enforcement law in 2010. Alabama, Georgia, Indiana, South Carolina, and Utah did the same in 2011. Federal courts quickly enjoined enforcement of key provisions of all these laws, and in 2012 the US Supreme Court struck down three of the four key provisions of Arizona's law (Arizona 2012). However, many states also have enacted laws beneficial to illegal immigrants, and the federal government has not blocked those laws. Thus, states have gone in different friendly and unfriendly directions in their treatment of illegal immigrants.

The controversy over illegal immigration makes it difficult to interpret surveys because advocates for illegal immigrants have blurred distinctions between illegal and legal immigrants by framing the issue as merely immigration. One cannot know, therefore, whether responses to questions about "immigrants" reflect public attitudes toward legal or illegal immigrants. Given the virtual absence of public controversy about legal immigration, question responses are probably influenced by individuals' attitudes toward illegal immigrants, most of whom are perceived to be Mexicans. Whites identify all Hispanics with illegal immigrants, whereas they are positive toward Asian immigrants (Abrajiano and Hajnal 2015).

This could be why nearly half (48 percent) of the respondents in the 2010 survey agreed either "strongly" or "somewhat" that there are too many immigrants in the country. Over half (63 percent) also said recent immigrants have different values from the majority of Americans, and 38 percent agreed that "immigrants should be encouraged to give up their customs and traditions" (see Table 6.2).

Nevertheless, compared to Canadian, German, and Spanish respondents, Americans were the least likely to say that immigrants have different values and should give up their customs and traditions. These responses seem consistent with our previous finding that Americans were the most likely to express attachment to their ethnic or ancestral group. Furthermore, 69 percent of Americans strongly or somewhat agreed that "people with different ethnic and religious backgrounds than the majority make an important contribution to" American culture, while 72 percent agreed that there are shared American values, and 64 percent reported shared values in their state. A 2015 survey found 65 percent of Democrats and 52 percent of Republicans saying that increasing the number of people of many different races, ethnic groups, and nationalities makes the United States a better place to live

Table 6.2

Immigration Attitudes

Agreement or disagreement with the following:	Strongly agree	Somewhat agree	Somewhat disagree	Strongly disagree	N/A
There are too many immigrants in my country	24.1%	23.6%	19.8%	19.3%	13.2%
Recent immigrants have different values from those of the majority of the country	24.0%	38.6%	18.7%	6.7%	11.9%
Immigrants should be encouraged to give up their customs and traditions	15.2%	22.7%	29.6%	23.1%	9.4%

Source: Association for Canadian Studies (2010).

(Pew 2015b). A 2016 survey found 57 percent of all registered voters saying that immigrants strengthen the United States because of their talents and hard work and 35 percent saying they are a burden because they take jobs, housing, and health care (Pew 2016a).

At the same time, among the four surveyed countries, Americans were the least likely (50 percent) to agree that "all children born in the United States should automatically be granted citizenship irrespective of their parents' citizenship status." This response is quite likely a reaction to illegal immigration and to news stories about so-called "anchor babies" and "birth tourists."

Combining the three items shown in Table 6.2 into a single scale of "immigration attitudes" and treating this scale as the dependent variable (where high scores represent more "pro" immigration attitudes), Table 6.3 sheds some light on demographic factors related to these views.

Demographic characteristics contributing to statistically significant *positive* scores on the immigration scale are female gender, higher lev-

Table 6.3

OLS Regression Model Explaining Immigration Attitudes as a Function of Various Socio-Demographic Variables

Dependent Variable = Scale of Immigration Attitudes (high score = positive attitudes)

Independent Variables:	B	Beta	Sig.
Born in US? (1 = yes, 2 = no)	.150	.013	NS
Gender	.429	.090	.010 (1 = male, 2 = female)
Age	-.103	-.152	.000
Income	.087 .199	.969NS Education .000	.294
Race	.409	.045NS (1 = white, 2 = Black)	
Hispanic?	.119	.011NS (1=yes, 2=no)	
Region (south = reference)			
North	.224 .105	.039NS Midwest .01	.579
West	-.008 .000	-.001NS Constant	4.506
R	.301		
R^2	.091	(.079 adjusted)	

Source: Association for Canadian Studies (2010).

els of education, and Midwest residency. Demographic characteristics contributing to *negative* scores are male gender and age. Of these factors, the most important are education and age. Higher-educated and younger Americans far more often reported positive immigration attitudes than did others.

Interesting also are the factors not related to the immigration scale.

Neither place of birth (born in the United States or not) nor race or Hispanic status contributes significantly to scale scores. Scores of respondents from the West are negative relative to the scores of respondents from all other regions, but the difference is not statistically significant.

Overall, Americans are supportive of immigration and receptive to immigrants, although they prefer high-skilled immigrants (Hainmueller and Hiscox 2010). Despite partisan divisions over immigration, there is a broad public consensus "about who should be admitted to the illegal immigration, and 40 percent of Americans express categorical opinions about whether or not illegal immigrants should have a path to legal status or citizenship (Wright, Levy, and Citrin 2014). Growing white movement into the Republican Party is due partly to illegal immigration. Whites living in states with a large Hispanic population identify as Republican and conservative more often than whites residing in other states (Abrajano and Hainal 2015). Even so, 60 percent of Republicans support a pathway to citizenship for illegal immigrants compared to 73 percent of Democrats and 57 percent of independents (Preston 2013). Anti-immigrant sentiment tends to flare up the most in places that experience a large, sudden increase in immigration, thereby making native residents receptive to national rhetoric that politicizes such change (Hopkins 2010).

Overall, all immigrants in the United States are assimilating at rates comparable to those of the past, although the naturalization rate is only about 50 percent, which is lower than in Australia, Canada, and many European countries, suggesting that many immigrants come to the United States for work but not citizenship (Waters and Pineau 2015). Historically, despite the prejudice and discrimination faced by many first-generation immigrants, the second and third generations ascended fairly rapidly into the elite sectors of American society. At least by the early 1970s, for example, the American elite had "become more ethnically heterogeneous than was true in the past, and it included individuals from all large ethnic groupings in the United States" (Alba and Moore 1982, 381).

Similarly, "Mexican Americans are not isolating themselves from the mainstream society and striving to establish a separate nation within the U.S." (Alba 2006, 293). Interestingly, Hispanics "with ties to their ancestral homelands are more likely to desire and seek out U.S. Hispanic officials, including 31 members of the U.S. Congress" (National Association of Latino Elected and Appointed Officials 2016). Univision, a Hispanic television network, is increasing its English-language programming because most Hispanics are now US-born. A 2012 study found that 88 percent of Hispanics followed at least some news in English compared to 78 percent who did so in 2006 (Hagey 2013). At the same time, in the Southwest, the *quinceañera*—a Hispanic celebration of a girl's fifteenth birthday—has replaced the Anglo sweet-sixteen party for many white, black, and Indian-American families (Lexington 2013). Receptivity to Hispanics is also evident in the popular Romeo Santos's infusion of traditional Latino sounds and subjects with elements of hip-hop and R&B (Hernández 2009) and in Cinco de Mayo—a celebration invented in the 1970s by San Francisco Hispanics who wanted to promote a pan-Hispanic holiday comparable to St. Patrick's Day for the Irish (dating back to 1762) and Columbus Day for the Italians (dating back to 1866). Hispanics include immigrants from more than twenty Spanish-speaking countries (Barlow and Naduau 2013).

Conclusion: Impacts on Federalism

Despite political polarization, which has reached an unprecedented level in the US Congress, and the various culture wars polarizing the country, there remains a strong underlying stability in public attachments to country, state, and locality and in the more middle-of-the-road issue positions held by most Americans. Unlike Belgium, Canada, and Spain, there are no competing national identities. Quite important, moreover, is that race, while an important factor in political polarization, is not a significant differentiator of attachment to country, state, or locality. Also, even though slightly more than half of Americans said that a state identity stronger than national identity would be "a problem for American unity," only 1 percent considered themselves to be from their state only, and only 5 percent said they were from their state but also from their country. This underlying attitudinal stability about fundamental matters mitigates the systemic divisiveness of political conflict that is significantly generated by elites and activists and also mutes calls for fundamental constitutional or statutory changes of the federal system. Despite Trump's winning of the electoral college vote while losing the popular vote, there is no movement to abolish or alter the electoral college mechanism of electing presidents.

The survey results also suggest a culture compatible with federalism as an expression of unity and diversity and with the United States as "compound republic," to use James Madison's phrase in *Federalist* 51, which is neither wholly confederal nor wholly national. Americans express high levels of attachment to their country and their shared language while simultaneously expressing high levels of attachment to their ancestral and religious groups.

Although attitudes toward immigrants are tainted by controversies over illegal immigrants, Americans are receptive, at least to legal immigrants, although a majority of Americans support a path to citizenship for illegal immigrants. While 63 percent said immigrants have different values from most Americans, 69 percent agreed that people with different ethnic and religious backgrounds than the majority make important contributions to American culture. These results suggest that, despite polarization among elites and activists over immigration policy, most Americans would support a compromise resolution of immigration issues that would not be punitive for illegal residents.

However, an important consequence of polarization for federalism has been frequent partisan gridlock in Congress, one result of which has been a failure to enact comprehensive immigration reform. As a result, the presidency has become the centre of immigration policy-making. President Obama pursued policies friendly to illegal immigrants, which stretched the limits of presidential authority and provoked revolts in many conservative states, including state lawsuits filed in federal courts seeking to block some of Obama's policies. The reverse has occurred under President Trump. Liberal Democratic state attorneys general filed lawsuits that convinced lower federal courts to block Trump's two executive orders limiting travel and immigration from some Muslim countries; and several hundred cities, mostly Democratic, declared themselves "sanctuary cities" whereby they refuse to cooperate with federal officials seeking to deport illegal aliens.

The structural impacts of polarization have been significant. With Congress so often gridlocked, the president and the Supreme Court have become the key drivers of federalism policy-making. However, because the Supreme Court can vacate presidential executive orders and agency rules, the Court is the *de facto* federalism kingpin and, thus, a crucial target of control for both parties. Quite tellingly, from 1789 to 1965, 68 percent of Supreme Court appointments were confirmed by acclamation in the Senate. None of the eighteen justices appointed since 1965 have been approved by acclamation. Polarization also has weakened the bargaining position of the states in the federal arena because it has divided their national lobbying associations, such as the National Governors Association. Although the association still functions, it has lost much of its vitality to the separate Democratic and Republican governors associations. Consequently, polarization has greatly weakened the shared rule aspect of federalism.

There is, therefore, intensified federal–state conflict between states controlled by the party in opposition to the party that controls the White House and/or Congress. In mid-2017, such party incongruence was most notable for the six states—California, Connecticut, Hawaii, Oregon, Maryland, and Rhode Island—where Democrats controlled the legislature and governorship. By contrast, the twenty-five states similarly controlled by Republicans enjoyed a largely cooperative relationship with Washington, DC. The polarization-driven desire of each party to completely control state governments, however, has intensified partisan gerrymandering (i.e., the drawing of election district boundaries to benefit one party over the other), which has substantially destroyed the historic representation of local territorial communities of interest in the US House of Representatives and state legislatures. Partisan polarization among the states also has generated divergent policy-making, especially on cultural issues such as abortion regulation, transgender lavatories, religious freedom, and marijuana legalization. Indeed, there is concerted effort, especially by conservative states, to regain control over some of the cultural issues that triggered national polarization.

References

Abrajano, Marisa, and Zoltan L. Hajnal. 2015. *White Backlash: Immigration Race, and American Politics.* Princeton: Princeton University Press.

Abramowitz, Alan. 2010. *The Disappearing Center: Engaged Citizens, Polarization, and American Democracy,* New Haven: Yale University Press.

Ahler, Douglas J. 2014. "Self-Fulfilling Misperceptions of Public Polarization." *Journal of Politics* 76 (3): 607–20.

Alba, Richard D. 1992. *Ethnic Identity: The Transformation of White America,* rev. ed. New Haven: Yale University Press.

———. 2006. "Mexican Americans and the American Dream." *Perspectives on Politics* 4 (2): 289–96.

Alba, Richard D., and Gwen Moore. 1982. "Ethnicity in the American Elite," *American Sociological Review* 47 (2): 373–83.

Allen, Danielle S. 2004. *Talking to Strangers: Anxieties of Citizenship since Brown v. Board of Education.* Chicago: University of Chicago Press.

Arceneaux, Kevin. 2005. "Does Federalism Weaken Democratic Representation in the United States?" *Publius: The Journal of Federalism* 35 (2): 297–311.

Arizona v. United States, 567 U.S. 387 (2012).

Autor, David, David Dorn, Gordon Hanson, and Kaveh Majlesi. 2016. "Importing Political Polarization? The Electoral Consequences of Rising Trade Exposure." Working Paper.

Baker, Wayne. 2005. *America's Crisis of Values: Reality and Perception.* Princeton: Princeton University Press.

Barber, Michael J. 2016. "Representing the Preferences of Donors, Partisans, and Voters in the US Senate." *Public Opinion Quarterly* 80 (Special Issue): 225–49.

Barker, David C., and Christopher Jan Carman. 2012. *Representing Red and Blue: How the Culture Wars Change the Way Citizens Speak and Politicians Listen.* Oxford: Oxford University Press.

Barlow, Julie, and Jean-Benoit Nadeau. 2013. "Cinco de Mayo No Hecho en México, Actually," *Wall Street Journal,* 3 May.

Bishop, Bill. 2009. *The Big Sort: Why the Clustering of Like-Minded America is Tearing Us Apart.* New York: Mariner Books.

Bowman, Carl Desportes. 2010. "The Myth of a Non-Polarized America." *Hedgehog Review* 12 (3): 65–77.

Brooks, Arthur C. 2016. "You're Stuck, America. Get a Move On!" *New York Times,* 21 May.

Brown v. Board of Education of Topeka, 347 U.S. 483 (1954).

Buchanan, Patrick J. 2017. *Nixon's White House Wars: The Battles That Made and Broke a President and Divided America Forever.* New York: Crown Forum.

Cahn, Naomi, and June Carbone. 2010. *Red Families versus Blue Families: Legal Polarization and the Creation of Culture.* New York: Oxford University Press.

Capps, Kriston. 2014. "Americans Love Local Government—They Just Don't Necessarily Want More of It," The Atlantic Media/Siemens State of the City Poll, 11 September. http://www.citylab.com/politics/2014/09/americans-love-local-governmentthey-just-dont-necessarily-want-more-of-it/379968/.

Citrin, Jack, and David O. Sears. 2014. *American Identity and the Politics of Multiculturalism.* New York: Cambridge University Press.

Cole, Richard L., and John Kincaid. 2000. "Public Opinion and America Federalism: Perspectives on Taxes, Spending, and Trust—An ACIR Update." *Publius: The Journal of Federalism* 30 (Winter/Spring): 189–201.

Cole, Richard L., John Kincaid, and Alejandro Rodriguez. 2004. "Public Opinion on Federalism and Federal Political Culture in Canada, Mexico, and the United States, 2004." *Publius: The Journal of Federalism* 34 (Summer): 201–21.

Cox, John Woodrow, Scott Clement, and Theresa Vargas. 2016. "New Poll Finds 9 in 10 Native Americans Aren't Offended by Redskins Name." *Washington Post*, 19 May. https://www.washingtonpost.com/local/new-poll-finds-9-in-10-native-americans-arent-offended-by-redskins-name/2016/05/18/3ea11cfa-161a-11e6-924d-838753295f9a_story.html.

Dionne, E. J., Jr. 2013. "Religion Challenges Left and Right," *Washington Post*, 5 August.

Djamba, Yanyi K., and Sitawa R. Kimuna. 2014. "Are Americans Really in Favor of Interracial Marriage? A Closer Look at When They Are Asked About Black-White Marriage for Their Relatives." *Journal of Black Studies* 45 (6): 528–44.

Dunkelman, Marc J. 2014. *The Vanishing Neighbor: The Transformation of American Community*. New York: W. W. Norton.

Fiorina, Morris P., and Samuel J. Abrams. 2010. *Culture War? The Myth of a Polarized America*, 3rd ed. New York: Longman.

Fischer, Claude S. 2010. *Made in America: A Social History of American Culture and Character*. Chicago: University of Chicago Press.

Friel, Brian. 2010. "Sorting the House." *National Journal* 42 (17): 32–7.

Gao, George. 2015. "How Do Americans Stand out from the Rest of the World?" Washington, DC: Pew Research Center. http://www.pewresearch.org/fact-tank/2015/03/12/how-do-americans-stand-out-from-the-rest-of-the-world/.

Gershon, Sarah Allen, and Adrian D. Pantoja. 2014. "Pessimists, Optimists, and Skeptics: The Consequences of Transnational Ties for Latino Immigrant Naturalization." *Social Science Quarterly* 95 (2): 328–42.

Gold, Howard J. 2015. "Americans' Attitudes Toward the Political Parties and the Party System," *Public Opinion Quarterly* 79 (3): 803–19.

Gutmann, Amy. 2003. *Identity in Democracy*. Princeton: Princeton University Press.

Hacker, Jacob S., and Paul Pierson. 2016. *American Amnesia: How the War on Government Led Us to Forget What Made America Prosper*. New York: Simon and Schuster.

Hagey, Keach. 2013. "As Young Hispanics Defect, Univision Polishes Its English." *Wall Street Journal*, 28 October.

Hainmueller, Jens, and Michael J. Hiscox. 2010. "Attitudes toward Highly Skilled and Low- skilled Immigration: Evidence from a Survey Experiment." *American Political Science Review* 104 (1): 61–84.

Hainmueller, Jens, and Daniel J. Hopkins. 2015. "The Hidden American Immigration Consensus: A Conjoint Analysis of Attitudes toward Immigrants." *American Journal of Political Science* 59 (3): 529–48.

Hall, Andrew B. 2015. "What Happens When Extremists Win Primaries?" *American Political Science Review* 109 (1): 18–42.

Haughney, Christine. 2014. "Pew Study Finds a Sharp Drop in Reporters at Statehouses," *New York Times*, 11 July.

Hernández, Deborah Pacini. 2009. *Oye Como Va! Hybridity and Identity in Latino Popular Music*. Philadelphia: Temple University Press.

Hernandez, Pablo, and Dylan Minor. 2015. "Political Identity and Trust." Working Paper No. 16-012, Harvard Business School, Cambridge, MA.

Hetherington, Marc J., and Jonathan D. Weiler. 2009. *Authoritarianism and Polarization in American Politics*. Cambridge: Cambridge University Press.

Hinchliffe, Kelsey L., and Frances E. Lee. 2016. "Party Competition and Conflict in State Legislatures." *State Politics & Policy Quarterly* 16 (2): 172–97.

Hochschild, Jennifer, and Vesla Mae Weaver. 2010. "'There's No One as Irish as Barack O'Bama': The Policy and Politics of American Multiracialism," *Perspectives on Politics* 8 (3): 737–59.

Hopkins, Daniel J. 2010. "Politicized Places: Explaining Where and When Immigrants Provoke Local Opposition." *American Political Science Review* 104 (1): 40–60.

Hunter, James Davison. 1991. *Culture Wars: The Struggle to Define America*. New York: Basic Books.

Huntington, Samuel P. 2004. *Who Are We? The Challenges to America's National Identity*. New York: Simon and Schuster.

Iyengar, Shanto, Guarev Sood, and Yphtach Lelkes. 2012. "Affect, Not Ideology: A Social Identity Perspective on Polarization." *Public Opinion Quarterly* 76 (2): 405–31.

Iyengar, Shanto, and Sean J. Westwood. 2015. "Fear and Loathing across Party Lines: New Evidence on Group Polarization." *American Journal of Political Science* 59 (3): 690–707.

Jacoby, William G. 2014. "Is There a Culture War? Conflicting Value Structures in American Public Opinion." *American Political Science Review* 108 (4): 754–71.

Jones, Jeffrey M. 2013. "U.S. Blacks, Hispanics Have No Preferences on Group Labels," Gallup Poll, 26 July. http://www.gallup.com/

poll/163706/blacks-hispanics-no-preferences-group-labels.aspx.

———. 2016. "U.S. Supreme Court Job Approval Rating Ties Record Low." Gallup Poll. http://www.gallup.com/poll/194057/supreme-court-job-approval-rating-ties-record-low.aspx?g_source=supreme+court+approval&g_medium=search&g_campaign=tiles.

Keck, Thomas M. 2014. *Judicial Politics in Polarized Times.* Chicago: University of Chicago Press.

Kelly, Stephen R. 2013. "Bonjour, America!" *New York Times,* 24 July.

Kennedy, John F. 1964. *A Nation of Immigrants.* New York: HarperCollins.

Kennedy, Ruby Jo Reeves. 1944. "Single or Triple Melting-Pot? Intermarriage Trends in New Haven, 1870–1940." *American Journal of Sociology* 49 (1): 331–39.

Kincaid, John. 1971. "The American Vocation and Its Current Discontents." *Publius: The Journal of Federalism* 1 (1): 115–40.

———. 2005. "Comparative Observations." In *Constitutional Origins, Structure, and Change in Federal Countries,* edited by John Kincaid and G. Alan Tarr, 409–48. Montreal and Kingston: McGill-Queen's University Press.

———. 2010. "United States of America." In *Diversity and Unity in Federal Countries,* edited by Luis Moreno and César Colino, 350–78. Montreal and Kingston: McGill-Queen's University Press.

———. 2016. "Territorial Neutrality and Cultural Pluralism in American Federalism: Is the United States the Archenemy of Peripheral Nationalism?" *Swiss Political Science Review* 22 (4): 565–84.

Kincaid, John, and Richard L. Cole. 2008. "Public Opinion on Issues of Federalism in 2007: A Bush Plus?" *Publius: The Journal of Federalism* 38 (Summer): 469–87.

———. 2011. "Citizen Attitudes toward Issues of Federalism in Canada, Mexico, and the United States." *Publius: The Journal of Federalism* 41 (1): 53–75.

Kirk, Russell. 1974. "The Prospects for Territorial Democracy in America." In *A Nation of States: Essays on the American Federal System,* 2nd ed., edited by Robert A. Goldwin, 43–66. Chicago: Rand McNally.

Konisky, David. 2011. "Public Preferences for Environmental Policy Responsibility." *Publius: The Journal of Federalism* 41 (1): 76–100.

Kruse, Kevin M. 2015. *One Nation Under God: How Corporate America Invented Christian America.* New York: Basic Books.

Ladewig, Jeffrey W. 2010. "Ideological Polarization and the Vanishing of Marginals: Retrospective Roll-Call Voting in the U.S. Congress."

Journal of Politics 72 (2): 499–512.

Levendusky, Matthew. 2009. *The Partisan Sort: How Liberals Became Democrats and Conservatives Became Republicans*. Chicago: University of Chicago Press.

Levitz, Jennifer. 2015. "Charm Offensive: Vermont Fights to Keep its Quaint Image." *New York Times*, 6 March.

Lexington. 2013. "The Power of a Party." *The Economist* 408 (3 August): 29.

Lopez, Mark Hugo. 2013. "Hispanic or Latino? Many Don't Care, Except in Texas." Research Center, October 28. http://www.pewresearch.org/fact-tank/2013/10/28/in-texas-its-hispanic-por-favor/.

Manseau, Peter. 2015. *One Nation Under Gods: A New American History*. Boston: Little, Brown.

Mason, Lilliana. 2015. "'I Disrespectfully Agree': The Differential Effects of Partisan Sorting on Social and Issue Polarization," *American Journal of Political Science* 59 (1): 128–45.

McCarthy, Justin. 2014. "Americans Still Trust Local Government More Than State," Gallup Poll, 22 September. http://www.gallup.com/poll/176846/americans-trust-local-government-state.aspx.

McCarthy, Justin. 2016. "Americans Still More Trusting in Local Over State Government." Gallup Poll, 19 September. http://www.gallup.com/poll/195656/americans-trusting-local-state-government.aspx.

National Association of Latino Elected and Appointed Officials. http://www.naleo.org/at_a_glance.

Newport, Frank. 2013. "In U.S., 87% Approve of Black-White Marriage, vs. 4% in 1958." Gallup Poll, 25 July. http://www.gallup.com/poll/163697/approve-marriage-blacks-whites.aspx.

Niebuhr, Reinhold, and Alan Heimert. 1963. *A National So Conceived*. New York: Charles Scribner's Sons.

Pew Research Center. 2014. "Political Polarization in the American Public." Washington, DC: Pew. http://www.people-press.org/2014/06/12/political-polarization-in-the-american-public/.

———. 2015a. "Public Trust in Government: 1958–2015," Washington, DC: Pew. http://www.people-press.org/2015/11/23/public-trust-in-government-1958-2015/

———. 2015b. "Beyond Distrust: How Americans View Their Government: Broad Criticism, but Positive Performance Ratings in Many Areas." Washington, DC: Pew. http://www.people-press.org/2015/11/23/beyond-distrust-how-americans-view-their-government/

———. 2016a. "Campaign Exposes Fissures over Issues, Values, and How Life Has Changed in the U.S." Washington, DC: Pew. http://www.people-press.org/2016/03/31/campaign-exposes-fissures-over-issues-values-and-how-life-has-changed-in-the-u-s/

———. 2016b. "A Wider Ideological Gap between More and Less Educated Adults." Washington, DC: Pew. http://www.people-press.org/2016/04/26/a-wider-ideological-gap-between-more-and-less-educated-adults/

———. 2017a. "Intermarriage in the U.S. 50 Years after *Loving v. Virginia*." Washington, DC: Pew. http://www.pewsocialtrends.org/2017/05/18/intermarriage-in-the-u-s-50-years-after-loving-v-virginia/

———. 2017b. "Public Trust in Government, 1958–2017." Washington, DC: Pew. http://www.people-press.org/2017/05/03/public-trust-in-government-1958-2017/

Poole, Keith T., and Howard Rosenthal. 1984. "The Polarization of American Politics." *Journal of Politics* 46 (4): 1061–79.

Preston, Julia. 2013. "In Report, 63% Back Way to Get Citizenship," *New York Times*, 25 November 25.

Putnam, Robert D. 2000. *Bowling Alone: The Collapse and Revival of American Community*. New York: Simon and Schuster.

Schildkraut, Deborah J. 2010. *Americanism in the Twenty-First Century: Public Opinion in the Age of Immigration*. New York: Cambridge University Press.

Stritikus, Tom T., and Eugene Garcia. 2005. "Revisiting the Bilingual Debate From the Perspectives of Parents: Policy, Practice, and Matches or Mismatches." *Educational Policy* 19 (November): 729–44.

Swift, Art. 2015. "Smaller Majority 'Extremely Proud' to Be an American," Gallup Poll. http://www.gallup.com/poll/183911/smaller-majority-extremely-proud-american.aspx.

Symposium on Immigration and National Identity. 2006. *Perspectives on Politics* 4 (2): 277–313.

Tavernise, Sabrina. 2016. "Life Spans of the Rich Leave the Poor Behind." *New York Times*. 13 February.

Taylor, Paul. 2016. "The Demographic Trends Shaping American Politics in 2016 and Beyond." Washington, DC: Pew, 27 January. http://www.pewresearch.org/fact-tank/2016/01/27/the-demographic-trends-shaping-american-politics-in-2016-and-beyond/.

Theriault, Sean M. 2008. *Party Polarization in Congress*. New York: Cambridge University Press.

Thompson, Lyke, and Richard Elling. 1999. "Let Them Eat Marblecake: The Preferences of Michigan Citizens for Devolution and Intergovernmental Service Provision." *Publius: The Journal of Federalism* 29 (1): 139–53.

Trippett, Frank. 1980. "The Busting of American Trust." *Time*, 20 October, 106.

United Stattes Census Bureau 2007. *Current Population Survey*, Annual Social and Economic Supplement, Updated. Washington, DC: U.S. Government Printing Office.

———. 2008. "An Older and More Diverse Nation by Midcentury," Press Release 14 August.

———. 2015. *Geographical Mobility: 2014 to 2015*. http://www.census.gov/hhes/migration/data/cps/cps2015.html.

US Department of Homeland Security. 2010. "Estimates of the Unauthorized Immigrant Population Residing in the United States: January 2010." Washington, DC: DHS Office of Immigration Statistics.

Vega, Tanzina. 2014. "Census Considers How to Measure A More Diverse America." *New York Times*, 2 July.

Voorheis, John, Nolan McCarty, and Boris Shor. 2015. "Unequal Incomes, Ideology and Gridlock: How Rising Inequality Increases Political Polarization." Unpublished paper, 21 August.

Waters, Mary C., and Marisa Gerstein Pineau. 2015. *The Integration of Immigrants into American Society*. Washington, DC: National Academies Press.

Wickett, S. Morley. 1906. "Canadians in the United States." *Political Science Quarterly* 21 (2): 190–205.

Wolfe, Alan. 1998. *One Nation After All: What Middle-Class Americans Really Think About … .* New York: Penguin.

Woodward, Kenneth L. 2016. *Getting Religion: Faith, Culture, and Politics from the Age of Eisenhower to the Era of Obama*. New York: Convergent.

Wright, Matthew, Morris Levy, and Jack Citrin. 2014. "Conflict and Consensus on American Public Opinion on Illegal Immigration." Unpublished Paper, 10 May.

Young, Ernest A. 2015. "The Volk of New Jersey? State Identity, Distinctiveness, and Political Culture in the American Federal System." Working Paper, Duke University, Durham, 24 February.

Zangwill, Israel. 1909. *The Melting-Pot*. New York: Macmillan.

7

Democracy, Public Safety, and Low Public Trust in Governments in Mexico

María Fernanda Somuano and Laura Flamand

Trust is key in any human relationship, even more so in arrangements where there is no absolute, hierarchical dominance, as in the governance of federal countries. Thus, the levels of trust and attachment of citizens to their governments are extremely consequential for both the operation of the federal system and the successful implementation of decentralization and intergovernmental policies.

There is a clear distinction between generalized and particular trust pointing to the need of establishing a more precise definition; namely, that trust is a three-part relationship involving a truster (e.g., citizens), a trustee (e.g., the government), and a specific context or domain over which trust is conferred (Kramer 1999, 574). In brief, trust is domain-specific and dependent on the attributes of the truster, the trustee, and the context.

In this chapter, we use public opinion surveys to explore levels of confidence and attachment of Mexicans to the federal, state, and municipal governments between 2009 and 2011. Using original survey data, we start by describing how trustful citizens are toward their governments in the federal arrangement; then we delve into the sources of such trust and the key role played by context.

The analysis is organized in four parts. First, we offer a brief review of the theoretical perspectives exploring the relationship between trust and democracy and of empirical work addressing public trust of gov-

Identities, Trust, and Cohesion in Federal Systems: Public Perceptions, edited by Jack Jedwab and John Kincaid. Montréal and Kingston: McGill-Queen's University Press, Queen's Policy Studies Series. © 2018 The School of Policy Studies, Queen's University at Kingston. All rights reserved.

ernments in multilevel systems. Second, we discuss the conditions under which the level of trust in governments is highly dependent on context. In the third section, we explore the levels of confidence and attachment of citizens to elected executives in Mexico's federal, state, and municipal governments. Especially, we emphasize the effects of region, identification with political parties, specific issues (i.e., public safety), and time on the varying and relatively unstable levels of trust and attachment in Mexico. Given that, compared to the citizens of the United States and Canada, Mexicans tend to be less trustful of the government in general and of local governments in particular, in this section we explore the reasons behind this behaviour. Finally, in the fourth section, we examine the implications of these heterogeneous levels of trust for the federal system as a whole.

Trust in Government and Democracy

Trust relates to beliefs, actions, and expectations. According to Claus Offe, "[t]rust is the belief that others, through their action or inaction, will contribute to my well-being and refrain from inflicting damage upon me" (Offe 1999, 47). Therefore, trust is a factor of paramount importance for solving the numerous collective action problems faced by citizens in modern social, economic, and political systems (Lubell 2007; Putman 2001).

Liberal democracy emerged from the distrust of traditional political authorities, and liberal innovations were created to check the discretionary powers implied in trust relationships; thus, "more democracy has meant more oversight of and less trust in authorities" (Warren 1999, 1). In fact, democratic mechanisms such as voting, freedom of speech and association, and separations of powers permit citizens to defy relations of trust, while restraining the discretion of the trusted and thus the potential harm in the remaining relations of trust (Warren 1999).

Other scholars, in contrast, have argued that trust enhances democratic processes (Brehm and Rahn 1997; Levi 1988; Uslaner 2002). These authors argue that in societies abundant in social capital, people not only create a larger number of civic associations but also participate in them more frequently and, consequently, develop bonds of trust. The central claim of these theorists is that social capital facilitates the establishment of democratic regimes and enhances their operation. For example, Putnam argues that "features of social life—networks, norms and trust—enable participants to act together more effectively to pursue shared objectives" (1995, 67). Putnam asserts that membership in horizontally ordered groups should be positively related with good government, and he tests his argument comparing the northern and southern Italian regions (1993).

Not all kinds of trust, however, are positive for democracy. Uslaner (1999) has argued that the kind of trust contributing to social capital may be generalized to people who are strangers as compared to trust that is particular (i.e., limited to a person's family or communal group). Particularized trust tends, in fact, to be attached to the types of group identities that are solidified against outsiders. Such groups, in turn, may increase factionalization and thus favour undemocratic solutions to conflicts. Generalized trust, in opposition, helps to build large-scale, complex, interdependent social networks and institutions and, therefore, becomes fundamental for developing social capital. Generalized trust, in addition, relates to a number of dispositions that underwrite democratic culture (e.g., tolerance for pluralism and criticism); in striking contrast, in non-democratic societies people tend not to trust each other. As happened in several Latin American countries under military rule, the pervasive culture of fear imposed by the authoritarian state explained why people did not trust strangers, giving credence to the assertion that "only in democracies is trust a rational gamble" (Uslaner 1999, 141).

Clearly, interpersonal trust is different from trust or confidence in institutions.[1] The relationship between trust in government or its institutions with democracy has been debated recently. Based on a careful analysis of the World Value Survey in forty-one countries, Inglehart (1999) discovered that trust in political institutions and elites is not as crucial for the long-term stability of democracies as interpersonal trust and subjective well-being.[2]

---

1. Hardin (1999) argues that it is illogical to speak of trust in the institutions of government because, in fact, citizens are not in a position to trust or not as they cannot possibly be aware of the relevant interests and circumstances of an institution. Furthermore, we cannot expect reciprocity from institutions; thus, it is not possible to trust them. From a different perspective, Offe (1999) suggests that trust in institutions may only exist when they are structured so that they might recur discursively to their constitutive norms. There are two basic strategies to build up trust in institutions: (1) the institutions develop an impeccable record in truth-telling, promise-keeping, fairness, and solidarity; and (2) the members of the community develop the habits and dispositions of extending trust to strangers by increasing the involvement of citizens in association life (Offe 1999).
2. Inglehart (1999) suggests that subjective well-being and interpersonal trust give

Cleary and Stokes investigate whether trust is necessarily beneficial for democracy and discover that democracy functions optimally when citizens consider their leaders fallible and thus realize the importance of constraining political institutions. They conclude that distrust, or what they call "a culture of skepticism," is positive for democracy (Cleary and Stokes 2006).

Even the most incredulous scholars, however, give trust the benefit of the doubt; they agree that at least a minimum level of citizen trust in their governments is necessary for the collective decisions and actions essential in democratic regimes. Consequently, we sum up briefly the reasons behind the purported democratic enhancing effects of trust. First, civic associations are schools of democracy teaching participants how to organize to pursue collective goals (Warren 2001). Second, a trusting citizenry permits democracy to operate better by encouraging cooperation with government in the provision of public goods and services (Putnam 2000). Third, communities with high levels of interpersonal trust free their governments from the role of enforcers and thus allow government officials to spend time and resources on other activities (Boix and Posner 1998). An active civic life, thus, encourages interpersonal expectations of cooperation; it heightens the belief that others will comply with the burdensome public demands critical for the functioning of democracy (Cleary and Stokes 2006).

As we have mentioned, trust is a crucial foundation for effective social, economic, and political life as it permits polities to solve collective action problems such as taxpaying, public security, and environmental policy (Lubell 2007). Following Lubell (2007), we integrate three theoretical approaches to explain trust in governments: the dominant, at least in political science, generalized trust (Rotter 1971), the transaction-cost approach (Levy 2000), and the advocacy-coalition framework (Sabatier and Jenkins-Smith 1993).

The generalized framework suggests that trust is based on the general predisposition of an individual to confide in other people or institutions. According to this theory, trust is a standing decision to give

---

place, first, to a general culture of political confidence sufficient to underwrite political opposition and transitions to power, and, second, to diffuse mass support for political institutions. In turn, this general culture and the diffuse mass support constitute a sound basis for the stability of democratic regimes. From our perspective, Inglehart does not provide a complete and persuasive argument for distinguishing between this diffuse mass support for political institutions and what other authors term "institutional trust."

most people the benefit of the doubt (Rahn and Transue 1998). In consequence, it is reasonable to measure this concept with questions such as "in general, would you say that most people can be trusted?" or "how frequently do you think you can trust the federal government to do what is right—always, most of the time, some of the time?" This framework, in general, is not particularly useful to explain the levels of trust in the case of thick or repeated relationships that tend to provide profuse information about the trustee (Lubell 2007).

The transaction-cost approach derives from the idea that, when trust is present, the costs associated with monitoring and enforcing cooperative agreements are reduced dramatically (Levi 2000). Trust is constructed throughout history on the basis of interactions; that is, the truster learns by experience who, how much, and in what circumstances to confide. In short, "trust is warranted when you believe someone with similar interests is willing and capable of keeping promises" (Lubell 2007, 239).

The transaction-costs approach also emphasizes the role of institutional structures in shaping policy trust and thus suggests that, in federal arrangements, citizens may develop different levels of trust in the federal, provincial, and local governments. In general, the greater the institutional distance[3] between a truster and a trustee, the higher the transaction costs of developing trust-based relationships (Lubell 2007).

The advocacy coalition framework posits that trust is a function of the similarity between the beliefs of the truster and those of the trustee (Leach and Sabatier 2005). People will confide in actors whom they believe have very similar beliefs and interests to their own. The expectations about the beliefs of a truster tend to be gleaned from stereotypes, reputation, and other public information more than from experience. For example, the survey question "do you think that municipal public servants consider the preferences and needs of people like you?" clearly links with this framework.

Is Trust in Government Context Dependent?

Most studies of trust in government start analyzing the overall confidence in government, in the orders of government, and then delve into the levels of trust in different policy areas. In what follows, we attempt

---

3. Institutional distance refers both to physical distance and to the uniform decisions adopted by the central governments affecting local jurisdictions (Lubell 2007).

to provide support for the hypothesis that trust is context dependent. Hence, to describe and study trust in governments, following Kramer (1999), we consider the three separate analytical elements discussed briefly in the introduction: the truster, the trustee, and the context.

We argue that it is reasonable to expect the levels of trust in government to vary according to (a) the individual characteristics of the truster (e.g., education, income, and party affiliation), (b) the order of government (i.e., federal, state, or municipal) or the institution (e.g., health ministry, board of elections, or the judiciary) that is to be trusted, and (c) the particular policy domain under contention (e.g., citizens may trust the central government more than the municipal order when their country is facing a health epidemic but may trust the municipal order the most when dealing with water provision).

Research Questions

In the political science literature, researchers approach the subject of trust in government employing three types of questions: the general ("how much do you trust the government?"), the personalistic ("do you trust the president?"), and the performance-oriented ("do you trust that the government is doing the right thing?").

Clearly, to inquire whether an individual trusts her current mayor or the local government is to ask about two different things, because the first question relates to interpersonal trust and the second one concerns institutional or organizational trust. Nevertheless, the findings of specific studies point to the fact that the interpersonal trust in the sitting officer influences a person's confidence in the institution as well (e.g., the level of confidence in the US federal government increased in the first years of the George W. Bush presidency when the presidential approval ratings rose after Bush's response to the terrorist attacks on 2001 and the cuts in the federal income tax; Cole, Kincaid and Rodriguez 2004).

Thus, levels of trust vary for the executive, legislative, and judicial branches of government. For example, in the United States, the office of the governor enjoys the highest level of public support, followed by state courts and then state legislatures (Kelleher and Wolak 2007, 712). Although overall the key explanatory variable for the levels of trust tends to be government performance, the performance measure for each branch is different by necessity as it relates to the executive, legislative, and judicial functions of government.[4]

Evidently, although surveys using these alternative approaches report different results, it has been shown that citizens who approve the performance of the government tend to trust the president or the government itself more.[5] Most experts seem to agree that the performance of the government is the key variable explaining levels of trust (e.g., Chanley et al. 2000; Safadi and Lombe 2011). Now, we add two layers of complexity to the questions: first, we introduce different orders of government because we are studying Mexico's federal system; second, we investigate whether context makes a difference for the levels of public trust and attachment.

Explanatory Variables

As we mentioned in the introduction, trust is domain-specific and dependent on the attributes of the truster, the trustee, and the context. Naturally, when examining the variables used to explore trust, it is possible to organize them around these three categories.

(1) Truster. The variables that tend to be used to portray the characteristics of the "trusting" individual are age, education, gender, income, race, and news consumption. For example, in the United States, Cole and coauthors report that support for the federal government increased notably among whites, Republicans, and college graduates in 2002 compared to their 1999 survey results (Cole, Kincaid, and Parkin 2002, 139).[6]

Regarding the characteristics of survey respondents, higher levels of education and income are negatively associated with trust in the na-

---

4. For the legislature, common measures are the number of bills approved or the fiscal burden; for the executive, the popularity of the governor and income inequality; and, finally, for the courts, confidence increases when judges are elected and with the number of cases overseen per judge.

5. Kincaid and Cole (2011), for example, suggest that in 2009 the decline in trust in the federal government among Americans could be explained by the souring of public opinion toward George W. Bush who had left office only three weeks before their survey.

6. The review of the literature reveals that, in general, the higher the income or the educational attainment, the lesser the trust in government, and that females tend to be more trusting than males (Safadi and Lombe 2011). In the empirical section of the chapter, using original survey data, we explore whether, in Mexico, the characteristics of the trustee indeed influence the levels of confidence in the federal, state, and municipal governments.

tional government (Safadi and Lombe 2011); by contrast, conservatives and those who position themselves toward the right of the ideological spectrum tend to be more trusting (Aydin and Cenker 2012).

(2) Trustee. What are the characteristics of the government defining the levels of trust and attachment? The literature seems to agree that the performance of the government is the key variable explaining levels of attachment and trust (e.g., Chanley et al. 2000, Safadi and Lombe 2011). There are, however, several ways of measuring performance, both perceived and actual, and they depend on the particular trustee and the context. For example, survey respondents seem to pay more attention to the levels of unemployment in times of economic crisis and when evaluating the executive branch than in times of economic growth or when assessing the legislature; as well, citizens tend to confide more in judges when they are elected and perceived as honest than when they are not (Kelleher and Wolak 2007).

The traits of the trustee have proved to be closely linked with the levels of trust in the government. Higher levels of perceived corruption, partisan conflicts (Kelleher and Wolak 2007), and political scandals (Chanley et al. 2000) are related to lower levels of confidence; in contrast, positive assessments of policy or governmental performance turn into higher levels of confidence (Safardi and Lombe 2011; Aydin and Cenker 2012).

(3) Context. The variables employed have a wide range from economic (e.g., income inequality) to political (e.g., divided government and party competition). Naturally, it is reasonable to anticipate levels of confidence to vary from one policy domain to another, but this has not been studied systematically.

Finally, in terms of the context, higher levels of crime or unemployment tend to be coupled with lower levels of trust (Kelleher and Wolak 2007); better current or prospective perceived economic performance are correlated with higher levels of confidence (Chanley et al. 2000; Kelleher and Wolak 2007).

Low Levels of Trust and Attachment to Governments in Mexico's Federal System

Comparatively, in multilevel arrangements, people tend to identify themselves primarily as citizens of their country rather than as world, provincial, or local community citizens (see Table 7.1 below). This is the case for all the countries included in Table 7.1. In all cases, individ-

Table 7.1

Percentage of Individuals Answering "Strongly Agree"

People have different views about themselves and how they relate to the world. Using this card, would you tell me how strongly you agree or disagree with each of the following statements about how you see yourself?: I see myself as a citizen of ...	Argentina	Brazil	Canada	Mexico	Spain	United States
The world	16.5	27.0	29.4	35.4	23.6	20.6
The country	36.9	32.5	45.0	49.6	49.9	61.2
The province/region	n.a.	n.a.	n.a.	n.a.	38.1	n.a.
The local community	35.0	30.6	31.1	33.9	38.7	31.1
Latin America	18.6	17.8	n.a.	22.4	n.a.	n.a.
North America	n.a.	n.a.	24.0	15.7	n.a.	30.5
Europe	n.a.	n.a.	n.a.	n.a.	18.2	n.a.

Note: n.a. = not available.

Source: World Value Survey 2005–8.

uals recognize themselves in the first place as citizens of a country. The fact that Mexicans show a higher level of attachment to their country than do Argentinians, Brazilians, or Canadians may prove the success of specific policies that Mexican governments have implemented to develop and reinforce national identity, specifically at the beginning of the twentieth century. Interestingly, Mexicans by far show more attachment to the world than do any of the other peoples listed in Table 7.1, who identify more with their local community. This result converges with recent studies that have shown that, even though 80 percent of Mexicans feel very proud of their country, also more than one-half of them (64 percent) have a very good or good opinion about foreigners. In fact, seven out of ten consider that foreigners living in Mexico contribute to the Mexican economy and bring with them innovative ideas (Schiavon et al. 2013).

As mentioned before, according to Table 7.1, people have higher levels of attachment to their country than their local community. Does this fact translate into higher levels of confidence in the federal government than in state and local governments? In what follows, we delve into this question by analyzing the relationships between attachment and trust in Mexico.

Relevant Background about the Mexican Federation

Mexico[7] is a highly unequal middle-income country characterized by widespread and persistent poverty.[8] Most socioeconomic indicators reveal deep regional heterogeneity. For example, even though the literacy rates of certain Mexican municipalities are similar to those of high-income countries such as Norway, in the predominantly rural and indigenous municipalities of the South the illiteracy rates of females are close to those of Mali, one of the poorest countries in the world (PNUD 2008).

Mexico's political system has long defied easy classification. In the 1950s and 1960s, political scientists in the United States defined the regime as a one-party democracy evolving toward a "true" (North

---

7. For background on Mexican federalism, see Wuhs (2013), Gutiérrez (2005), González (2006), and Graizbord (2009). Also, Domínguez and Lawson (2004), Magaloni (2007), Merino (2003), and Ortega (2008) analyze, from different perspectives, the transition to democracy in Mexico.

8. In 2012, in Mexico, the per capita gross national income was US$8,590, the Gini index of income distribution was 47.2, and 51.3 percent of the population was below the national poverty line (World Bank 2013a; World Bank 2013b).

Atlantic-style) democracy (O'Donnell et al. 1986; Smith 1991). During the 1980s and 1990s, however, Mexico seemed to move to the rapidly expanding category of hybrid part-free/part-authoritarian system that does not conform to classical typologies (Pye 1990). Mexico was thus characterized by competitive (though not necessarily fair and clean) elections in which governments often engaged in undemocratic practices (e.g., electoral fraud and selective repression of dissidents). At the time, the hegemonic *Partido Revolucionario Institucional* (PRI) seemed committed to maintaining political stability and labour discipline rather than to expanding democratic freedoms, protecting human rights, or mediating class conflicts.

From a normative perspective, the Mexican government appears to be organized much like the government of the United States: a presidential system, three autonomous branches of government (i.e., executive, legislative, and judicial), and federalism with considerable autonomy of the state and municipal orders of government. In practice, however, the political system in Mexico is very far from the American model. Until the late 1980s, both houses of the federal legislature were controlled continuously for some seventy years by the PRI, and decision-making tended to be highly centralized. The president, operating with few restraints on his authority, dominated the legislative and judicial branches.

In Mexico, since the late 1930s and until very recently, the central government dominated both states and municipalities in the fiscal, administrative, and political realms. During the PRI's hegemony, states operated mostly as delegates of the federal government in their territory, and municipalities as agents of their respective state government. PRI local officials tended to bend to the wishes of their hierarchical superior within the party (either governor or president) in order to further their own political careers and to avoid dismissal from gubernatorial or municipal office (Domínguez 1999; Ward and Rodriguez 1999).

Since the early 1980s, electoral victories by the opposition in municipal and state elections, and considerable gains in both federal legislative chambers, marked the beginning of a democratization of the system. The definitive transition from the hegemonic party system to a moderate pluralism (Sartori 1992) occurred with the presidential election of 2000 when, for the first time in modern Mexican history, the PRI lost the presidency.

With democratization and especially after the election of President Vicente Fox (*Partido Acción Nacional*, PAN) in 2000, political intergovernmental relations in Mexico have been transformed considerably. State governments have progressively become more influential and relevant decision-makers at the national level. Governors from political parties in opposition to the party of the president have been the most active and demanding in their interactions with the federal government (Flamand 2004) and also the most prone to adopt an independent stance from that of their national party leaders (Langston 2006).

In the fiscal realm, nevertheless, intergovernmental relations in Mexico are still largely characterized by the dependence of state governments on federal largesse. Despite the fact that the income of state governments in real terms almost tripled in the 1996–2010 period, state governments are still highly dependent on federal transfers, both conditional and unconditional.[9]

In the last twenty years, furthermore, state governments have been the main recipients of devolved functions resulting from decentralization (e.g., education and health services as well as the management of natural resources). In most cases, particularly in education, decentralization has merely signified the transfer of administrative responsibilities without decision-making power or sufficient financial resources. State governments, for example, must accept yearly increases in the wages of state teachers because these are not negotiated in the states but by the federal government (between the National Union of Education Workers and the federal ministry of education). As a result, massive and disruptive teachers' strikes and other protests are common, such as major demonstrations mounted in 2013 against President Enrique Peña Nieto's proposed education reforms.

Despite these decentralizing tendencies, the federal government continues to be the main tax collector, while subnational governments levy an extremely limited number of taxes. This last fact clearly illustrates the degree to which subnational governments are dependent on (and vulnerable to) the actions of the federal government.

Mexico is thus a highly unequal and heterogeneous country in the process of consolidating a federal democratic system which, as we discuss in the rest of the chapter, proves to be a most interesting case to explore the determinants of the levels of citizen trust toward the three orders of government in a rather unstable context.

In a most provocative comparative analysis of the levels of trust in

---

9. In 2010, federal transfers represented 81 percent of the total income of an average state, while the share of own-source revenue was only 9 percent (INEGI 2012).

government in the three North American federal countries, Richard Cole, John Kincaid, and Alejandro Rodriguez (2004) and Kincaid and Cole (2011) use original survey data to discover, first, the level of government citizens trust the most and, second, which country exhibits the strongest federalist culture. We briefly review their most significant findings for the Mexican case as they are a necessary prelude to the original empirical study presented in this chapter.

The study indicates that, overall, Mexicans tend to trust their governments less when compared to the respondents in Canada and the United States. There is, however, an interesting change, as Mexicans tended to trust local government the most in 2004 but federal authorities by 2009. Kincaid and Cole (2011) presume that this change relates to the increase in drug trafficking violence at the local level throughout the period. The study discovers, in addition, that Canada exhibits the most robust federal political culture, followed by the United States and then Mexico.[10]

Descriptive Analysis

The findings of our data analysis coincide with those of Kincaid and Cole for 2009. Considering levels of trust and also perceptions of government efficacy and government responsiveness, both the federal government and the president receive the highest grades. The share of citizens reporting a great deal of confidence in the president is four percentage points larger than the share saying they trust their governor a great deal, and almost double the share declaring they trust the municipal president a great deal (see Table 7.2).

Regarding the perception of government performance, the majority considers the federal government to be the most efficient order when dealing with public safety. Furthermore, most citizens declared the president to be the public official who takes into account the needs of the people the most when compared to governors and municipal presidents. Six out of every ten survey respondents, however, stated that neither the federal nor the state or municipal officials consider the needs of the people when taking decisions.

---

10. The questions posed to survey respondents to address the "federalist culture" are: (1) "a federal form of government is preferable?"; (2) "a country in which everyone speaks the same language is preferable?"; (3) "having a strong leader in government is preferable?"; and (4) "when making decisions, government is better off limiting discussion?"

Table 7.2

Confidence, Effectiveness, and Responsiveness: The National Government

1. Level of confidence

	President	Governor	Municipal president
Not at all	16.8	18.2	24.4
Not very much	30.3	33.1	36.3
Quite a lot	37.0	36.3	30.1
A great deal	14.8	10.8	7.4
Do not know/Not available	1.0	1.5	1.8

2. Effectiveness in dealing with public security

	Federal government	State government	Municipal government
Very ineffective	17.8	18.1	23.5
Somewhat ineffective	25.1	28.1	29.6
Somewhat effective	42.8	41.1	36.4
Very effective	11.8	9.0	6.9
Do not know/Not available	2.4	3.8	3.7

3. Do these authorities take into account people's needs when they make decisions?

	President	Governor	Municipal president
Yes	40.1	38.4	32.7
No	56.9	57.9	63.3
Do not know/Not available	2.9	3.7	3.9

Source: USAL-Colmex (2011).

The most interesting finding of this initial analysis is that there are extremely acute differences among survey respondents across states. We explore, in particular, Guanajuato, Mexico City, and Veracruz (see Table 7.3). We chose these states for two reasons. First, the survey we used is representative at the state level only in these cases; second, they illustrate the vast variation across Mexican regions in aspects such as level of democracy,[11] governing party,[12] and socioeconomic indexes.[13]

Regarding confidence, the respondents from Guanajuato are the most trusting (six out of ten trust the federal, state, and municipal government quite a lot or a great deal) followed by the citizens of Veracruz and Mexico City. Furthermore, an average citizen of Mexico City or Veracruz trusts the state government more than the municipal; in Guanajuato, however, citizens trust both subnational governments about the same. It is important to underscore that we do not suggest that these three states represent the entire variation across Mexican states, but they do illustrate that the perceptions of citizens tend to vary in different contexts.

Note interestingly that, in line with the Kincaid and Cole speculation, the level of confidence seems to be closely associated with the effectiveness of each order of government in maintaining public safety. The citizens of Guanajuato offer the most positive evaluation in this respect, followed by those of Veracruz and Mexico City. Similarly, trust appears to be related to responsiveness, as the survey respondents of Guanajuato perceive all three orders of government to be more responsive than do those of Veracruz and Mexico City.

These initial findings suggest that confidence in the three orders of government varies prominently in the states included in this study, and it seems to be closely linked to the perceptions of effectiveness and re-

---

11. According to the IDD-Mex 2012 (Democratic Development Index), the three states are characterized by different levels of democracy. The Index considers two dimensions: respect to political rights and civil liberties; and institutional quality and political efficacy. The state with the highest value of the composite index is Guanajuato, followed by the Mexico City and Veracruz.
12. At the time of the survey, Mexico City was governed by the leftist PRD; Guanajuato by the right-oriented PAN; and Veracruz by the former dominant party at the federal level until 2000, the PRI.
13. In terms of socioeconomic variables, in 2011, the Federal District has the highest GDP (in US dollars) per capita ($11,009) and percentage of urban population (99.7 percent), whereas Guanajuato is in the middle of the table ($6,010 and 69.7 percent respectively) and Veracruz is in the low section of the table ($4,722 and 60.6 percent respectively). See http://www.inegi.org.mx.

Table 7.3

Confidence, Effectiveness, and Responsiveness: The State Governments

1. Level of confidence
Proportion of citizens saying they trust the official "quite a lot or a great deal"

	Federal government	State government	Municipal government
Mexico City	45.8	44.5	33.3
Guanajuato	68.1	58.6	57.1
Veracruz	60.0	54.8	34.3

2. Effectiveness in dealing with public safety
Proportion of citizens saying the official is "somewhat or very effective"

	Federal government	State government	Municipal government
Mexico City	46.6	46.0	44.1
Guanajuato	70.5	64.8	56.0
Veracruz	55.1	53.5	44.5

3. Do these authorities take into account people's needs when they make decisions?
Proportion of citizens responding "yes"

	Federal government	State government	Municipal government
Mexico City	46.6	46.0	44.1
Guanajuato	70.5	64.8	56.0
Veracruz	55.1	53.5	44.5

Source: USAL-Colmex (2011).

sponsiveness of each order of government. Naturally, these findings open the door for future research exploring the relation between performance and confidence in the other twenty-nine states.

Data and Methodology

To explore the sources of trust in the federal, state, and municipal governments, we analyzed data from the University of Salamanca-El Colegio de México Survey 2011 (USAL-Colmex 2011). The survey was administered face to face to a sample of 2,900 adults (eighteen years and older). The sample is a probabilistic, stratified, clustered and multistage sample with oversamples in three states: Guanajuato, Mexico City, and Veracruz.

Our dependent variable is the level of trust in the three different orders of government. Confidence toward the three orders of government is measured on a four-point scale; in this initial analysis, we created a dichotomous variable by coding the two lowest categories as 0s and the two highest as 1s.[14] Then we estimated several logistic models to explain the levels of trust in each order of government in the national sample and in three states with oversamples.

We included variables that the literature has proved influence the levels of confidence in governments. For ease of presentation, we organized the variables in three groups: *group effects* (i.e., party identification and membership in trade unions or religious, human rights, or environmental organizations), *perceptions* (e.g., of the economy and of government performance), and *sociodemographic* (e.g., gender, age, and income). We begin with the following hypotheses:

1. Individual partisan affiliation influences confidence in different orders of government; that is, citizens tend to be more trusting of governments headed by their preferred party.
2. The causal role of being a member of an organization is debated by researchers. On one hand, membership in organizations may increase the level of confidence in governments via the formation of social capital inside the organizations. On the other, from this perspective, individuals create organizations to work out problems that governments are unable to solve. In this perspective,

---

14. Somuano and Flamand (in preparation) explore the database with an *ordered probit* model to address the fact that the dependent variable is both categorical and ordinal.

membership in organizations tends to be negatively associated with trust in government.
3. Higher levels of confidence are associated with positive retrospective or pocketbook perceptions of the economy.
4. Satisfaction with democracy and the perception of low levels of corruption in the national government have a positive effect on levels of trust in the federal, state, and local governments.
5. A positive evaluation of the performance of the president, the governor, or the municipal president is also related to higher levels of trust toward each order of government.

We estimated three logistic models to explain the levels of confidence in the president, the governors and the municipal presidents with the national sample (see Table 7.4). Regarding *group effects*, as expected, being a member of a civic or social organization increases the probability of trusting the president, the governor, and the municipal president. In addition, given that President Felipe Calderón (2006–12) was a member of the *Partido Acción Nacional* (PAN), those who identified with the *Partido Revolucionario Institucional* (PRI) or the *Partido de la Revolución Democrática* (PRD) or who were independents were less likely to trust him, relative to PAN identifiers.

With respect to *perceptions*, individuals reporting low levels of corruption in the national government were more likely to trust the president, the governor, and the municipal president. A plausible explanation is that the consumption of national news may influence local life, especially when related to corruption scandals. This suggests, in fact, that media consumption is one of the channels through which national phenomena affect perceptions and evaluations of state and municipal officials.

Citizen evaluations of government performance, as expected, are the variables most influencing the levels of confidence in the president. Those reporting that federal public safety policies are effective, those that consider that the president takes into account their needs, and those who overall deliver a positive evaluation of the president are more likely to trust him.

The results of the models explaining levels of confidence in governors and mayors are markedly similar. Party identification does not seem to explain the levels of confidence in governors or municipal presidents. Being an independent, however, does have a negative impact on trust for both governors and municipal presidents relative to the reference

... continued on page 204

Table 7.4

Citizen Trust in the Three Orders of Government in the National Sample (Logit Models)

	President		Governor		Municipal president	
	Coefficient (st. error)	p value	Coefficient (st. error)	p value	Coefficient (st. error)	p value
Sociodemographics						
Gender	-0.061	0.507	-0.025	0.799	0.023	0.830
	-0.092		-0.099		-0.107	
Age	0.004	0.214	0.000	0.913	-0.003	0.400
	-0.003		-0.003		-0.004	
Education level	0.019	0.450	0.011	0.690	-0.011	0.701
	-0.025		-0.027		-0.029	
Income	0.029	0.140	-.0052	0.015	-0.014	0.534
	-0.020		-0.021		-0.022	
Indigenous	-0.247	0.218	0.004	0.987	-0.016	0.950
	-0.201		-0.230		-0.252	
Employed	0.137	0.142	-0.042	0.672	0.050	0.646
	-0.094		-0.100		-0.109	
Religiosity	0.086	0.015	0.013	0.728	0.041	0.970
	-0.035		-0.038		-0.042	

continued...

Table 7.4, continued

Citizen Trust in the Three Orders of Government in the National Sample (Logit Models)

	President		Governor		Municipal president	
	Coefficient (st. error)	p value	Coefficient (st. error)	p value	Coefficient (st. error)	p value
Group effects						
Membership in organization	0.241 -0.093	0.010	0.372 -0.100	0.000	0.403 -0.105	0.000
Priista	-0.246 -0.123	0.045	-0.094 -0.126	0.455	-0.009 -0.130	0.943
Perredista	-0.610 -0.158	0.000	-0.037 -0.164	0.821	-0.265 -0.178	0.137
Other	-0.422 0.344	0.220	-0.237 -0.377	0.531	-0.018 -0.432	0.967
Independent	-0.433 -0.119	0.000	-0.219 -0.125	0.080	-0.277 -0.132	0.036

continued…

Table 7.4, continued

Citizen Trust in the Three Orders of Government in the National Sample (Logit Models)

	President		Governor		Municipal president	
	Coefficient (st. error)	p value	Coefficient (st. error)	p value	Coefficient (st. error)	p value
Economic perceptions						
Retrospective national	0.442	0.001	-0.234	0.084	0.197	0.162
	-0.133		-0.135		-0.141	
Retrospective pocketbook	-0.182	0.183	0.379	0.007	0.345	0.017
	-0.137		-0.141		-0.145	
Political and social perceptions						
Satisfaction with democracy	0.107	0.002	0.028	0.450	0.122	0.002
	-0.034		-0.037		-0.040	
National corruption	-0.419	0.000	-0.342	0.000	-0.508	0.000
	-0.087		-0.093		-0.099	
Victim	-0.104	0.240	-0.010	0.920	-0.090	0.930
	-0.089		-0.095		-0.099	

continued...

Table 7.4, continued

Citizen Trust in the Three Orders of Government in the National Sample (Logit Models)

	President		Governor		Municipal president	
	Coefficient (st. error)	p value	Coefficient (st. error)	p value	Coefficient (st. error)	p value
Perceptions on government performance						
Effectiveness of security policies	0.737 -0.088	0.000	0.790 -0.094	0.000	0.666 -0.099	0.000
Take into account people's needs	0.920 -0.090	0.000	0.850 -0.095	0.000	0.548 -0.101	0.000
Performance approval	0.773 -0.095	0.000	0.305 -0.047	0.000	0.269 -0.046	0.000
Corruption of local authorities					0.118 -0.151	0.433
Constant	-1.501 -0.332	0.000	-1.358 0.380	0.000	-1.255 -0.416	0.000

continued...

Table 7.4, continued

Citizen Trust in the Three Orders of Government in the National Sample (Logit Models)

	President		Governor		Municipal president	
	Coefficient (st. error)	p value	Coefficient (st. error)	p value	Coefficient (st. error)	p value
Nagelkerke R^2	0.282		0.202		-0.136	
Overall prediction	69.9%		66.0%		65.2%	
Number of observations	2320		2337		2027	

Source: USAL-Colmex (2011).

category of PAN.

For governors, a better retrospective pocketbook economic perception increases the probability of trusting in this official. In contrast, individuals considering that both the national and their personal economic situations have improved tend to be more trustworthy of their municipal presidents.

Finally, positive perceptions about the effectiveness of the state or municipal security policies, the overall performance of the governor or the municipal president, and the idea that they take into account the needs of the citizens increase the likelihood that citizens trust their governor or their mayor.

Now, in order to explore whether context influences the levels of trust in government, we estimated logistic models for the three Mexican states oversampled in the survey. Thus, Table 7.5 presents the results of the determinants of trust in the president in three different states: Mexico City (governed by the PRD), Guanajuato (governed by the PAN), and Veracruz (governed by the PRI).

Noticeably, context has a decisive effect on the levels of citizen trust in the president. In the case of the Mexico City, membership in organizations exerts a positive and significant effect on the level of confidence in the president; this is not the case, however, for Guanajuato and Veracruz.

Regarding retrospective national economic perceptions, the variable has a positive and significant effect in Veracruz but not in Mexico City nor in Guanajuato. The findings across the three states, comparing the effects of satisfaction with democracy, perception of national corruption in the national government,[15] and having been the victim of a crime, emphasize the fact that confidence in the president seems to originate

---

15. In Guanajuato and Veracruz, perceptions of corruption in the national government are also significantly related to confidence in the president. In Guanajuato, as expected, the perception of corruption is negatively related to trust (i.e., the higher the levels of perceived corruption in the country, the lower the level of confidence in the president); in contrast, in Veracruz the relationship is positive (i.e., the higher the levels of perceived corruption, the higher the levels of trust). This may have to do with the escalation in drug violence in the state of Veracruz. Just a month before our survey was carried out, thirty-five dead bodies were dumped by suspected drug traffickers near the city's biggest shopping mall. This terrible fact may have had a positive effect on people's levels of support and confidence in President Calderon's security strategy, independent of other concerns such as corruption or economic issues. Clearly, this assertion needs to be studied more deeply for verification.

… continued on page 209

Table 7.5

Citizen Trust in the President in Three Mexican States (Logit Models)

	Mexico City		Guanajuato		Veracruz	
	Coefficient (st. error)	p-value	Coefficient (st. error)	p-value	Coefficient (st. error)	p-value
Sociodemographics						
Gender	.0220	0.423	-0.266	0.333	-0.197	0.474
	-0.275		-0.275		-0.275	
Age	-0.003	0.733	0.003	0.744	-0.008	0.448
	-0.009		-0.009		-0.010	
Education level	-0.102	0.151	0.005	0.949	-0.019	0.805
	-0.071		-0.082)		-0.077	
Income	-0.016	0.815	0.116	0.079	0.202	0.106
	-0.066		-0.066		-0.125	
Indigenous	-0.633	0.510	-0.774	0.623	-0.735	0.101
	-0.961		-1.572		-0.448	
Employed	0.372	0.190	0.325	0.254	0.286	0.308
	-0.284		-0.285		-0.280	
Religiosity	0.125	0.227	-0.081	0.478	0.060	0.589
	-0.104		-0.114		-0.112	

continued...

Table 7.5, continued

Citizen Trust in the President in Three Mexican States (Logit Models)

	Mexico City		Guanajuato		Veracruz	
	Coefficient (st. error)	p-value	Coefficient (st. error)	p-value	Coefficient (st. error)	p-value
Group effects						
Membership in organization	0.632	0.020	0.237	0.359	-0.207	0.505
	-0.272		-0.258		-0.310	
Priista	-0.091	0.843	-0.167	0.592	-0.567	0.137
	-0.461		-0.312		-0.381	
Perredista	-0.411	0.357	0.469	0.428	-0.577	0.377
	-0.446		-0.591		-0.653	
Other	0.335	0.664	0.093	0.918	-1.888	0.147
	-0.771		-0.095		-1.301	
Independent	-0.520	0.205	0.060	0.857	-0.780	0.038
	-0.410		-0.330		-0.377	

continued…

Table 7.5, continued

Citizen Trust in the President in Three Mexican States (Logit Models)

	Mexico City		Guanajuato		Veracruz	
	Coefficient (st. error)	p-value	Coefficient (st. error)	p-value	Coefficient (st. error)	p-value
Economic perceptions						
Retrospective national	0.100	0.809	0.470	0.212	0.886	0.043
	-0.414		-0.376		-0.438	
Retrospective pocketbook	-0.205	0.601	-0.733	0.046	-0.207	0.629
	-0.395		-0.367		-0.428	
Political and social perceptions						
Satisfaction with democracy	0.265	0.014	0.017	0.869	0.059	0.614
	-0.108		-0.102		-0.118	
National corruption	-0.406	0.157	-0.646	0.010	0.500	0.067
	-0.286		-0.252		-0.273	
Victim	-0.844	0.001	-0.032	0.902	-0.187	0.532
	0.263		-0.256		-0.299	

continued…

Table 7.5, continued

Citizen Trust in the President in Three Mexican States (Logit Models)

	Mexico City		Guanajuato		Veracruz	
	Coefficient (st. error)	p-value	Coefficient (st. error)	p-value	Coefficient (st. error)	p-value
Perceptions on government performance						
Effectiveness of security policies	0.737 -0.088	0.000	0.737 -0.289	0.011	0.687 -0.274	0.012
Take into account people's needs	0.920 -0.090	0.000	0.884 -0.256	0.001	1.058 -0.268	0.000
Performance approval	0.773 -0.095	0.000	0.885 -0.304	0.004	0.070 -0.138	0.611
Constant	-1.225 -1.023	1.023	-0.652 -0.968	0.968	-0.379 -1.054	0.719
Nagelkerke R²	0.402		0.248		0.221	
Overall prediction	73.5%		75.4%		72.9%	
Number of observations	400		400		400	

Source: USAL-Colmex (2011).

from different sources with two key exceptions. These are both perceptions regarding government performance: first, the effectiveness of security policies; and second, the responsiveness of the president. These
two variables are statistically significant and positively related with
levels of confidence in the president in the three states.

In order to assess whether the predictors of confidence in the president are similar to those of the governor (representing a different trustee in a different order of government), we estimated three additional
models where the dependent variable is the level of confidence in the
governor, one for each of the three states under analysis (see Table 7.6).

Just as in the national sample, in the case of Mexico City, religiosity
relates positively to trust. This is consistent with research showing that
high levels of religiosity enhance both interpersonal and institutional trust (Brañas-Garza et al. 2009). Regarding political and social perceptions, those more satisfied with democracy, those perceiving lower
levels of national corruption, those regarding public safety policies as
effective, and those considering that they have a responsive governor
tend to be more trusting in this official.

In Guanajuato, the factors determining whether citizens confide in
their governor are membership in organizations and variables related
to performance evaluation of the state government (e.g., effectiveness
of security policies, responsiveness, and overall performance approval).

Finally, in Veracruz, victimization has a negative effect; those reporting having been a victim of a crime tend to trust the governor less. In
addition, a couple of performance variables are significantly and positively related to trust: the effectiveness of security policies and the responsiveness of the state executive.

Even though the statistical analysis offered in the models reveals that
trust in the president, the governors, or the municipal presidents is context dependent, overall the key explanatory variables are perceptions
of government performance. In particular, the effectiveness of security
policies and the extent to which the official takes into account the needs
of the people when taking decisions are the key forces behind trusting
or not trusting.

... continued on page 215

Table 7.6

Citizen Trust in the Governor in Three Mexican States (Logit Models)

	Mexico City		Guanajuato		Veracruz	
	Coefficient (st. error)	p-value	Coefficient (st. error)	p-value	Coefficient (st. error)	p-value
Sociodemographics						
Gender	-0.005	0.987	0.198	0.510	-0.323	0.305
	-0.327		-0.301		-0.315	
Age	-0.023	0.030	0.002	0.842	-0.002	0.854
	-0.011		-0.010		-0.012	
Education level	-0.113	0.183	-0.026	0.770	-0.016	0.863
	-0.085)		-0.090		-0.094	
Income	0.015	0.857	0.113	0.123	0.188	0.151
	0.081		-0.073		-0.131	
Indigenous	-1.751	0.081	22.790	0.999	-0.448	0.411
	-1.003		-40192.97		-0.544	
Employed	0.123	0.732	0.304	0.330	0.370	0.272
	-0.359		-0.311		-0.337	
Religiosity	0.299	0.025	0.102	0.411	-0.014	0.914
	-0.133		-0.124		-0.132	

continued...

Table 7.6, continued

Citizen Trust in the Governor in Three Mexican States (Logit Models)

	Mexico City		Guanajuato		Veracruz	
	Coefficient (st. error)	p-value	Coefficient (st. error)	p-value	Coefficient (st. error)	p-value
Group effects						
Membership in organization	0.159 -0.335	0.635	0.582 -0.293	0.047	-0.256 -0.360	0.477
Priista	-0.183 -0.559	0.744	-0.366 -0.341	0.284	0.454 -0.409	0.267
Perredista	0.149 -0.548	0.786	-0.479 -0.662	0.470	0.360 -0.755	0.633
Other	-0.308 -0.932	0.741	-0.853 1.353	0.529	-0.628 -1.574	0.690
Independent	-0.491 -0.487	0.314	-0.347 -0.368	0.346	0.220 -0.412	0.594

continued…

Table 7.6, continued

Citizen Trust in the Governor in Three Mexican States (Logit Models)

	Mexico City		Guanajuato		Veracruz	
	Coefficient (st. error)	p-value	Coefficient (st. error)	p-value	Coefficient (st. error)	p-value
Economic perceptions						
Retrospective national	-0.424	0.359	-0.141	0.736	-0.483	0.296
	-0.462		-0.419		-0.462	
Retrospective pocketbook	0.389	0.371	0.238	0.563	0.255	0.596
	-0.434		-0.411		-0.482	
Political and social perceptions						
Satisfaction with democracy	0.278	0.034	-0.016	0.894	-0.196	0.173
	-0.131		-0.118		-0.144	
National corruption	-0.776	0.027	-0.151	0.612	0.405	0.189
	-0.352		-0.298		-0.308	
Victim	-0.136	0.670	0.394	0.170	-0.635	0.063
	-0.319		-0.287		-0.341	

continued...

Table 7.6, continued

Citizen Trust in the Governor in Three Mexican States (Logit Models)

	Mexico City		Guanajuato		Veracruz	
	Coefficient (st. error)	p-value	Coefficient (st. error)	p-value	Coefficient (st. error)	p-value
Perceptions on government performance						
Effectiveness of security policies	0.785 -0.318	0.013	0.973 -0.314	0.002	0.978 -0.316	0.002
Take into account people's needs	0.650 -0.312	0.037	0.605 -0.292	0.038	1.215 -0.327	0.000
Performance approval	0.183 -0.161	0.256	0.603 -0.181	0.001	0.095 -0.179	0.594
Approval of Calderon	-0.070 0.159	0.658	-0.131 -0.175	0.454	-0.086 -0.168	0.608
Constant	0.191 -01.323	0.885	-2.873 -1.242	0.021	-0.060 -1.295	0.963

continued...

Table 7.6, continued

Citizen Trust in the Governor in Three Mexican States (Logit Models)

	Mexico City		Guanajuato		Veracruz	
	Coefficient (st. error)	p-value	Coefficient (st. error)	p-value	Coefficient (st. error)	p-value
Nagelkerke R²	0.270		0.273		0.240	
Overall prediction	71.4%		76.3%		73.2%	
Number of observations	400		400		400	

Source: USAL-Colmex (2011).

Conclusions

Despite the variations in the findings of Kincaid and coauthors throughout time (2004, 2010), in both surveys Mexicans are the least trusting toward their governments in North America. Furthermore, the Latinobarometer polls of 2009, 2010, and 2011 consistently rank Mexico at the bottom of the list of Latin American countries regarding the satisfaction of citizens with democracy.[16] In 2013, moreover, Mexicans are the most unsatisfied with democracy among the citizens of Latin America. What are the sources of this generalized and time-persistent distrust?

The analysis presented in this chapter reveals that the key explanatory variables for the levels of trust for officials in the three orders of government in the Mexican federation are performance related: particularly, the effectiveness of public safety policies and their responsiveness to the needs of the citizens. Apparently, Mexicans tend to consider their governments mostly ineffective and thus not trustworthy; however, as we have shown in the chapter, there is variation across orders of government and states.

Especially revealing is the fact that variables such as membership in organizations, party identification, assessments of the state of the economy, satisfaction with democracy, national corruption, and crime victimization are statistically significant only in specific contexts (i.e., in specific states).

In Mexico City, for example, membership in a union or a non-governmental organization increases the probability that a citizen trusts the president. In Guanajuato, perceiving low levels of corruption in the national government turns out to be crucial, while in Veracruz the retrospective evaluation of the state of the economy is key. In short, even when deciding to trust or not trust the same person, such as the president, context seems to make a significant difference in these states.

Similarly, when deciding whether or not to trust their governor, citizens from Mexico City are clearly influenced by how satisfied they are with democracy and by their perceived level of corruption in the national government. In contrast, in Guanajuato, beyond government performance, the key variable is membership in an organization. Final-

---

16. The specific question posed to interviewees is "How satisfied are you with the way in which democracy works in your country?" Interestingly, in 2013, barely 20 percent of those interviewed agree with the statement that "Mexico is governed for everyone's benefit," thus clearly revealing that most Mexicans consider that government officials do not pursue the common good.

ly, in Veracruz, the most influential determinant of trust is whether the respondent had been the victim of a crime recently.

Even though the statistical models reveal that trust in the president, the governors, or the municipal presidents is context dependent, in general the crucial forces behind trusting or not trusting are perceptions of government performance: the effectiveness of security policies and the extent to which the official takes into account the needs of the people when taking decisions.

Although, in the Mexican case, the secession of a state has not been considered a threat in recent times, we briefly focus on the positive and negative consequences of these low levels of trust and attachment for the operation of a democratic federal system in Mexico.

Recentralizing Tendencies?

As we discussed at the beginning of the chapter, democratic mechanisms (e.g., the checks and balances of presidential and federal systems) serve to limit the authority of specific actors in the political arena. For example, the authority of the Supreme Court prevents state governments from implementing laws with unconstitutional provisions, and the federal government may not modify the Constitution without the approval of the majority of the state legislatures.

In several areas, since at least 2003, there have been significant, although subtle, recentralizing tendencies in Mexico. Basic education and health services for the uninsured were decentralized to the states in the 1990s; however, federal programs (such as *Oportunidades*, *Seguro Popular*, and *Escuelas de Calidad*) have progressively imposed on state governments specific and restrictive rules for their operation.

Given that Mexicans tend to trust the federal government more than their state or municipal authorities, these recentralizing tendencies may enjoy wide popular support and thus further weaken the possibility of state and local governments checking the powers of the federation. In a country as heterogeneous and complex as Mexico, subnational policies are very much needed to tend to specific and different needs across the territory and also as laboratories of policies that may later be extended to other states or to the nation as a whole.

Is Trust in Government Officials Related to Satisfaction with a Democratic Regime?

For specific social tasks, trust may generate means of social coordination when other instruments such as government regulation or market forces are not capable of doing so (Offe 1999). The studies reviewed in the first part of this chapter show that Mexico is in a clear disadvantage with respect to Canada and the United States in this regard (Kincaid et al. 2011) and thus reveal somewhat dim prospects for a consolidation of the democratic system in Mexico.

Recent studies have shown that Mexicans' satisfaction with democracy has declined over recent years. The Latinobarometer of 2006 showed that 41 percent of Mexicans were satisfied with the democracy of their country; in 2009, this perception declined to 28 percent. In 2011, the percentage of satisfaction with democracy decreased even more, down to 23 percent, and in 2013 the same percentage dropped to 21 percent. Among all the Latin American countries, only Honduras had a lower level of satisfaction in 2013 than Mexico (18 percent). Interestingly, whereas in the entire continent the main reasons of dissatisfaction are the economic situation, crime, and unemployment, in Mexico the reasons are related to income distribution and security. Since both indexes have definitely not improved but indeed have worsened during recent years, this decline in satisfaction with democracy will definitely not cease with the return of the PRI to the executive power (Moreno 2013; *The Economist* 2013).

We have seen that, in general, trust in government officials is related to satisfaction with a democratic regime, although there are variations. Using the national survey, we found that satisfaction with democracy is positively and significantly associated with trusting the president and the municipal presidents but not the governors. Using the state surveys, satisfaction is a variable increasing the probability of having confidence in the president and the governor in Mexico City but not in Guanajuato or Veracruz.

As we have already discussed, the most consistent and robust finding of this research is that the main determinants of trust across the orders of government in Mexico are performance related. Thus, the relationship between government performance and satisfaction with democracy may be mediated by trust. In this regard, because trust relates to government performance, and performance to satisfaction with democracy, we can expect low levels of trust to weaken both Mexican democracy and government integrity (see Table 7.7).

In fact, most political analysts conclude that for democracy to blossom in Mexico in the next twenty years governance needs to be strengthened: in particular, clearly enforcing the rule of law, increasing

Table 7.7

Correlations between Perception of Performance of Government Officials at Different Levels of Government and Satisfaction with Democracy (National Sample)

Perception of good performance and satisfaction with democracy	Tau c	Gamma
President	0.272***	0.379***
	-0.020	-0.026
Governor	0.169***	0.242***
	-0.020	-0.028
Municipal president	0.166***	0.216***
	-0.021	-0.026

*** significant at 0.001 level

Source: USAL-Colmex (2011).

the accountability of public servants and politicians (i.e., by consolidating the checks and balances across branches and levels of government), and also empowering citizens. In the realm of federalism, subnational governments need to be transformed at least in two crucial areas: fiscal responsibility, given that they tend to spend mostly federal transfers and not own-source income, and civil service, because a large number of state and municipal public officials lack the indispensable professional qualifications and expertise to perform their jobs.[17]

Low levels of satisfaction with democracy may increase the legitimacy of other types of regimes among the citizenry or, at least, increase their support for centralizing or authoritarian decisions. Therefore, one of the current greatest challenges of elected politicians in Mexico in the three orders of government is to build and restore the link of trust between citizens and government authorities.

---

17. In this regard, at the end of 2013 the national Congress approved a constitutional reform that now allows the re-election of municipal presidents. This is a very welcome reform as it gives mayors a longer period to learn the trade and deliver results, thus placing their political future more in the hands of voters than in the purses of political bosses.

References

Brehm, John, and Wendy Rahn. 1997. "Individual-Level Evidence for the Causes and Consequences of Social Capital." *American Journal of Political Science* 41 (3): 999–1023.

Boix, Carle, and Daniel N. Posner. 1998. "Social Capital: Explaining Its Origins and Effects on Government Performance." *British Journal of Political Science* 28 (4): 686–93.

Brañas-Garza, Pablo, Máximo Rossi, and Dayna Zaclicever. 2009. "Individual's Religiosity Enhances Trust: Latin-American Evidence for the Puzzle." *Journal of Money, Credit and Banking* 41 (2/3): 555–66.

Cleary, Matthew, and Susan Stokes. 2006. *Democracy and the Culture of Skepticism: Political Trust in Argentina and Mexico.* New York: Russell Sage Foundation.

Cole, Richard, and John Kincaid. 2000. "Public Opinion and American Federalism: Perspectives on Taxes, Spending, and Trust: An ACIR Update." *Publius: The Journal of Federalism* 30 (1): 189–216.

Cole, Richard L., John Kincaid, and Alejandro Rodríguez. 2004. "Public Opinion on Federalism and Federal Political Culture in Canada, México, and the United States." *Publius: The Journal of Federalism.* 34 (3): 201–21.

Domínguez, Jorge I. 1999. "The Transformation of Mexico's Electoral and Party Systems, 1988–1997: An Introduction." In *Toward Mexico's Democratization: Parties, Campaigns, Elections, and Public Opinion,* edited by Jorge I. Dominguez and Alejandro Poire, 1–23. New York: Routledge.

Domínguez, Jorge, and Chappell Lawson, eds. 2004. *Mexico's Pivotal Democratic Election. Candidates, Voters and the Presidential Campaign of 2000.* Palo Alto, CA: Stanford University Press.

Flamand, Laura. 2004. "The Vertical Dimension of Government. Democratization and Federalism in Mexico." PhD diss. University of Rochester, NY.

González, Manuel. 2006. "United Mexican States." In *Distribution of Powers and Responsibilities in Federal Countries,* edited by Akhtar Majeed, Ronald L. Watts, and Douglas Brown, 181–206. Montreal and Kingston: McGill-Queen's University Press.

Gutiérrez, Juan. 2005. "United Mexican States." In *Constitutional Origins, Structure, and Change in Federal Countries,* edited by John Kincaid and George A. Tarr, 208–38. Montreal and Kingston: McGill-Queen's University Press.

Graizbord, Boris. 2009. "United Mexican States." In *Local Government and Metropolitan Regions in Federal Systems*, edited by Nico Steytler, 200–33. Montreal and Kingston: McGill-Queen's University Press.

Hardin, Russell. 1999. "Do We Want to Trust in Government?" In *Democracy & Trust*, edited by Mark E. Warren, 22–41. New York: Cambridge University Press.

Inglehart, Ronald. 1999. "Post-modernization Erodes Respect for Authority, But Increases Support for Democracy." In *Citizens: Global Support for Democratic Governance*, edited by Pippa Norris, 236–56. Oxford: Oxford University Press.

———. 1999. "Trust, Well-Being and Democracy." In *Democracy and Trust*, edited by Mark E. Warren, 88–121. New York: Cambridge University Press.

Instituto Nacional de Geografía e Informática [INEGI]. 2012. *Finanzas públicas estatales y municipales*, México: INEGI. http://www.inegi.org.mx/est/contenidos/proyectos/registros/economicas/finanzas/.

Kelleher, Cristine A. and Jennifer Wolak. 2007. "Explaining Public Confidence in the Branches of State Government." *Political Research Quarterly*, 60: 707–721.

Kincaid, John, and Richard L. Cole. 2011. "Citizen Attitudes Toward Issues of Federalism in Canada, Mexico and the United States." *Publius: The Journal of Federalism* 41 (1): 53–75.

Kramer, Roderick. 1999. "Trust and Distrust in Organizations: Emerging Perspectives, Enduring Questions." *Annual Review of Psychology* 50: 569–98.

Langston, Joy. 2006. "The Changing Party of the Institutional Revolution. Electoral Competition and Decentralized Candidate Selection." *Party Politics* 12 (3): 395–413.

Leach, William, and Paul Sabatier. 2005. "To Trust an Adversary: Integrating Rational and Psychological Models of Collaborative Policymaking." *American Political Science Review* 99 (4): 491–503.

Levi, Margaret. 1988. *Of Rule and Revenue*. Berkeley: University of California Press.

———. 1996. "Social and Unsocial Capital." *Politics and Society* 24 (1): 45–55.

Magaloni, Beatriz. 2008. *Voting for Autocracy: Hegemonic Party Survival and its Demise in Mexico*. Cambridge, MA: Cambridge University Press.

Merino, Mauricio. 2003. La transición votada: Crítica a la interpretación del cambio político en México. México: Fondo de Cultura Económica.

Moreno, Alejandro. 2013. "Razones de la insatisfacción," *Reforma*. http://busquedas.gruporeforma.com/reforma/Documento/Impresa.aspx?id=5022014 | InfodexTextos&tit=&text=Razones+de+la+insatisfacci%f3n&url=https://hemerotecalibre.reforma.com/20131110/interactiva/RENF20131110-012.jpg.

Offe, Claus. 1999. "How Can We Trust our Fellow Citizens?" In *Democracy and Trust*, edited by Mark E. Warren, 42–87. New York: Cambridge University Press.

Ortega, Reynaldo. 2008. *Movilización y democracia: España y México*. México: El Colegio de México.

Programa de las Naciones Unidas para el Desarrollo México [PNUD]. 2008. *Índice de Desarrollo Humano Municipal en México 2000–2005*. México: PNUD.

Putnam, Robert D. 1993. *Making Democracy Work: Civic Traditions in Modern Italy*. Princeton: Princeton University Press.

———. 1995. "Bowling Alone: America's Declining Social Capital." *Journal of Democracy* 6 (1): 65–78.

———. 2000. *Bowling Alone: The Collapse and Revival of American Community*. New York: Simon and Schuster.

Pye, Lucian W. 1990. "Political Science and the Crisis of Authoritarianism." *American Political Science Review*, 84 (1): 3–19.

Rotter, Julian. 1971. "Generalized Expectancies for Interpersonal Trust." *American Psychologist 35* (1): 1–7.

Sabatier, Paul, and Hans Jenkins-Smith. 1993. *Policy Change and Learning: An Advocacy Coalition Approach*. Boulder, CO: Westview Press.

Safadi, Najwa, and Margaret Lombe. 2011. "Exploring the Relationship Between Trust in Government and the Provision of Social Services in Countries of Globa South: The Case of Palestine." *Journal of Social Service Research*. 37 (4): 403–11.

Schiavon, Jorge, David Crow, Gerardo Maldonado, Rodrigo Morales, and González Guadalupe. 2013. "Mexico, the Americas and the World, 2012–2013. Foreign Policy: Public Opinion and Leaders." Working Paper, CIDE, Mexico City. http://repositorio-digital.cide.edu/handle/11651/885.

The Ecomomist. 2013. "The Latinobarómetro Poll: Listen to Me." *The Economist*. https://www.economist.com/news/americas/21588886-slightly-brighter-picture-democracy-not-liberal-freedoms-listen-me.

Uslaner, Eric. 1999. "Democracy and Social Capital," in *Democracy and Trust*, edited by Mark E. Warren, 121–50. New York: Cambridge University Press.

———. 2002. *The Moral Foundations of Trust.* New York: Cambridge University Press.

Ward, Peter, and Victoria Rodríguez. 1999. "New Federalism, Intra-Governmental Relations and Co-Governance in Mexico." *Journal of Latin American Studies* 31 (3): 673–710.

Warren, Mark. 1996. "Deliberative Democracy and Authority." *American Political Science Review* 90 (1): 46–60.

———. 1999. "Introduction." In *Democracy and Trust*, edited by Mark E. Warren, 1–21. New York: Cambridge University Press.

World Bank. 2013a. "Mexico. World Development Indicators." http://data.worldbank.org/country/mexico#cp_wdi.

———. 2013b. "Gini Index. Data." http://data.worldbank.org/indicator/SI.POV.GINI.

Wuhs, Steven. 2013. "Mexico: From Centralized Authoritarianism to Disarticulated Democracy?" In *Routledge Handbook of Regionalism and Federalism*, edited by John Loughlin, John Kincaid, and Wilfried Swenden, 190–208. Oxford, UK: Routledge.

8

Challenging the Irrevocable Decline: Democratic Satisfaction, National Cohesion, and Federal Political Culture in Australia (2008–2014)

A. J. Brown and Jacob Deem

Introduction

Like many Western democracies, Australia has experienced a decline in popular trust in elected institutions. However, interpreting reasons and possible solutions through surveys of public attitudes is difficult, given susceptibility to changes in political climate, electoral cycles, and media discourse. Yet, if different elements of public opinion track differently over a given period, especially if they span recognized categories of diffuse and specific factors, it may be possible to identify reforms that might address falling trust and thus improve to the health of the political system. This chapter uses results from the first four Australian Constitutional Values Surveys (2008, 2010, 2012, and 2014) to examine the role of different factors in public opinion—particularly evidence that elements of federal political culture are holding constant, even when satisfaction in democracy and in the federal system is suffering declines. The results challenge assumptions that Australia's system works well as a stable recipe for national political cohesion, but they also provide a

Identities, Trust, and Cohesion in Federal Systems: Public Perceptions, edited by Jack Jedwab and John Kincaid. Montréal and Kingston: McGill-Queen's University Press, Queen's Policy Studies Series. © 2018 The School of Policy Studies, Queen's University at Kingston. All rights reserved.

new basis for believing that strengthening and improving federalism is one important option for addressing this and thus for bolstering public trust in governance overall.

How are we to interpret evidence of declining trust in political institutions? Further, is it possible to identify specific areas of reform—to institutions or political practice—which, if addressed, might arrest or ameliorate such decline? We approach these questions through two prisms in order to understand the dynamics of public trust and political cohesion in Australia. The first prism is the general search in political science for better means of distinguishing between the factors that explain empirically measured levels of public trust in government. The second is the particular contribution that the study of federal political culture might play in that search—requiring, by definition, a focus on elements of public attitudes that span a spectrum from diffuse sociological considerations to more specific judgments of the extent to which political practice, institutional design, and constitutional structures are serving the needs of communities at their different spatial configurations.

We use national public opinion evidence from the first four Australian Constitutional Values Surveys to explore these questions.[1] The surveys consisted of stand-alone twenty-minute telephone interviews conducted of national samples of adults in May 2008, March 2010, October 2012, and September 2014.[2]

The first part of the chapter reviews the mix of factors that might in-

1. The 2008 and 2010 Australian Constitutional Values Surveys were made possible by the Australian Research Council (ARC) through Discovery Project 0666833, led by Griffith University, with Charles Stuart University, the University of Melbourne, and the University of New England; the 2012 Survey was funded by Griffith University and the University of New South Wales; and the 2014 Survey was funded by ARC Discovery Project DP140102682, led by Griffith University with the University of New South Wales, the University of Sydney, Australian National University, Lafayette College, and the University of Texas. The authors thank the ARC, project colleagues, and John Davis (Newspoll Limited; now OmniPoll Limited) for contributions to questionnaire design. Further project details are available at http://www.griffith.edu.au/federalism.
2. The twenty-minute stand-alone telephone interviews were conducted of 1201, 1100, 1219, and 1204 adult participants (2008, 2010, 2012 and 2014 respectively). Participants were sampled in a quasi-random fashion, with random digit dialing and within-household screening questions employed to ensure a random sample from quotas set in capital and non-capital stratum. Cross-referencing with data from the Australian Bureau of Statistics indicated that the samples were generally representative of the overall Australian population.

form public opinion with respect to trust at any given time and provides some background to Australian political culture, identity, and cohesion. We also suggest that whereas explanatory factors are widely accepted as falling into two major categories—"diffuse" and "specific"—they may be better understood as falling on a continuum rather than into binary categories. The second part presents three key, contrasting results for the overall state of Australian public attitudes toward government over the period. Satisfaction with the way democracy is working is experienced as steady then falling sharply; satisfaction with the way the federal system is working is experienced as a slight but important decline; while support for federalist principles of institutional design, or particular elements of federal political culture, remains constant. These results suggest quite different types of factors at work on public trust. They raise the question: if the basic picture of what citizens value in their federal political institutions is remaining steady over a given period, what is causing these differential shifts in their confidence in democracy and their general system? In particular, how do perceptions of the different spatial scales and orders of government, and relations between them, influence overall trends in public trust?

The third part of the chapter addresses this question by examining the recent decline in confidence in democracy. Here, a focus on the various levels of government confirms that falling trust in democracy in the period is driven by a fall in specific support for democratic practice and outcomes at the national level. Nevertheless, important implications are revealed for the health of the overall structure of government, which present not as problems of national cohesion but as problems nonetheless. The fourth part investigates declining satisfaction with the system as a whole, again by examining perceptions of the various levels but also relating back to federal political culture, issues of identity and attachment, and further data regarding citizens' preferences for the future of their federation. Gradual decline in faith in the federal system coincides with majority support for change, whether from a belief that federalism has failed or, more likely, that the system is not federal enough.

Conclusions are drawn regarding the mix of factors affecting the gradual decline in trust in Australia's federal system. The analyses confirm a composite picture in which part of the problem can be attributed at least indirectly to specific, short-term political events, policy shifts, and leadership behaviour, but most of it can be attributed to intermediate factors involving the nature and performance of structures and institutions, transcending incumbent governments. Further, perceptions and preferences are in part driven by entirely diffuse factors of political identity and attachment regarding scales of political organization, which present as both a problem and an asset for reform. We conclude that while perhaps little can be done to avoid volatility in short-term political behaviour and negative public reactions thereto, addressing the structure and operations of longer-term institutions to make them more federal, in line with most value preferences, is likely to have a positive influence on these intermediate and diffuse bases of trust. These results affirm the significance of federal reform as an issue for study and policy debate, while also shedding light on the complex interplay between different factors of trust.

Background: Specific Support, Diffuse Support, and Australian Political Culture

Despite the importance of citizen support for democracy, political science still struggles with the relation between general support for democratic institutions and specific support for incumbent governments. Exploring the "crisis of regime" in the United States during the early 1970s, David Easton (1975) identified the distinction between "diffuse" and "specific" support. Specific support refers to citizens' attitudes toward, and level of satisfaction with, the current government. Diffuse support is deeper, and reflects wider evaluations of the political system. While a government may attract little specific support, the institution of representative government may still be perceived positively. According to Easton (1975, 436), "political discontent is not always, or even usually, the signal for basic political change."

Easton's differentiation of diffuse and specific support has taken on renewed significance in Australia, as in other countries (e.g., Norris 1999; Aydin and Cenker 2012), as efforts are made to explain declines in trust in government. As a general measure of political health, "trust" (and like concepts such as "faith," "confidence," and "satisfaction") remain multifaceted and context dependent (Dunn 1998; Uhr 2005). Almost by definition, in democratic leadership, sustaining trust is "permanently problematic" (Kane and Patapan 2012, 83). Political trust serves to link individuals with the institutions that serve them, but the myriad factors that actually *explain* it represent "a complex miasma in need of fresh and varied consideration" (Denemark and Niemi 2012)—hence the importance of analyses that break down how overall evidence of trust and cohesion relate to the specific scales and structures at which, and through which, citizens and government actually interact. Falling trust may not be all negative: for example, if it indicates growing proportions of "critical citizens" (Norris 1999). Nevertheless, empirical study remains underpinned by the risks that too much disenchantment poses for the goals and stability of a democratic society (Doorenspleet 2012). Therefore, it is important to try to identify the different causes of fluctuations in trust—and especially, in Australia, to see if the current federal structure of governance is working as a bulwark of overall trust, identity, and cohesion, or is undermining these, or is simply irrelevant to them. We will see that risks of too much disenchantment loom large in Australian citizens' perceptions of the spatial structure of their democracy.

In any such inquiry, different results on different measures of public opinion also point to there being different factors at work. Accepting Easton's distinctions, some of these likely relate to levels of specific support for the government, arising either through individuals' assessments of incumbent governments' ability to meet their articulated demands or through perceptions of an incumbent government's general performance (Easton 1975, 438–9). On the first, if a citizen makes a demand of the government (in a personal capacity or indirectly through interest groups), the perceived extent to which this demand is met will influence their evaluation of the government. On the second, even if citizens are "unable to see their present conditions as a product of identifiable actions (or lack of actions) by the authorities, they may nonetheless be pre-disposed to hold the government responsible for their plight" (Easton 1975, 439).

At the same time, we expect to find that some results relate to levels of diffuse support—being a more durable, basic form of support, which Easton again attributes to both direct and indirect influences: direct experience and socialization. The latter assumes that childhood and adult socialization create lasting attitudes toward political institutions, evident even in the rituals and symbols surrounding political institutions and public office, which "have long been presumed to contribute in one way or another to the reservoir of more deeply rooted [sentiments]" (Easton 1975, 446). This kind of diffuse support can therefore be thought of as a complex social phenomenon—part of the psychology of all citizens (e.g., Gerrig et al. 2009; Nelson and Fivush 2004)—providing the basis of their political culture. By political culture, we mean a citizenry's body of "collective assumptions" about

governing institutions and processes, embedded in wider power relationships and woven into their assumptions about life (Smith 2001).
However, there are clearly relations between sources of specific support
and diffuse support because the latter is also shaped by direct experi-
ences. Support for government as an institution (as opposed to specific
support for an incumbent government) "may be a product of spill-over
effects from evaluations of a series of outputs and of performance over
a long period of time" (Easton 1975: 446). Prolonged specific attitudes,
or their aggregate, may eventually have an impact on underlying diffuse support, including erosion of support for an institution if citizens
are discontented with the specific government(s) or decision-makers
controlling that institution over an extended time.

Australia is a particularly interesting country in which to study these
combinations, for two reasons. First, empirical study of public attitudes
is revealing because Australian political culture entails a historically
high level of public expectations about the performance of democracy.
As primarily a postcolonial, immigrant society descended from British traditions, its political development through the second half of the
nineteenth century provided much opportunity for democratic inno-
vation of global significance (e.g., Trollope 1873; Hancock 1930). High
liberal democratic standards and ideals of public policy, established in
colonial politics during this period, were then also embedded in expectations of the new nation's federal order of government when the
colonies reunited as a federation from 1901.

Second, inquiry into the relation between territorial distributions of
power and trust in government is particularly apposite in Australia because its federation is stereotypically seen as a model of stability and
cohesion. For many, the choice of federal design was necessitated by
the degree of political independence developed by the colonies from
their separations during the 1820s to 1850s (e.g., Irving 1999a, 2). In fact,
the picture is richer than this because the idea of a single Australian nation or dominion "had been in the minds of officials ... even before the
division of the colonies" (Irving 1999b, 2), prompting British colonial
policymakers to introduce federal principles at the outset, in light of
North American developments, creating the world's first "top-down,"
deliberately created federation (Brown 2004; 2012c). Either way, the legitimacy of a federal structure is based more on functional dictates of
geographic scale, dispersal, and the role of regional political autonomy
in colonial development than on any need to bind fully independent
polities or socio-cultural groups (Galligan 1995). Claims that Austra-

lia's relative lack of territorial cultural diversity undermine the case for federalism have been contested, first on the basis that imperatives of regional self-determination and political diversity are enough (Holmes and Sharman 1977) and more recently using evidence that cultural and socio-economic diversity are of growing relevance (Aroney et al. 2012). Nevertheless, the federation was founded on a strong philosophy of cultural and political homogeneity, respect for British unitary ideals, and a strong sense of cohesion.

These fundamentals are reflected today in the overall pattern of Australian citizens' attachment to the spatial scales at which their governing institutions are organized—primarily an "indirect diffuse" variable as an element of the attitudinal mix, using Easton's categories. Table 8.1 presents the results for citizen "belonging" and "attachment" to different spatial scales from the 2008, 2012, and 2014 Australian Constitutional Values Surveys, compared with equivalent "attachment" results for Germany, Canada, and the United States.

These results highlight important questions about the best ways of measuring this variable. In Australia, different results were obtained when citizens were asked about their sense of "belonging" to particular scales in 2008 (arguably prioritizing emotional, historical, and cultural ties), as against how strongly "attached" they felt to the same scales in 2012 (arguably prioritizing physical and economic ties, a citizen could have no sense of belonging and yet feel irrevocably "attached," for example, if economically trapped). These results suggest the need for an approach to measuring political identity that properly accounts for both sets of elements (Brown and Deem 2014). Further differences may stem from the fact that the US, Canadian, and German surveys measured attachment to political scales alongside a long list of other items, whereas the Australian questions were restricted to political scales. Nevertheless, the contrasting order of the scales commanding greatest to least attachment shows each country to be distinctive. Like citizens in the United States, Australian citizens' national attachment ranks as very strong, but at the subnational level, unlike the United States and even more so Canada, Australians' local attachment competes with and may outrank state attachment—a pattern more akin to Germany. As a "diffuse" variable, this pattern of identification, including the vexed question of "regional" attachment, emerges as significant below.

This discussion of factors also suggests a need for ongoing debate about the best ways to categorize them. Whereas Easton's initial distinction between diffuse and specific support was intended to explain

Table 8.1

Sense of Attachment/Belonging to Nation, State, Local Compared (Percentages)

%	Germany	Canada	USA	Australia		
	2010	2010	2010	2008	2012	2014
Strength of ...		Attachment		Belong-ing	Attach-ment	Attach-ment
Nation						
Very strong	47.3	58.0	67.0	64.4	78.1	73.3
Quite strong	36.6	29.0	25.0	25.7	19.4	21.7
Subtotal	83.9	87.0	92.0	90.1	97.5	95.0
Not very/at all[a]	15.5	12.0	7.0	9.9	2.4	4.6
State	Lander	Province	State	State	State	State
Very strong	35.9	46.0	40.0	43.0	50.1	47.5
Quite strong	41.6	42.0	40.0	38.8	39.5	42.2
Subtotal	77.5	88.0	80.0	81.8	89.6	89.7
Not very/at all[a]	22.0	11.0	18.0	18.2	10.1	10.1
Region[b]						
Very strong				40.1 [c]	51.6	46.5
Quite strong				39.9 [c]	39.5	40.6
Subtotal				80.0 [c]	91.1	87.1
Not very/at all[a]				20.0 [c]	8.7	7.0
Local						
Very strong	42.4	37.0	34.0	39.8	54.1	51.2
Quite strong	38.2	45.0	40.0	39.3	37.9	39.1
Subtotal	80.6	82.0	74.0	79.1	91.9	90.3
Not very/at all[a]	19.1	18.0	25.0	20.9	7.8	9.1

Notes: [a]Not very/not at all strong given as two items in a four-point scale in ACS surveys and 2012 Australian survey but as a single item in a three-point scale in

continued

Table 8.1, continued

Sense of Attachment/Belonging to Nation, State, Local Compared (Percentages)

2008 Australian survey. [b] "Region" defined as "an area that is bigger than your local area, but smaller than the whole of" the respondent's state/territory. [c] 2008 regional belonging only asked of those who identified as living in a region, presented as percentage of those; 2012 and 2014 regional attachment asked and presented as percentage of all respondents. "Don't know" responses omitted.

Source: Germany, Canada, and USA: Association for Canadian Studies (2010); and authors' 2008, 2012, and 2014 Australian Constitutional Values Surveys (question not asked in 2010 Australian survey).

why citizens could still trust democracy even when a particular regime was corrupt, subsequent patterns of generally declining trust appear to require a more nuanced diagnosis. The connections between specific and diffuse support have become more important, especially the way in which specific political choices and practices impact on overall values and preferences—not only in terms of the "outputs" of specific incumbent governments, or many governments, but the effects of choices of institutional design on governing practices that transcend the decisions of any or all specific incumbent governments. Here, a focus on the territorial and spatial bases of multi-level governance becomes crucial because these diffuse variables can be presumed to be important for citizens' views on whether different orders of government have sufficient power and capacity to perform desired roles, are configured or structured sufficiently to represent and maximize their interests, or are capable of effective cooperation or competition.

The design and functionality of multi-level governance is thus more than simply a cultural artefact, and yet it is not directly or entirely within the control of any single elected regime to improve. It becomes a "conditioning quality" of the democratic system, key to understanding how the system performs and how citizens form their judgments of its performance, irrespective of its "defining properties" (see Alexander, Inglehart, and Welzel 2011, 59). Such conditioning qualities occupy a complex middle ground in which Easton's distinctions between diffuse and specific factors tend to collapse. Accordingly, in discussing the different variables below, we suggest it may be better to see the range of factors as occupying a continuum rather than hard categories.

Three Differences Across Time: A Cliff, a Slide, and a Flat Line

Studies repeated over time (i.e., 2008–14) are especially useful because they not only track whether trust is rising or declining but can better allow both specific and diffuse causes to be identified or more reliably speculated upon. Moreover, three key results show that support for different features of government has moved in different ways and at different rates. By examining these differences, it is possible to identify specific as against diffuse dimensions of support for political institutions as well as begin to identify more realistically what interventions might result in changed patterns of support.

Satisfaction with Democracy

Democracy plainly lies at the heart of Australian political institutions. General public perceptions of the effectiveness of the democratic system are therefore fundamental to understanding both identity and trust. In the Australian Constitutional Values Surveys, participants were asked: "On the whole, how well do you think democracy works in Australia today?" They were offered responses on a five-point Likert Scale, with the results shown in Figure 8.1.

Consistent with the nation's history, the generally high level of Australian satisfaction with democracy is a "distinctive characteristic" of the political system (McAllister et al. 2012, 7). Nevertheless, the results show a dramatic fall in democratic satisfaction from 2008 and 2010 (80.8 percent and 82.3 percent respectively, with no statistically significant difference) to 2012 (73.1 percent) and again to 2014 (69.0 percent). A one-way analysis of variance (ANOVA) confirms this decline as statistically significant.[3] Other studies, including the Australian Election Study, confirm that, while remaining high by international standards, overall satisfaction with democracy is at its lowest point since 1998 and that the fall corresponds with a rising proportion of citizens identifying the need for "better government" among their current concerns (McAllister et al. 2012, 7; McAllister and Peitsch 2011).

The nature of the decline, however, makes it logical to look to specific events between March 2010 and October 2012, when the above data, taken together, indicate the major fall occurred. The key event prompt-

---

3. $F\ (3,\ 4623) = 31.180,\ p < .001.$

Figure 8.1

"How Well Do You Think Democracy Works in Australia?"

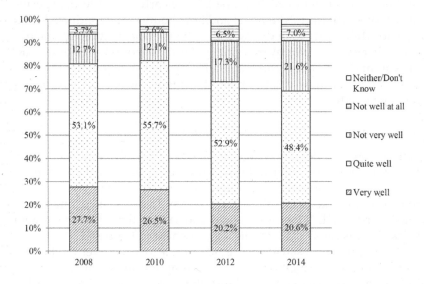

Source: Australian Constitutional Values Surveys (2008, 2012, 2014).

ing many to question the workability of democracy in this period was the surprise removal of the nation's sitting prime minister (Kevin Rudd) as leader of his party in June 2010. A bitterly fought federal election followed in August 2010, resulting in a hung Parliament and a protracted sense of political instability while a knife-edge minority government was negotiated, whose legitimacy then continued to be widely attacked in many media—all unconventional events, especially for the federal level of politics (e.g., Rourke 2010). Even after the incumbent minority government was replaced at the 2013 election, federal politics remained bitter, likely contributing to the further declines captured in the 2014 results. In September 2015, history repeated when the new prime minister (Tony Abbott) was also replaced as party leader. While public reaction appeared more supportive of this move, at least initially, future surveys will show whether this either further eroded, or served to help restore, faith in democracy.

Irrespective, while satisfaction with "the way democracy works" is sensibly regarded as capturing a wide range of variables, the major decline experienced in 2010 can be fairly clearly traced to the specific factors of Kevin Rudd's removal and how politics was conducted from 2010 to 2014, rather than diffuse ideas about democracy as a principle. This will be tested later by examining attitudes about the conduct of affairs at this level of government relative to others—a question that also throws light on how citizens relate to different levels of government more generally.

Satisfaction with the Three-Levelled Federal System

Satisfaction with democracy has dropped in Australia, but this democracy is federal, not unitary. To measure perceptions of the system as a whole, independently of its democratic qualities, participants were reminded that theirs is a three-level system (federal, state, and local). They were asked: "How well would you say the three-levelled system works in Australia?" The results are presented in Figure 8.2.

The graph shows satisfaction gradually decreasing over the period, which a one-way ANOVA revealed to be significant, if small in effect.[4] Linear contrasts showed that the decline from 2008 to 2010, and the overall difference from 2008 to 2014, were significant ($p = .016$ and $.010$ respectively) but not significant between 2010 and 2012 or between 2012 and 2014. The pattern can therefore be characterized as a slow decline that, while small in relative terms, highlights a trend that will only become worse if unaddressed. Overall, satisfaction is also plainly lower for the working of this system than it is for democracy in general. Therefore, the functionality of the federal system is an issue of greater concern to more citizens than the functionality of democracy per se. This in itself challenges basic assumptions that the federal system works as a cornerstone of Australians' usually positive view of democracy or as an optimum recipe for political stability and cohesion. It also helps explain why federal reform is an ongoing issue of policy importance in Australia (for an update, see Deem, Hollander, and Brown 2015).

Most importantly for present purposes, however, this falling satisfaction with the federal system appears to bear some relationship to attitudes toward democracy. Satisfaction with the working of democracy

---

4. $F(3, 4669) = 4.812$, $p = .002$.

Figure 8.2

"How Well Does the Three-Levelled System Work in Australia?"

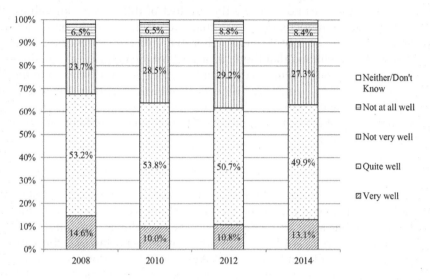

Source: Australian Constitutional Values Surveys (2008, 2012, 2014).

and the federal system was moderately and significantly correlated in each year.[5] Further, the increasing strength of the correlations suggests that there may be corroding or spillover effects from Rudd's removal in 2010. The variables are by no means inextricably linked, however. The differences in the patterns and rates of falling satisfaction with democracy and the federal system suggest that, despite some overlap, satisfaction with democracy can operate at least partly independently of satisfaction with the federal system, and vice versa.

The more gradual fall in perceptions of federal workability—which, unlike dissatisfaction with democracy, was already underway before 2012—reinforces this result. It appears to represent a fall in more diffuse support, given that it is difficult to point to specific causes of this more

---

5. 2008 $r = .363$; 2010 $r = .378$; 2012 $r = .432$, 2014 $r = .457$, $p < .001$ all years.

general decline. If there are causes, they are likely a mix of specific and diffuse effects or effects that are difficult to categorize as entirely specific or diffuse, being neither entirely the product of specific regimes or electoral outcomes nor entirely the product of diffuse societal values. This result strengthens our sense that such factors should be understood as falling on a continuum rather than into hard categories; it increases the likelihood that there are aspects of the nature and functioning of the federal system—"conditioning qualities," as discussed in the previous section—which are influencing public perception. The results again raise the question of whether concern is concentrated upon particular levels of government, or upon relations between them, or upon some other factors.

Citizen Attachment to Federal Institutional Design Principles

If satisfaction with the federal system is generally lower than satisfaction with democracy, and in gradual decline over the period, is this because public support for federalism itself is falling? The question is made doubly relevant by recognition that, notwithstanding the supposed inevitability and stability of Australia's federation, popular attitudes toward federalism have long been described as "love-hate" (Galligan 1995: 9, 53–62), adding pressure to the calls for reform noted above. Are citizens becoming less happy with the *federal* elements of this system, with its performance, or with the way it is structured?

We can answer the first question by measuring key aspects of federal political culture—in particular, citizen attachment to federalist principles of institutional design. In our surveys, participants were provided with four different institutional features of a system that "has different levels of government," commonly associated with federalism, and asked to indicate how desirable they considered each to be (see Table 8.2).

From these items, a composite measure was created by grouping respondents in logical combinations of answers, as shown in Table 8.3 below (see Brown 2012a, 2012b). This approach is part of a continuing effort to find and test internationally relevant measures of citizen attachment to federalism (see Brown et al. 2016). In the initial Australian studies here, participants who thought that all four features are desirable were defined as "Strong Federalists." Participants who thought all features are undesirable were classed "Strong Non-Federalists." Next, people who thought that division of power and different laws (legal di-

Table 8.2

Federal Political Attachment Measures of ACVS (Percentages)

%		Desirable (very/ somewhat)	Undesirable (somewhat/ very)	Neither/ don't know
Having power divided up between different levels of government	2008	68.5	25.4	6.2
	2010	67.5	26.9	5.5
	2012	69.3	24.1	6.6
	2014	72.9	22.5	4.6
Allowing different laws in response to varying needs and conditions in different parts of Australia	2008	59.3	36.1	4.6
	2010	56.3	40.7	3.3
	2012	55.5	41.5	3.0
	2014	62.2	33.7	4.1
Being able to elect different political parties at different levels of government	2008	75.9	19.2	5.0
	2010	81.7	15.2	3.1
	2012	78.1	16.6	5.3
	2014	78.7	17.4	3.9
Different governments arguing over who is responsible for a particular problem	2008	19.1	77.2	3.8
	2010	20.9	75.9	3.3
	2012	17.3	79.1	3.5
	2014	23.2	73.9	2.9

Source: Australian Constitutional Values Surveys (2008, 2010, 2012, 2014).

versity) are desirable were classed as "Clear Federalists," even if one or both of the other features were thought undesirable. "Clear Non-Federalists" were the opposite: they thought division of power and legal diversity are undesirable, regardless of response to the other two features. People who thought that division of power, but not legal diversity, is desirable were categorized as "Conflicted Federalists," while "Conflicted Non-Federalists" saw desirability in legal diversity but not division of power. These categories are given the label "conflicted" due to the apparent conflict between the two outlooks (legal diversity often presupposes at least some division of power, and to a large extent division of power provides legal diversity).

These results show that in the case of federalism *in principle*, public attitudes are more love than hate. Around two-thirds of the respon-

Table 8.3

Citizen Attachment to Federal Design Principles in Australia (Percentages)

	2008 (n = 1201)	2010 (n = 1100)	2012 (n = 1219)	2014 (n = 1204)
1. Strong Federalists	10.0	11.7	10.3	13.3
2. Clear Federalists	34.6	32.0	33.5	38.4
3. Conflicted Federalists	21.6	22.2	24.1	19.3
Subtotal—federalists	66.1	66.0	67.9	71.0
4. Conflicted Non-federalists	12.0	9.8	8.6	9.2
5. Clear Non-federalists	8.7	11.3	9.0	8.7
6. Strong Non-federalists	4.1	4.6	5.8	4.2
Subtotal—non-federalists	24.7	25.7	23.4	22.1
Don't know	9.2	8.3	8.6	6.8
	100.0	100.0	100.0	100.0

Source: Australian Constitutional Values Surveys (2008, 2010, 2012, 2014).

dents are federalists, compared with only about 25 percent who are non-federalists (see also Brown 2012a, 2012b). If there is internal conflict in values, it lies in the substantial proportion that lies in the "conflicted" bands (about 33 percent). This means that, although the majority of Australians hold federalist values, only around 44 percent can be called "strong" or "clear" federalists.

However, the most striking result is the uniformity and consistency over the four-year period; there is no decline in this "in principle" support for federalism. The responses regarding the desirability of the features, and the results in combination, were the same in all surveys. Analysis of variance confirms that there is no significant difference in the breakdown of federalists and non-federalists across time.[6]

6. $F(3, 4720) = .533, p = .660$. Linear contrasts revealed no significant differences from year to year (p values: 2008 v 2010 = .799; 2010 v 2012 = .440; 2012 v 2014 = .108; 2008 v 2014 = .366.

These results confirm that citizen attachment to federal principles was stable across the period, notwithstanding that significant change was occurring in attitudes toward democracy in general and the performance of the federal system. Despite these changes, the citizenry's attitudes regarding what they valued or sought from the political system remained unchanged. This constancy suggests that these attitudes combine to make up a diffuse variable, reflecting a range of norms, expectations, and desires deeply embedded in the society rather than being susceptible to specific short-term or immediate factors, or even intermediate ones. However, attachment to federal principles is plainly different from the question of how the federal system is actually performing. It further raises the question: if these expectations are stable, what is driving the declines in confidence?

Effectiveness and Cohesion: Which Level, All Levels, or Relations between Them?

The three contrasting results above show that, to understand public trust in Australia, we must measure it not simply in aggregate but with respect to government at each of its levels. Our surveys asked participants to nominate the level of government they considered to be the "most effective at its particular job," followed by next most effective, with the remaining level automatically classified as the least. While other results also provide insights, this measure of relative effectiveness enables us to identify support factors relevant to each level. Figure 8.3 presents the results for the least effective level. Most notable is the plummet in opinion about the federal level, shown as the large jump in citizens who rate this as the least effective. This result corresponds with the drop in satisfaction with democracy. A significant, if weak, relationship was found between these two variables.[7] This item was not included in the 2014 survey. People who were disenchanted with the way democracy operates were thus likely to be the most dissatisfied with the federal level. This supports the earlier hypothesis that the bulk of the decline in perceptions of how democracy works is attributable to the specific political events at the federal government level from mid-2010.

By contrast, the rating of local government was negatively correlated with dissatisfaction with democratic functioning.[8] On its surface, this

---

7   . 2008 r = .127, p< .001; 2010 r = .090, p = .003; 2012 r = .092, p = .001.
8. 2008 r = -.097, p = .001; 2010 r = -.132, p < .001; 2012 r = -.163; p < .001.

Figure 8.3

Least Effective Level of Government

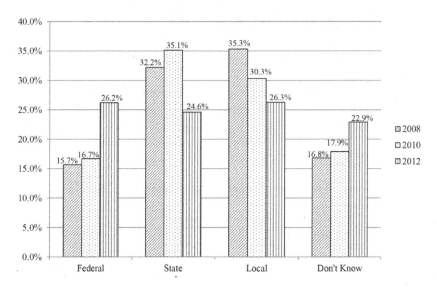

Source: Australian Constitutional Values Surveys (2008, 2010, 2012).

indicates that people who thought local government was the least effective tier were more likely to be satisfied with how well democracy is
working. However, the better interpretation is probably that those who
did not have the same adverse reaction to the political events at the
federal level simply retained greater faith in both democracy and the
federal level, and they so turned their concerns regarding effectiveness
upon the other levels. In other words, the effectiveness of local government simply does not play a significant role in people's judgments
about how well democracy is working. If they consider federal and
state governments to be more effective, they are more likely to think
that democracy is working well.

The result with respect to state government reinforces this. Here,
there was no significant relationship one way or another between rating state government as the least effective and satisfaction or dissat-

isfaction with democracy. This indicates that even if disenchantment with the performance of state government may relate to other things, it is not driving disenchantment with democracy per se. This result is consistent with qualitative evidence collected as part of the 2008 survey: that, relative to the other levels, more citizens judge state governments on the practical outcomes of the major policy and functional areas they deal with (e.g., health delivery, primary and secondary education, most on-ground transport, and most law and order) than on issues of democratic quality, political identity, representation, and inclusiveness (see Brown 2008, 458).

These results have three important implications for understanding the fall in democratic satisfaction and the general decline in satisfaction with the federal system. First, the fall in democratic satisfaction in 2010, clearly attributable to the federal government, confirms specific factors at play. However, this also reveals something about the impacts of such a fall on the effective functioning of the system as a whole. This is because, secondly, it is clear that Australian citizens are forming their primary views on the quality of democracy based on what is occurring at the federal level rather than on state or local levels. The importance of the federal level resonates with the earlier evidence of the strength of belonging or attachment that citizens attached to Australia, the nation, as a political scale. It is consistent with Australia's "thick" national identity and cohesion.

The third implication is that the fall in confidence in the federal level represents a serious issue for the overall health of the system. Consistent with Australia's "thick" national identity, citizens look to the federal government to make the entire system work better or to overcome the deficiencies in the other two levels of government, whose absolute performance—especially that of state governments—remains relatively poor. This is emphasized by the fact that, between 2010 and 2012, state elections brought changes of government in Australia's three most populous states (New South Wales, Queensland, and Victoria), in the first two cases with landslide defeats of long-term incumbents. The low satisfaction with state government remained unchanged. The sense that falling support for the federal level leaves many citizens with no level in which to have faith is reinforced by a notable increase in "don't know" responses to the question in Figure 8.3. The proportion of respondents unable to nominate who they thought most effective jumped from 12 percent in 2008 and 2010 and to 17 percent in 2012; meanwhile, the proportion who could not decide who was least effective jumped from 17 percent to 23 percent. Additionally, the correlation became stronger over the period between falling satisfaction with the overall system and the decline in performance/confidence for the federal level,[9] whereas this correlation weakened for the state and local levels.

Importantly, problems with the working of the federal system do not present as an issue of national cohesion. It will be remembered from Table 8.1 that Australians' sense of attachment to the nation in 2012 remained very strong, notwithstanding the fall in perceived performance of the national government. Indeed, bivariate correlations show only a weak correlation between citizens' "belonging" or "attachment" to a specific spatial scale and their perception of performance/confidence for the level of government at that scale, as shown in Table 8.4.

The weakness of these correlations, and the variation between positive and negative associations, indicates that a sense of belonging or attachment to an area is unlikely to influence perceptions regarding performance of that area's government. Citizens do not take a more positive view of government simply because they identify strongly with their nation, state, or locality. Similarly, government performance does not appear to influence attachment. This explains comparatively high levels of attachment to Australia as a nation, despite a decrease in satisfaction with the performance of the federal government.

Equally, whatever problems are driving falling satisfaction with democracy or the federal system are not perceived by citizens as soluble through national fracture or dissembling of the federation as a nation. Historically, the high point of such fractious responses to the system's functioning occurred in the 1930s when a majority of citizens in the "latecomer" state to the federation, Western Australia (WA), agitated to secede. While WA remains one of the states with the greatest falls in satisfaction with the system, it is also one of the states in which Australian identity runs most strongly, and, despite occasional posturing by leaders, there is little support for secession. Asked about alternative preferences for the future of the system in 2014, only 12 percent of Western Australians preferred "a system that allows a state to become an independent nation" (followed by around 5 percent or less in other states). For comparison, in response to the equivalent question in Spain, Catalonian support for this option was around 23 percent (2011), while other research puts direct support for Catalonian independence at 30

9. 2008 r= -.305, p <.001; 2012 r= -.344, p <.001.

Table 8.4

Bivariate Correlations between "Belonging/Attachment" and "Performance/Confidence" for Spatial Areas

	Federal level	State level	Local level
2008 (Strength of belonging/performance)	.118**	.128**	.076**
2012 (How strongly attached/trust and confidence to do a good job)	.096**	.047	.069*
2014 (How strongly attached/trust and confidence to do a good job)	-.068**	.006	-.038**

Notes: * p <.005; ** p <.001

Source: Australian Constitutional Values Surveys (2008, 2012, 2014).

percent (Grau Creus 2012).[10]

Instead, citizen concern with the federal system's operation is directed at the system itself. The system cannot be escaped, even if there was desire to do so; yet there is falling confidence in either the way it is structured, the way it is functioning, or both. There is a close relation between falling satisfaction overall and a growing proportion of citizens who believe that the ability for different levels "to collaborate on solutions to problems" is a desirable feature of the system but is not being achieved well in practice. In 2008, 48 percent of all participants felt that the current system failed to deliver adequate collaboration between levels, increasing to 52 percent in 2010 and 56 percent in 2012, a significant shift,[11] before settling down at 50 percent in 2014. This trend is moderately and significantly correlated with growing dissatisfaction with the overall system.[12] This is notwithstanding that most of the same

10. We thank Mireia Grau Creus of the Institut d'Estudis Autonòmics, Government of Catalonia, for her assistance in the translation and framing of our question.
11. 2008 v 2012, F (2, 3249) = 4.614, p = .003.
12. 2008 r = -.259; 2010 r = -.204; 2012 r = -.269, p (all years) <.001.

citizens voted in the state elections, mentioned above, to change their governments to ones of a different political party to the federal government. Despite these electoral changes, as shown earlier in Table 8.2, there is also no real increase in the proportion of citizens seeing it as desirable to have arguments between different levels of government, either nationally or in any individual state—even those whose new governments have espoused "competitive" over "cooperative" federalism. These results support arguments that improved machinery and processes of intergovernmental cooperation are a real and present need (see Appleby et al. 2012; Kildea et al. 2012).

Or Is It the Structure? Reform Preferences and Public Trust

At the same time, the above results suggest that the falling support for Australia's federal system relates to fundamental issues of structure—that is, diffuse factors regarding whether the design of the system is constant with preferred principles—not simply intermediate factors regarding the way those structures operate or the specific factors relating to incumbent governments. The basic view of citizens in terms of desirability of federalist design principles remains unchanged, but there is movement in their preferences regarding the future. Our surveys asked participants whether they thought the structure of the system should be the same in the future, "say 20 years from now," or different, with preferences defined by the number and type of levels of government, and numbers of units at subnational levels (for previous 2008 and 2010 results, see Brown 2012a, 2012b, 2012c). Figure 8.4 displays the number of people who would keep the current system or reform it in one of a number of major ways.

Some of the reform preferences are dramatic. Consistent with long-standing debates noted earlier (see, e.g., Galligan 1995; Brown 2004; Brown 2012c), the most strongly supported options entail abolishing the state governments and replacing them with a new tier involving a greater number of "regional" governments. Creation or recognition of this regional level, whether in place or in addition to the state level, was supported by 32.2 percent, 42.2 percent, 40.4 percent, and 40.7 percent of citizens in 2008, 2010, 2012, and 2014 respectively. Support for reform exists across the country. Even in the most conservative state (WA), the 2014 total of those who preferred the current system plus those who did not know was only 39 percent. Support for reform is strongest in the most populous states (New South Wales, Queensland, and Victoria),

Figure 8.4

Federal Reform Preferences

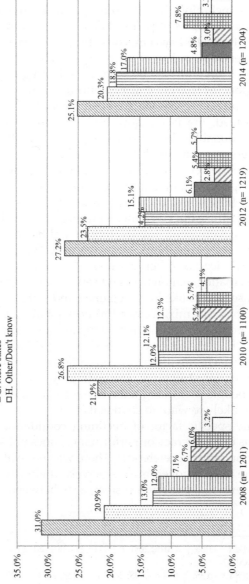

A. Status quo (current three levels, same number of States)
B. Abolish/replace states (with regional or local or both)
C. Keep Fed & State govt, but fewer States, or abolish or replace local
D. Four tiered system (Fed, State, Regional, Local)
E. No Federal govt
F. Federal govt only (no other levels)
G. More states
H. Other/Don't know

Source: Australian Constitutional Values Surveys (2008, 2010, 2012, 2014).

especially the first two, being also large geographically.

We know, from the 2008 and 2010 surveys, that these preferences do not reflect a majority desire to get rid of federalism per se, nor simply to reduce the number of levels of government (Brown 2012a). Most citizens, including those favouring reform, retain high support for federalist principles of political design and maintain that Australia needs a multi-levelled system, consisting of at least two, but probably three, or even four, orders of government. These two factors are themselves related, as confirmed by a significant and growing correlation between support for federalist design and the number of levels of government respondents would like to see in the future.[13]

Instead, the issues surround the nature and configuration of the subnational levels. Moreover, the state variations suggest these reform preferences may be the product of particular conditions, which again are neither entirely specific (related to incumbent governments and their policies) nor entirely diffuse (related to sociology). They most likely flow from citizen experience of intermediate factors, being somewhat diffuse but nevertheless direct, such as the challenges of a single state government, irrespective of politics or policy, managing large, dispersed populations, and associated large, dispersed bureaucracies and services; or other qualities of governmental interaction related to participation, remoteness and servicing of community needs; as well as diffuse factors like local, regional, and state identity.

To test this mix, we need to understand the relation of such reform preferences to satisfaction with the operation of the current system. In each of the four years, there was a significant correlation between dissatisfaction with the three-levelled system (Figure 8.3) and popular support for structural reform (Figure 8.4)—meaning, unsurprisingly, that people who thought the current system was not working well were more likely to want to change it.[14]

The specific factor of declining confidence in the federal level, in terms of democracy or performance, does not seem to have had an impact on reform preferences. There was no relationship between the fall in the federal government's perceived effectiveness and support for it as a level in a preferred system; only between 5 percent and 12 percent

---

13. 2008 r = -.068, p = .018; 2010 r = -.116, p <.001; 2012 r = -.103, p <.001, 2014 r = -.248, p <.001.
14. 2008 r = -.195; 2010 r = -.198; 2012 r = -.229; 2014 r = .231, p (all years) <.001.

of participants would abolish the federal level,[15] with the proportion of these falling in the final period of surging national dissatisfaction. Similarly, the fact that local and state governments benefited from the fall in federal government support, by rising in specific ratings of relative effectiveness, does not guarantee diffuse support for them as institutions. Despite the significant fall in the perceived ineffectiveness of local government relative to the other levels (Figure 8.3),[16] Figure 8.5 shows no rise in absolute terms in the proportion of citizens who would retain local government at all in their preferred future scenario; a very large proportion say they would not.

State government also experienced a significant improvement in the relative effectiveness rating between 2010 and 2012, but absolute confidence remained low, suggesting that improvement was effectively by default. This is confirmed by structural reform preferences. Opinions of the state level in 2010 were not significantly different from those in 2008; yet in 2010, significantly ($p = .001$) more people supported abolishing or replacing the states in a national system (26.8 percent, up from 20.9 percent). Further, this desire subsided in 2012 and 2014 (returning to 20 percent support for abolition or replacement in 2014), but confidence in state government remained unchanged.

When it came to absolute (rather than relative) judgments regarding the performance of a particular level, however, a slightly different picture emerged. These correlations are shown in Table 8.5.

This common-sense result confirms that relatively low support for the retention of either the state or local level of government (or both) in a future scenario relates to a significant degree to citizens' views of the performance of the existing level. The proportion of citizens prepared to abolish or replace state government thus aligns with the fact that, on average, it is seen as the most poorly performing level. A further result from the analysis of support for federalist political design confirms the extent to which problems at the state level lie at the root of reform sentiment. In no year was there any relation between that support and perceived relative effectiveness of either the federal or local levels. However, a negative weak correlation was found between support for federalism and the relative effectiveness of state government.[17]

---

15. 2008 = 7.1%; 2010 = 12.3%; 2012 = 6.1%; 2014 = 4.8%.
16. $F_{(2, 3517)} = 12.355$, $p < .001$.
17. 2008 $r = -.083$, $p = .004$; 2010 $r = -.073$, $p = .015$; 2012 $r = -.066$, $p = .021$; 2014 $r = -.166$, $p < .001$.

Figure 8.5

Federal Reform Preferences for Retaining Local Government

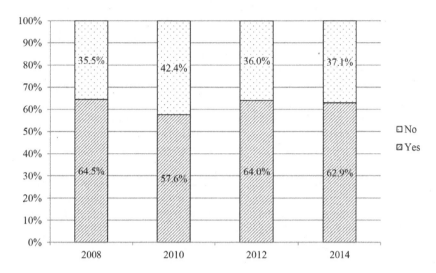

Source: Australian Constitutional Values Surveys (2008, 2010, 2012, 2014).

This means that stronger federalists, far from seeing states' rights as the cornerstone of the federal system, were more likely to view the states as the least effective tier of government.

Together, these results tend to confirm that it is the policy and structural challenges faced by the state level, in the experience of citizens, that drive underlying tensions in the federal system. In fact, other than perhaps WA residents, most citizens do not necessarily see their state government as the bulwark and embodiment of effective federalism; if anything, despite being federalists, most see the states as something of a problem. The result also reinforces that citizens' views are based on more than simply the specific factor of their support for incumbent governments; such views also relate to more intermediate and diffuse judgments regarding performance of the structure. Rather than federalism being the problem, it appears that the system is not federal enough. The fact that large proportions of citizens also identify with

Table 8.5

Bivariate Correlations between "Performance/Confidence" for a Level, and Retention of that Level of Government in Preferred Future Structure

	Federal level	State level	Local level
2008 (performance/retention)	.079*	.289**	.212**
2012 (trust and confidence to do a good job/retention)	.091*	.154**	.213**
2014 (trust and confidence to do a good job/retention)	.176**	.227**	.233**

Notes: * $p <.005$; ** $p <.0$

Source: Australian Constitutional Values Surveys (2008, 2012, 2014).

their "region" more strongly than their state (Brown and Deem 2014), even when the former has no recognized elected political institutions, reinforces the tensions and underscores the instability of the federal system in practice.

These results confirm the complexity of the mix of factors underpinning the gradual decline in faith in the federal system, support for structural reform, and the relation between them. Overall, declining satisfaction remains impacted upon, indirectly, by highly specific factors such as falling confidence in the federal level, at least because the citizenry plainly looks to the strength of the federal level to overcome perceived inadequacies in the system. It is also affected by the specific performance of the state and local governments, but apparently less in the specific sense of incumbent responsibility introduced by Easton (1975) and more in an indirect, diffuse, or intermediate way, stemming from weaknesses in institutions—including systems of cooperation and the capacity of at least some state governments to meet policy and functional challenges—with these perceptions more strongly felt in some states than in others, irrespective of incumbent governments and their policies. Finally, in the same states, it may be affected by highly diffuse factors, such as a mismatch between scales of government and those with which the community identifies.

Further, these analyses show that some support for reform relates directly to perceptions of problems or weaknesses, although much also is found among those not outwardly dissatisfied with the current system. Many of those articulating reform preferences are satisfied with the current system and even with democracy. This may indicate a high political capacity in the Australian community to grapple with the challenges exposed by these tensions in the system. As identified by its leading historian, the Australian federation itself was the product of a "utopian moment" in which sufficient dissatisfaction with current institutions was matched by sufficient confidence in the ability to move to better ones (Irving 1999). While the tensions in Australian public trust do not present as challenges to national cohesion, they present as pervasive challenges to the long-term stability of the federal system if this more gradual, underlying disenchantment continues to grow. The question to be pursued is not whether, but what kind of, reforms to federal institutions and practices should be undertaken to rebuild and bolster citizens' relationships with their governing structures.

Conclusions

This study has examined different declines in trust in Australian political institutions against a backdrop of stable support for a federal system in principle, as well as how structural reform may arrest such negative trends. In particular, satisfaction with the way democracy works, reactions to Australia's current three-levelled federal system, and citizen support for federal principles served as key areas for investigation, using results from the Australian Constitutional Values Surveys. These topics have been considered in light of how they may fall on a continuum of support, from specific short-term attitudes on one of the spectra to sources of deep-set diffuse support on the other. Cultural or political identification with the various spatial scales of community in Australia, which differ in comparison to those in the United States, Canada, and Germany, presented as an important diffuse background variable.

Primary results included a sharp fall in satisfaction with the way democracy works in Australia; a gradual decline in satisfaction with the current three-levelled federal system in a manner largely independent of the decline in democratic satisfaction; and, despite this turbulence, an unchanging landscape of attachment to federalism in principle. Comparison of these results using attitudes toward each level of government identified declining ratings of federal government effectiveness as an important factor in falling democratic satisfaction. This had several implications, including the problem that disenchantment with federal performance represents for the overall health of the system. Given the nature of the perceived institutional and structural deficiencies of the system, the extent to which the federal government is relied upon to make the entire system "work" leaves many citizens with no institution in which to place their faith.

At the same time, the apparent contradiction between falling support for the federal system and stable attachment to federalist design principles highlights diffuse structural reform preferences. While confidence in the current federal system may be declining, most citizens do not see federalism itself as at fault. Rather, concerns appear to stem from the performance, nature, and configuration of subnational levels of government, particularly the state level, as a result of the size and structure of states and not simply their incumbent governments or policies. Reform preferences are confirmed to be driven by a complex mix of specific, intermediate, and diffuse factors. Identification of the different ingredients of this complexity enables a clearer picture of the different reform paths that might positively address the underlying causes of declining public trust. It confirms that federal reform will remain an important topic for study and deliberation in Australia. In a society with fine democratic traditions, the study of public attitudes is also confirmed as pivotal to an effective understanding of how political institutions should respond.

References

ABC Radio. 2013. "Federal Labor's 'Splash' Effect on WA Election." *ABC Radio Australia*, 10 March. http://www.radioaustralia.net.au/international/2013-03-10/federal-labors-splash-effect-on-wa-election/1099396.

Alexander, Amy C., Ronald Inglehart, and Christian Welzel. 2011. "Measuring Effective Democracy: A Defence." *International Political Science Review* 33 (1): 41–62.

Appleby, Gabrielle, Nicholas Aroney, and Thomas John, eds. 2012. *The Future of Australian Federalism: Comparative and Interdisciplinary Perspectives*. Melbourne: Cambridge University Press.

Aroney, Nicholas, Scott Prasser, and Alison Taylor. 2012. "Federal Diversity in Australia: A Counter-Narrative." In *The Future of Austra-*

lian Federalism: Comparative and Interdisciplinary Perspectives, edited by Gabrielle Appleby, Nicholas Aroney, and Thomas John, 272–99. Melbourne: Cambridge University Press.

Aydin, Aylin, and Cerem I. Cenker. 2012. "Public Confidence in Government: Empirical Implications from a Developing Democracy." *International Political Science Review* 33 (2): 230–50.

Brown, A. J. 2004. "One Continent, Two Federalisms: Rediscovering the Original Meanings of Australian Federal Political Ideas." *Australian Journal of Political Science* 39 (3): 485–504.

Brown, A. J. 2008. "In Pursuit of the 'Genuine Partner': Local Government and Federal Constitutional Reform in Australia." *University of New South Wales Law Journal* 31 (2): 435–66.

Brown, A. J. 2012a. "Measuring the Mysteries of Federal Political Culture in Australia." In *Tomorrow's Federation: Reforming Australian Government*, edited by Paul Kildea, Andrew Lynch, and George Williams, 310–31. Sydney: Federation Press.

Brown, A. J. 2012b. "From Intuition to Reality: Measuring Federal Political Culture in Australia." *Publius: The Journal of Federalism* 43 (2): 297–314.

Brown, A. J. 2012c. "Mapping Federal Political Culture and Support for Political Reform in the World's First 'Top Down' Federation: The Strange Case of Australia." Panel: Implications of Public Attitudes for Boundaries of National, Regional and Local Power in Federal and Non-Federal Systems, Triennial Meeting, International Political Science Association, Madrid, Spain:, 8–11 July.

Brown, A. J., and Jennifer Bellamy, eds. 2007. *Federalism and Regionalism in Australia: New Approaches, New Institutions?* Canberra: ANU E Press.

Brown, A. J., and Jacob Deem. 2014. "A Tale of Two Regionalisms: Improving the Measurement of Regionalism in Australia and Beyond." *Regional Studies* 50 (7): 1154–69.

Brown, A. J., John Kincaid, Jacob Deem, and Richard L. Cole. 2016. "Measuring Citizen Attachment to Federal Principles: Results from Australia, Canada, the United States, Germany, and Great Britain," International Political Science Association, World Congress of Political Science, Poznan, Poland, July.

Cole, Richard L, John Kincaid, and Alejandro Rodriguez. 2004. "Public Opinion of Federalism and Federal Political Culture in Canada, Mexico and the United States, 2004." *Publius: The Journal of Federalism* 34 (3): 201–21.

Deem, Jacob, Robyn Hollander, and A. J. Brown. 2015. "Subsidiarity in the Australian Public Sector: Finding Pragmatism in the Principle." *Australian Journal of Public Administration* 74 (4): 419–34.

Denemark, David, and Richard G. Niemi. 2012. "Political Trust, Efficacy and Engagement in Challenging Times: An Introduction." *Australian Journal of Political Science* 47 (1): 1–10.

Doorenspleet, Renske. 2012. "Critical Citizens, Democratic Support and Satisfaction in African Democracies." *International Political Science Review* 33 (3): 279–300.

Duchacek, Ivo. 1987. *Comparative Federalism: The Territorial Dimension of Politics*. New York: University Press of America.

Dunn, John. (1988) 2000. "Trust and Political Agency." In *Trust: Making and Breaking Cooperative Relations*, edited by Diego Gambetta and Basil Blackwell 1988; electronic edition 2000, 73–93. Oxford: University of Oxford.

Easton, David. 1975. "A Re-Assessment of the Concept of Political Support." *British Journal of Political Science* 5 (4): 435–57.

Galligan, Brian. 1995. *A Federal Republic: Australia's Constitutional System of Government*. Melbourne: Cambridge University Press.

Gerrig, Richard, Philip Zimbardo, Andrew Campbell, Steven Cummings, and Fiona Wilkes. 2009. *Psychology and Life* (Australian ed.). Frenchs Forest, Australia: Pearson Education Australia.

Grau Creus, Mireia. 2012. "From Saints to Sinners: Changes in Public Opinion of the Autonomous-Community Governments of Spain," Paper for Triennial Meeting, International Political Science Association, Madrid, Spain, 8–11 July.

Hancock, William K. 1930. *Australia*. London: Benn.

Holmes, Jean, and Campbell Sharman. 1977. *The Australian Federal System*. Sydney: Allen & Unwin.

Irving, H., ed. 1999a. *The Centenary Companion to Australian Federation*. Melbourne: Cambridge University Press.

Irving, Helen. 1999b. *To Constitute a Nation: A Cultural History of Australia's Constitution*. Melbourne: Cambridge University Press

Kane, John, and Haig Patapan. 2012. *The Democratic Leader: How Democracy Defines, Empowers and Limits its Leaders*. Oxford: Oxford University Press.

Kildea, Paul, Andrew Lynch, and George Williams, eds. 2012. *Tomorrow's Federation: Reforming Australian Government*. Sydney: Federation Press.

Kincaid, John, and Richard L. Cole. 2016. "Citizen Evaluations of Federalism Performance and Feelings of Regional Equity and Subordination in Four Federal Polities." *Publius: The Journal of Federalism* 46 (1): 51–76.

———. 2011. "Citizen Attitudes toward Issues of Federalism in Canada, Mexico, and the United States." *Publius: The Journal of Federalism* 41 (1): 53–75.

McAllister, Ian, and Juliet Pietsch. 2011. *Trends in Australian Political Opinion: Results from the Australian Election Study, 1987–2010*, Canberra: Australian National Institute for Public Policy and ANU College of Arts and Social Sciences, Australian National University.

McAllister, Ian, Juliet Pietsch, and Adam Graycar. 2012. *Perceptions of Corruption and Ethical Conduct: ANU Poll Report No. 13*, Research School of Social Sciences, Australian National University, October. http://www.anu.edu.au/anupoll.

Macintyre, Stuart. 1999. *A Concise History of Australia*. Melbourne: Cambridge University Press.

Nelson, Katherine, and Robyn Fivush. 2004. "The Emergence of Autobiographical Memory: A Social Cultural Development Theory." *Psychological Review* 111 (2): 486–511.

Norris, Pippa. 1999. *Critical Citizens: Global Support for Democratic Governance*. Oxford: Oxford University Press.

Rourke, Alison. 2010. "Australia Faces Hung Parliament as Julia Gillard's Labor Party Suffers Losses." *The Observer*, 21 August. http://www.guardian.co.uk/world/2010/aug/21/australian-election-hung-parliament-likely.

Smith, Rodney. 2001. *Australian Political Culture*. Frenchs Forest, Australia: Pearson Education.

Trollope, Anthony. 1873. *Australia* (Selections of *Australia and New Zealand*, Chapman & Hall, London), P. D. Edwards and R. B. Joyce (eds), University of Queensland Press, Brisbane, 1967.

Uhr, John. 2005. *Terms of Trust: Arguments Over Ethics in Australian Government*. Sydney: UNSW Press.

9

German Federalism: On the Way to a "Cooperative Centralism"?

Henrik Scheller

Germany has a long tradition of federalism extending far back in history (Ziblatt 2004; Broschek 2011). This tradition has always been characterized by a discrepancy between the attitudes of the public to its federalism and the reform ideas of the (political) elites. While the public has a strong desire for an equality of living conditions, solidarity, social cohesion, and cooperation between the orders of government, academic discourse is shaped by calls for wide-ranging federalism reforms, which are oriented toward the American model of "dual federalism." Against this background, this chapter contrasts public attitudes on key aspects of the federal system with long-lasting academic recommendations for reform. Light will be shed on the general perception of the federal system as a whole, the division of powers, and in particular the issue of joint decision-making (*Politikverflechtung*) between the orders of government—all issues that have been repeatedly interrogated in various surveys. A further aspect of these polls is the question of the extent to which solidarity or competition shall be realized between the federal and *Land* governments—a question that is highly controversial in politics and academia (especially in the fiscal equalization debate), though public perceptions are quite different. The German public prefers a pragmatic and cooperative approach instead of normative concepts when it comes to solving major political challenges faced by the *Länder* and the Federal Republic. I therefore argue that dogmatic de-

mands by German federalism researchers for an extensive disentanglement of competences and financial responsibilities of the federal and
Land governments run the risk of undermining the legitimacy of the
federal system as a whole. At the same time, they obscure the need for
new and old forms of cooperation, which are important for any federal
state.

In recent history, the prolonged deliberation of two commissions appointed by the *Bundestag* and *Bundesrat*, which met from 2003 to 2009,
was an expression of the complexity of the reform discussion. The debate occurred originally in 1998 during the last political controversy
about fiscal equalization. That debate was shaped once more by the
long-lasting critique of the clunkiness of joint decision-making necessities in German federalism. The veto power of the *Länder* in the *Bundesrat*, the loss of competences by *Länder* parliaments, the compounded
tax system, and many forms of mixed financing structures between the
Bund and the *Länder* have been most criticized over decades. Against
this background, the first of these commissions was charged with the
"modernization of the federal system" in general, though especially the
constitutional division of powers; the second commission dealt with
the "modernization of fiscal relations between the federal and state levels." Since 2009, the states' prime ministers have been negotiating again
a reform of the fiscal equalization scheme.

All these debates have been dominated by models and reform proposals dating back to the 1960s. Moreover, since the federalism debate in
Germany is significantly influenced by economists, the main emphasis
of the discourse still lies on possible ways to optimize the efficiency of
joint decision-making structures of the federal and *Land* governments.
Idealized models of the economic theories of democracy and federalism (Downs 1957 and 1965; Olson 1969; Tullock 1976; Oates 1972 and
1988; Musgrave 1969; Ostrom 1990) usually act as the benchmark for
this line of argumentation (Scheller 2005, 75; Seitz 2008, 154; Fuest 2008,
119; Kronberger Kreis 2000; Bertelsmann Stiftung 2000). One example is
the "disentanglement and competition paradigm." Critics of the existing federalism demand increased competition between the federal and
state governments and greater autonomy for both. Other suggestions
for reform that often arise in this context include the call for a modification of the *Länder's* boundaries, a reduction of equalization transfers,
independent sources of income for the *Länder* in form of autonomous
taxation powers, and a tightening of the *Länder's* and municipalities'
debt restrictions.

To date, however, no majority in the political arena has been reached in order to implement these proposals. Moreover, the flat-out demand for the "disentanglement" of federal coordination and cooperation structures replaces the discourse centred around normative models and recurrent themes in the German federalism debate. The general preference for disentangling the functions of the different jurisdictions takes the place "of a political cultural framework" (Benz 2005, 207). Serious attempts to justify the future necessity of federalism from a political and cultural perspective (i.e., for reasons of legitimacy, efficient problem-solving, and historical path-dependency) are few and far between, although German federalism already faces the initial impacts of global challenges. The extraordinary financial situation of the East German *Länder* since reunification in 1990, combined with the highly visible consequences of demographic change and the lack of democratic legitimacy in the European multi-level system, creates further problems, which have been drawn into the disentanglement discussion. Commenting on the negotiations surrounding the First Federalism Reform, which occurred between 2003 and 2006, therefore, Benz spoke about the dilemma of a "disentanglement trap" (*Entflechtungsfalle*) because the demand for a far-reaching separation of federal and *Land* functions became one of the foremost drivers of this process (Benz 2008). Thus far, political necessities and specific features of individual policy fields have played only a subordinate role in the debates.

In light of this discrepancy, the question arises to what extent perceptions of the problem in the academic sphere actually coincide with the attitudes of the populace. It is thus assumed that a discrepancy exists between the scientific reform suggestions and the demands of the public with respect to the provision of nationwide services. The present analysis thereby faces the problem that surveys covering federal problems are rare in Germany. Often, opinion surveys only implicitly touch on the federal dimension in the context of specific political issues. Therefore, this study must resort to analyzing surveys that are quite a bit older than usual. Admittedly, Germans' attitudes toward the federal system appear relatively stable compared to still older data sets and, for the most part, are not subject to short-term fluctuations. This analysis is thus substantially supported by a survey by the Bertelsmann Stiftung from the year 2008 conducted by the Institute for Applied Social Sciences,[1] by various data sets from the somewhat conservative Institut für

---

1. The representative survey was developed by the Bertelsmann Stiftung and

Demoskopie Allensbach from 2007, and by a survey of the Association for Canadian Studies from September 2010.

Acceptance of the Federal System

In order to investigate the extent to which the understanding of the problems of German federalism encountered in politics and academia correspond to the perceptions of its citizens, it first makes sense to inquire into the overall acceptance of the federal system. In the September 2007 survey from the Institut für Demoskopie Allensbach, participants were asked the following question: "Everything considered, do you find you have more advantages because Germany's *Länder* have their own governments, or is it more of a disadvantage?"[2] Of those surveyed, 33 percent said they perceived "more advantages," while 20 percent stated that they saw "more disadvantages." The responses "neither" and "undecided, I don't know" were chosen by 34 and 13 percent of respondents, respectively. These figures alone already begin to reflect Germans' ambivalent feelings about the federal system. Notably, the 2007 approval rates were worse than those from 1995, while disapproval rates remained about the same. In 1995, 42 percent answered that they saw "more advantages" in the existence of independent *Länder*, while only 8 percent perceived "more disadvantages" (Köcher 2009, 159).

---

carried out in each single state by the Institute for Applied Social Sciences. The target group and survey population consisted of Germans eighteen years or older living in a private household with a land-line telephone connection. The survey was carried out by telephone between 23 October and 9 December, 2007, using CATI (Computer Assisted Telephone Interview) technology. The goal was to access citizens' opinions in each German state, resulting in sixteen separate polls. Either 250 or 251 respondents were queried in each state, yielding a total of 4,015 interviewees. The design of the survey's telephone queries (i.e., calls to households with a varying number of members and telephone connections) means that not all members of the survey population could be interviewed with the same degree of probability. These discrepancies were accounted for by carrying out adjustments (i.e., the results were weighted to compensate for discrepancies and align the survey structure to reflect the key socio-demographic characteristics of the actual distribution). In order to generate representative findings for the federal level, the individual results were subsequently weighted proportionally by state. This weighting yielded an effective population of 1,537 (i.e., the interviews with 4,015 subjects correspond to a nationwide survey of 1,537 Germans).

2. The wording of all questions was translated from German into English by the author.

There also was a wide range in approval rate variability when all sixteen German *Länder* are examined side by side. Above all, Bavaria (46 percent), Baden-Württemberg (44 percent), Schleswig-Holstein, and Hamburg (both 39 percent) showed higher approval rates than the so-called new *Länder* of Saxony (20 percent), Mecklenburg-Western Pomerania (19 percent), Brandenburg (16 percent), and Saxony-Anhalt (11 percent) (Köcher 2009).[3] These numbers coincide somewhat with those from the Association for Canadian Studies from September 2010. According to that survey, 30.4 percent of 1,000 respondents stated that they "somewhat agree" with the statement "Federalism has more advantages than disadvantages for my *Land*." Only 8.6 percent said "strongly agree." In contrast, around half of those surveyed said that they "somewhat disagree" (25.2 percent) or "don't know/I prefer not answering" (25.7 percent). Just 10.1 percent "strongly disagree" with the statement (Association for Canadian Studies 2010, 30). All in all, Germans' approval of the federal system is far from unanimous.

Acceptance of the federal system can also be assessed through citizens' identification with their individual *Land*. The 2008 survey by the Bertelsmann Stiftung (see Figure 9.1 below) showed that people identified most strongly with their immediate community (39 percent). Far fewer identified with the federal level (32 percent), the European Union (14 percent), or, finally, their *Land* (11 percent). In Berlin and Lower Saxony, respondents identified with the federal and local levels to roughly the same degree, while identification with the federal level predominated in Bremen and Hesse.[4] Against this background, then, the survey findings are unsurprising when it comes to the question of which order of government should play a greater role in the future. Above all, those interviewed said they would like to see a larger role accorded to the federal and local levels. This preference can be found most frequently in eastern Germany and Bavaria and Saarland in eastern Germany. This wish, however, does not consistently correlate with the identification and satisfaction respondents demonstrate for the various levels. In ten of the sixteen *Länder*, respondents tended to want the European Union

---

3. This is opposite to the findings in chapter 4 about the Canadian case: There the municipalities are the level with least attachment for Canadians, as well as the finding in chapter 5 about Mexico. There, the national level is the most powerful draw on identity for many countries.

4. The survey's question with regard to the identification with the various political levels was "Which level do you identify with most closely: your city or town, your state, Germany, or Europe?" (Bertelsmann Stiftung 2008, 13).

Figure 9.1

Primary Political Identification by Level of Government (%)

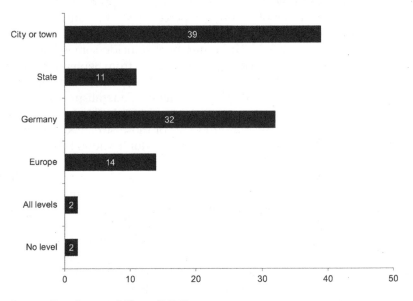

Source: Bertelsmann Stiftung (2008).

(EU) to play a greater role as opposed to the *Land* governments. Yet, interviewees were more hesitant to prefer the European level in four eastern *Länder* (Saxony, Thuringia, Mecklenburg-Western Pomerania, and Saxony-Anhalt) along with Bavaria and Saarland. Finally, in Hamburg, Berlin, Schleswig-Holstein, and Hesse, respondents preferred a greater role for the European Union than for the national level (Bertelsmann Stiftung 2008, 19).

With this information, it becomes clear why, when discussing the key characteristics they associate with their home *Land*, residents feel that *Land* politics and governance—whether in the North, South, East, or West—play a notably subordinate role. For example, in Saarland, Thuringia, Brandenburg, and Saxony-Anhalt, only one respondent in a hundred said that he or she identified with his or her *Land* on matters of state-level politics. For the majority, identifying characteristics were instead ascribed to a completely different level. In Schleswig-Holstein, Mecklenburg-Western Pomerania, and Thuringia, for example, between 34 and 42 percent of those surveyed mentioned "the environment and friendly people" as outstanding characteristics of their *Land*. In contrast, residents of Baden-Württemberg, Bavaria, and Hesse identified with their *Land* through its economic performance. "Culture and history" were mentioned by only 22 percent of respondents (Berlin). Further, results in North Rhine-Westphalia and Lower Saxony revealed an issue of particular concern when it comes to *Land* politics. One in four interviewees in North Rhine-Westphalia did not ascribe any distinguishing characteristics to their *Land*; in Lower Saxony, the figure was even higher at 27 percent.[5]

In contrast to the public's relatively weak identification with their *Land*, the results for the European level are quite surprising. It is notable, for example, that in Bremen, Berlin, Saarland, Lower Saxony, Hesse, North Rhine-Westphalia, Schleswig-Holstein, Hamburg, and Rhineland-Pfalz, the EU is considered to be even more important than the *Land*. Relatively speaking, only interviewees in Germany's eastern and southernmost regions are skeptical of the EU. These findings for these regions can undoubtedly be ascribed to fears regarding centralization that have both historical and regional roots in the *Länder* in question. In Germany's eastern *Länder*, for example, skepticism regarding Europe can be traced back to East Germany's centralist tendencies, while in Bavaria the phrase "Bavaria in Germany and Europe" (in that order) has become a standard feature of political discourse. Respondents' identification with the EU is strongest in North Rhine-Westphalia (21 percent) and weakest in Mecklenburg-Western Pomerania (7 percent). Interviewees in Mecklenburg-Western Pomerania identify even more closely with their *Land* than with the federal level (Bertelsmann Stiftung 2008).

One aspect of the public's ambivalence toward federalism in Germany can be seen in the relationship between identification with individual states and satisfaction with each *Land's* political performance.

---

5. The survey's question with regard to the state-level politics was "In your opinion, what are the outstanding characteristics of the *Land* in which you live, in comparison to other *Länder*?" Multiple responses possible (Bertelsmann Stiftung 2008: 16).

Contrary to expectations, satisfaction with each political level is not correlated with the degree of identification at that level, with the exception of very positive results for the local level. Moreover, as shown above, respondents identified least with the state level. On the other hand, states' performance is given better marks compared to the national and European levels. Given these contradictions, it can only be assumed that political debate at the state level needs to be communicated in a manner that is even more transparent and straightforward than has been the case. One reason for the lack of clarity here might well be the varied regional offerings within the German media landscape, which is home to *Land* radio and television broadcasters as well as diverse regional newspapers.

The Association for Canadian Studies' research also attests to citizens' rather conservative rating of *Land* politics. Given the question "Overall, how much trust and confidence do you have in the following to do a good job?", only 6.8 percent responded that they had a "great deal" of trust in their *Land* government. Otherwise, 39.9 percent of respondents had only a "fair amount" of trust in their state, 33.9 percent said "not very much," 15.4 percent said "none at all," and 4.0 percent said, "I don't know / I prefer not answering" (Association for Canadian Studies 2010, 49).

The contradiction between identification and satisfaction with the individual levels increases when respondents are asked whether Germany's *Länder* should continue to exist in their present form. Despite their low level of identification with the states, when asked whether the existence of *Länder* is justified in light of the work done at the federal and EU levels a full 25 percent of all respondents said "no." Agreement on this point ranges from some 19 percent (Rhineland-Pfalz and Mecklenburg-Western Pomerania) to 29 percent (North Rhine-Westphalia and Saxony-Anhalt) (Bertelsmann Stiftung 2008). This trend is consistent with findings in which residents of Mecklenburg-Western Pomerania identify most strongly with their state, while 25 percent of those in North Rhine-Westphalia feel they do not identify with their state at all. The findings are even more striking when the possibility of a fusion between the respondent's own state and a neighbouring state is presented. A majority of interviewees in Berlin, Hamburg, Schleswig-Holstein, Rhineland-Pfalz, Bremen, Lower Saxony, Saarland, and Saxony-Anhalt (listed in order of the most positive responses first) said they could imagine merging with a neighbouring state. Especially in the North (a small majority of residents in Mecklenburg-Western Pomerania say they would not like to merge), reactions are consistently positive to this proposal across state lines. The inclusion of Rhineland-Pfalz and Saarland in this group is also understandable from a geographical standpoint. At the same time, the fusion of Berlin and Brandenburg is only supported by a majority of respondents in Berlin and not in Brandenburg. These findings are in alignment with repeated calls for redrawing *Land* lines, particularly in response to fiscal policy considerations (Ottnad and Linnartz 1997, 175). Many would like to see political bodies created that are more equal in terms of economic resources in order to reduce the considerable disparities between the country's states and to increase competition among them. Political leaders regularly dismiss such calls, saying that the public does not in fact support them.

Joint Decision-Making as a Cause of Limited Identification?

Germany is a federation of semi-autonomous states. The sharing of responsibilities between the nation and its states is carried out by means of a functional division of tasks. According to this division, the federal level takes precedence in legislation. The states are then entrusted almost exclusively with executing the laws passed by the federal government. This arrangement makes forms of joint decision-making unavoidable. This is because legislation alone, which does not also fully address how the laws should be implemented, can hardly solve any problem adequately. According to Article 50 of the Basic Law, the *Bundesrat* must assist the federal government in states' administrative matters. A certain degree of complexity is inherent in this arrangement, which is over sixty years old. Further complications involve conflicts regularly arising between the federal and state levels, which in some cases can lead to gridlock. For this reason, joint federal–state decision-making structures—regarded as either obligatory or voluntary cooperation—are often seen as a central reason for the (putative) reform resistance inherent in German federalism. In the past, critics have repeatedly pointed out that these structural peculiarities of the political system have increased continuously since the Federal Republic was founded in 1949. Additionally, a number of authors have described distinctive tendencies toward unitarism (Hesse 1962; Abromeit 1993). Using metaphors such as a "one-way street," the alleged "congenital defect of the federal system," or a "joint decision-making trap" (*Politikverflechtungsfalle*), these authors declare a degree of stasis and inflexibility in the intergovernmental political system, which stands in clear opposition to innumerable reforms within the federal and state levels (Scheller and Schmid 2008).

Political processes in the last few decades have become more and more complex, opaque, and time consuming. The succession of political reform measures in a given policy field appears to have accelerated due to a decreasing half-life of laws. Legislative improvements seem to be required at increasingly shorter intervals. Tax laws as well as labour market and health policies are the most prominent examples. Scharpf has already pointed out that this can have two causes. One reason could be due to the specific features of the federal system, though a particular constellation of federal actors can enhance any inherent tendency toward self-blockades ("performance is following federal structure"). However, another cause could be the complexity of individual regulations. In this case, political negotiation and decision-making processes are shaped by the specific structures of single problems, which have to be solved politically ("performance is determining federal structure"). Already in 1976, Scharpf came to the almost banal observation that "multi-level problems" cannot be solved optimally by "single-level decision-making structures" (Scharpf 1976, 29). One fundamental conclusion of the joint decision-making theory (*Politikverflechtung*), therefore, emphasizes that the economic principle of fiscal equivalence must remain only an ideal because the group of people making political decisions will only rarely be congruent with those who have to bear the costs for these decisions or profit from their implementation.

German citizens' attitudes toward cooperation in the country are, in contrast to researchers' claims, surprisingly pragmatic. In the Bertelsmann Stiftung's 2008 survey, respondents were asked to agree or disagree with the following statement: "The German states should work together and not enter into competition with one another." The five possible answers ranged on a scale from "I agree completely" to "I do not agree at all." Altogether, 88 percent of respondents nationwide said they "somewhat agree" with this statement (Bertelsmann Stiftung 2008, 25). There was no state with consent rates less than 80 percent. Agreement was highest in Saxony-Anhalt at 96 percent and lowest in the net-contributor state of Bavaria with 83 percent. These attitudes provide evidence for a deeply rooted consciousness of solidarity, which seems to be a fundamental feature of the German political culture. These results seem to be contradictory with regard to the comparable high approval rates to the question whether the interviewees wish to see a change of the boundaries of the *Länder*. However, the historical experience gives evidence that a majority of people that had to decide in a polling booth about a concrete merger of two *Länder* always voted against it.

One question on the Association for Canadian Studies' September 2010 survey was formulated a bit differently; yet the results confirmed that Germans considered cooperation between federal and state executives to be necessary and even capable of making improvements. Participants were given a statement suggesting that cooperation exists between the levels in matters of policymaking: "The national and state governments are working well together." Just 2.9 percent and 22.1 percent of those surveyed answered that they "strongly agree" or "somewhat agree" with this statement, respectively. By contrast, 37.5 percent and 21.1 percent of those interviewed said they "somewhat disagree" or "strongly disagree." Another 16.4 percent, however, answered "don't know/I prefer not answering." If one looks at these results together with another question from the survey, the Germans' ambivalence toward the federal system becomes clear. Upon being presented with the statement "The national government interferes in regional decision-making," 13.6 percent and 38.8 percent of interviewees answered that they "strongly" or "somewhat agree." On the other hand, 25.7 percent answered that they "somewhat disagree," while just 6.4 percent "strongly disagree" and 15.5 percent "don't know/I prefer not answering." Thus, intervention by the federal government in *Land* affairs seems to be viewed critically (Association for Canadian Studies 2010, 27, 33).

Beyond the necessity of cooperation as perceived by the public, it becomes apparent that the political reform debate goes in the opposite direction. Although certain "glocal challenges" such as climate change and demographic change seem to be managed effectively only through joint decision-making structures allowing collaboration between the different levels of government, German legislators implemented exactly the opposite approach with the First Federalism Reform from 2006. The Basic Law's newly created Article 84, para. 1, and Article 85, para. 1, expressly forbid the federal government from transferring any of its tasks to the local level. These new stipulations reinforce the basic principle that, in Germany, federal and local authorities may not stand in direct relationship to each other because municipalities are legally part of their respective *Länder*. From a general governance point of view, these rules seem questionable because recent experience in diverse policy fields has shown that collaboration between both levels appears inevitable.[6] The so-called "cooperation ban" was eased in December 2014 as lawmakers decided that, particularly in university education, some cooperation between the federal and local levels is indispensable. The *Bund* can therefore provide financial programs for universities, which have to be co-financed by the *Länder*. Due to the constitutional two-layer structure of the federation, the formal implementation of such federal–state programs makes it necessary that the *Länder* forward the money to the municipalities and the universities.

Coherence or Diversity in Federal Policymaking?

The question as to the purpose of intergovernmental cooperation requires of survey participants a certain basic knowledge of how the federation functions. With the multilayered complexity of negotiation arrangements between federal, state, and local levels, this is not unproblematic—particularly because the EU is wielding greater and greater influence on Germany's legislation. In this light, questions are better posed for participants regarding the implementation of individual policies, which allows for a consideration of their desire for uniform nationwide regulations, their acceptance of state-specific regulations, and the legal diversification that results. Taken together, it appears that all the surveys from the recent past show that a majority of the public approves of national regulation in a variety of policy areas. This approval is another indication of the distinctive ideals of homogeneity and "equivalent living conditions" (*Einheitlichkeit der Lebensverhältnisse*) in the Federal Republic as a whole.

That the constitutional principle of the "uniformity of living conditions" in the Federal Republic (Article 72, para. 2, of the Basic Law) has been of such importance for the political and public debate for decades is quite remarkable for two reasons. First, constitutional lawyers largely agree that this formulation does not require the *Bund* or the *Land* governments to provide specific public services. This lies solely within the political discretion of the legislator, if he or she grants social goods. Second, the formula was modified as part of the constitutional reform in 1994. The phrase "uniformity of living conditions" as a condition for

---

6. In the discussion of the highly complex implementation of Germany's Hartz-IV law (governing social assistance programs), a public debate has ensued for the first time on whether cooperation between the federal and local levels in the area of local administration of employment programs, known as Job Centers, should be written into the Basic Law.

the usage of the competing legislation by the *Bund* was changed into the formulation "that the establishment of equivalent living conditions throughout the federal territory or the maintenance of legal or economic unity renders federal regulation necessary in the national interest." For unknown reasons, however, the lawmaker missed harmonizing this formulation with Article 106, para. 3, of the Basic Law, which still stipulates the "uniformity of living standards throughout the federal territory" as one criterion for the distribution of fiscal equalization transfers.

Against this background it is no wonder that a relative majority of the population in both old and new *Länder* rejects the existence of "great differences between the states" in areas such as administrative policy, cultural affairs, and education—issues that belong under the original states' jurisdiction (Grube 2001, 110). The 2008 Bertelsmann Stiftung survey pointed out that a clear 85 percent majority cutting across political party lines said it prefers that uniform tax rates be maintained throughout the country. The range of responses varied only slightly, between 79 percent for FDP (Free Democratic Party) supporters and 87 percent for SPD (Social Democratic Party) supporters (Bertelsmann Stiftung 2008, 26).[7] These results reveal a clear majority opposed to the calls repeatedly made within the federalism debate to give states more freedom to set their own tax rates. In light of efforts to harmonize tax rates across Europe, such calls must be seen as questionable to begin with. The results are also ambivalent when it comes to the issue of reducing public debt, a topic that was discussed intensively in the Second Federalism Commission from 2006 to 2009. Two possibilities exist for policymakers dealing with budget issues; namely, reducing public debt through increased taxes or reduced expenditures, including lower levels of social assistance. The findings of the Bertelsmann Stiftung survey show that a majority of the public rejects tax increases, even if these serve to reduce public debt. Of particular interest are areas in which higher taxes might be relatively acceptable for reducing debt, such as tax increases on tobacco and alcohol products, which met with the greatest public approval to the extent that they actually serve this purpose. Approval decreases progressively when respondents are asked about corporate, inheritance, wealth, income, social assistance, and value added taxes. Interviewees clearly distinguish between types

---

7. The survey's question with regard to uniform tax rates in all German *Länder* was: response of "I agree" to the statement "Tax rates should remain the same in all German *Länder* in the future" (Bertelsmann Stiftung 2008: 26).

of taxes and are not absolutely opposed to tax increases per se.

It is not just in the areas of fiscal and budget policy that a majority of Germans desire standardized national regulations. A similar picture arises in the context of comparable standards in kindergartens, schools, and universities—although education matters are formally subject to the cultural sovereignty (*Kulturhoheit*) of the *Länder*. Given Germany's relative lack of natural resources, as well as the demographic shifts that will affect it in coming years, increased investment in this area seems to be virtually unavoidable (in light of the rising number of university students, the increasing number of immigrants, the necessity of life-long learning, etc.). Against this background, and in order to ensure an efficient use of resources, increased focus is being placed on ways to compare the various states' university and school systems. Under the current legal framework, these are almost exclusively the responsibility of *Land* governments. Throughout the country, 91 percent of those queried felt that it is the responsibility of the federal government to ensure that uniform standards are in place.[8] Interviewees particularly in the eastern states and in Bremen (94 to 97 percent) felt this should be the case. Somewhat lower levels of agreement can be found in Bavaria, Berlin, and Baden-Württemberg. It should also be noted that, even in Bavaria, which focuses on state-level issues, 88 percent of respondents endorsed this idea (Bertelsmann Stiftung 2008, 22). These results are approximately comparable with the findings from the Institut für Demoskopie Allensbach's November 2008 survey. Here, participants were asked, "The individual states are almost exclusively responsible for education laws; the national government hardly plays a role. Do you approve or disapprove of this arrangement?" Only 20 percent of those surveyed answered, "I approve," while 51 percent said, "I disapprove." Another 29 percent remained undecided or did not respond. It is interesting that mostly East Germans, at 73 percent, versus 46 percent of West Germans, clearly rejected federalism in education (Köcher 2009, 542). The stronger support among East German *Länder* for standardized national regulations and fiscal transfer arrangements does not only stem from their relatively poor fiscal position. This West–East divide can still

---

8. The survey's question with regard to uniform national educational standards was: response of "I agree" or "I disagree" to the statement "It is the responsibility of the federal government to ensure uniform standards for kindergartens, schools and universities." Figures are in percentages, ranked according to the difference between agreement and disagreement (Bertelsmann Stiftung 2008, 22).

be traced back to the considerable financial disparities between old and new states. However, cultural differences also play an important role; in the former GDR, the idea of the "centralized state" and the "equality of all people" were much more marked by the prevailing socialist state ideology. Political cultural research shows that such attitudes become weaker only after decades.

These public attitudes about the legislative role of the federation and the states in education policies, too, stand in distinct contrast to the discussions that took place as part of the First Federalism Commission, during which the *Länder* insisted on maintaining decision-making responsibility for education matters by insisting on their "cultural sovereignty." The federal government, conversely, insisted on its own authority when it comes to university admissions and university degrees, as well as quality assurance. As a consequence, these unbridgeable differences between federal and state political leaders meant that the First Federalism Commission ended inconclusively in December 2004, an impressive example of the questionable situation that arises when policy-related necessities are dissociated from operative legal frameworks. The issue of assigning responsibilities to various actors at different levels, which derives almost exclusively from a desire for "disentanglement," became a prime goal of reform efforts and thereby eclipsed substantive aspects and questions of how it might be possible to ensure quality standards as well as uniform and therefore comparative structures nationwide. The conflict between the federal and state levels thus exemplifies the entire federalism debate in Germany.

The desire for legislative coherence that is as comprehensive as possible is also expressed in the survey conducted by the Institut für Demoskopie Allensbach in September 2007. Participants were asked: "Please take a look at these cards. Which of these do you think should be regulated uniformly nationwide and which should be controlled by the individual states?" For all sixteen policies, a majority of over 50 percent favoured nationwide regulation. At the top was the "establishment of a legal alcohol limit" for drivers (92 percent), "tax rates" (90 percent), and the "regulation of school diplomas" (83 percent). Even for tasks currently falling under *Land* jurisdiction, a majority still supported uniform regulation. These included "food inspection and authorization" (77 percent), "outfitting and organization of police" (74 percent), "rules and regulations for higher education" (74 percent), and the "creation of openings for childcare for children under 3 years of age" (52 percent) (Köcher 2009, 160).

270   Henrik Scheller

Competition or Solidarity?

Fiscal equalization is debated regularly. The equalization scheme consists of four steps: two vertical and two horizontal components that build on each other.[9] It is structured in this way to make sure the financial power of states that lie under the national average is increased to give them around 99 percent of the average. Currently, there are four donating states (Bavaria, Baden-Württemberg, Hessen, and Hamburg) and twelve recipient states, first and foremost the East German states (Saxony, Saxony-Anhalt, Thuringia, Mecklenburg-Western Pomerania, Brandenburg, and Berlin), which are particularly weak financially because their original financial power before equalization was only roughly 50 percent that of the average. Nevertheless, economists in particular recommend a radical simplification of the four-step equalization system, along with a reduction of the distribution levels in order to strengthen the autonomy of the *Länder* as well as competition between them. However, basic structural reforms are still controversial. This is hardly surprising. A number of states would barely be able to survive without allocations from the equalization system. This explains why not only the horizontal equalization transfers between states but also the vertical financial allocations from the federal government to the *Länder* were enacted on the basis of constitutional regulations institutionalized during the Great Financial Constitutional Reform of 1969 and have not been substantially modified since then (Articles 106 and 107 of the Basic Law).

With this in mind, the question arises as to how German citizens assess the solidarity created through the financial equalization scheme. In the 2008 survey by the Bertelsmann Stiftung, interviewees were asked to express their acceptance or rejection of the following statement: "Germany has an equalization scheme for redistributing public funds. Rich states provide additional financial resources to poor states. This should continue to be the case." The five answer possibilities ranged on a scale from "agree completely" to "do not agree at all." The results are clear. Altogether, 74 percent of all Germans said they "somewhat agree." In nearly all states—including net-contributor states—this widespread agreement on the fiscal equalization system reached far more than 70

---

9. The reform of the fiscal equalization system between the Federal Government and the Länder, which was negotiated successfully in 2017, includes that the transfer system will consist of only three stages from 2020.

Figure 9.2

Percentage Agreeing with Equalization Scheme for Redistributing Public Funds

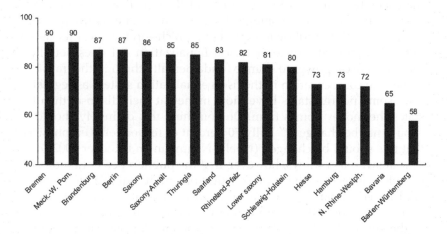

Source: Bertelsmann Stiftung (2008).

percent (see Figure 9.2). Agreement was highest in Mecklenburg-Western Pomerania and the deeply indebted Bremen at 90 percent. Even in Baden-Württemberg, agreement with this statement was still 58 percent, which was the lowest overall (Bertelsmann Stiftung 2008, 24). Analogous to the German welfare state, it must be stated that the "institutional core" of not only the social safeguarding systems but also the fiscal equalization system apparently seems to enjoy an exceptionally high, long-term, and stable acceptance (Roller 2002, 14; Bönker and Wollmann 2000, 514). Also from the longitudinal perspective, the high level of public confidence in the fiscal equalization system is fairly stable. Moreover, older surveys also show that agreement of East Germans was always higher than that of West Germans (Noelle-Neumann and Köcher 1997, 830; Noelle-Neumann and Köcher 2002, 715). This reflects the more strongly ingrained ideals of equality and justice in the East German population, influenced not least by their socialization in the former GDR (Greiffenhagen 1998, 49, 174).

This whole ambivalence, which characterizes the attitudes of Germans toward their federal system, as well as their fiscal constitution, is also mirrored by an older survey. So, the answers change fundamentally and become further differentiated if the question has to do with the concrete fiscal distribution effects of the equalization system and possible financial disadvantages for one's own state. However, it all has to do with the following question, which—in technical terms—is not stated correctly, since the Fiscal Equalization Act does not allow the states' fiscal power to change fundamentally through the transfers: "After the compensation in the fiscal equalization system as regulated now, some poorer states have more money at their disposal than the states the money comes from. Do you think this definitely should or should not be changed?" Fully 70 percent of respondents emphasized that this should be changed (Noelle-Neumann and Köcher 2002, 715). This answer also shows, however, that the public's perception of such complex subjects as the fiscal constitution and its equalization scheme is distorted in part by the media because the contexts are not always represented correctly or are connected in inappropriate ways. Thus, in the survey by the Institut für Demoskopie Allensbach in September 2007, the following question was posed: "There are states such as Saarland and Bremen that have particular financial difficulties. What is your opinion? Should the other states and the federal government support these highly indebted states through fiscal equalization, or should a nationwide upper debt limit for these states be introduced to legally force them into frugality?" In this case, as well, 57 percent answered that an "upper debt limit" should be introduced. Only 25 percent were in favour of fiscal equalization, and 18 percent remained undecided (Köcher 2009, 162). The question is posed incorrectly, inasmuch as the federal government cannot legally force states to introduce a debt brake because states as such also have fiscal autonomy. According to the jurisprudence of the federal Constitutional Court, both layers of government carry a certain obligation to assist in the case of "national emergencies" in order to help extremely financially weak states.

Similarly problematic is a statement put forth in the 2010 survey by the Association for Canadian Studies asking Germans to assess the following: "The national government does not transfer a fair amount of equalization payments to my state." Only 12.8 percent of respondents "strongly agree" and 25.7 percent "somewhat agree." In contrast, 17.1 percent "somewhat disagree," 8.1 percent "strongly disagree," and 36.3 percent said "don't know / I prefer not answering" (Association for Canadian Studies 2010, 29). In particular, the last figure indicates that the suggestive nature of this *ex negativo* question is problematic because the average citizen is ultimately unable either to understand the complex budget structure of a regional administrative body or to judge what a "fair amount of equalization payments" is. Moreover, the acceptance of vertical transfers from the federal to state level has only limited compatibility with the expectations of the general public, according to whom the states are considered to lack much political importance, and yet govern autonomously—even when their budgets are actually a combination of funds out of the compounded tax system and multiple unrelated allocations.

The constitutional clauses (Article 72, para. 2, and Article 106, para. 2, of the Basic Law) promulgating "equivalent living conditions" (*Gleichwertigkeit der Lebensverhältnisse*) and "uniformity of living conditions" (*Einheitlichkeit der Lebensverhältnisse*) have left a particular mark on Germany's political culture, even if these concepts are not official governance objectives and are not enforceable by law in material terms (Scheller 2005, 243). Abstract as the clause is, it provides little information as to which areas of life require national standards and which do not. All the same, a significant majority of Germany's citizens seems to have a clear idea of what is meant. For example, the desire for comparable living standards across Germany is particularly strong in the eastern states, with 46 percent to 59 percent of interviewees there saying they would prefer this. In all other states as well (with the exception of Hesse and Saarland), most people would like to see equal living standards achieved throughout Germany (see Figure 9.3). In second place, respondents say they would like to see equal standards at the European level as well. In Hesse and Saarland, the European level is the level most often cited as appropriate for equal/comparable living standards (Bertelsmann Stiftung 2008).

The high degree of approval for solidarity between the federal and state levels is accorded even more significance through the relatively weak support for competition among the states. Economists in particular repeatedly express a preference for market-like competition among the various orders of government as an appropriate management model for Germany's federal system. In terms of the question of where competition should be promoted (i.e., among major corporations, among EU member states, among local jurisdictions, or among Germany's *Länder*) competition among the states receives the lowest approval, except in Bavaria, Baden-Württemberg, and Saxony-Anhalt. The notion of interstate competition is most strongly endorsed in Saxony-Anhalt

Figure 9.3

State-by-State Support for Comparable Living Standards (%)

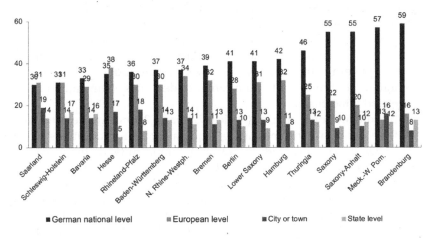

Source: Bertelsmann Stiftung (2008).

and Bavaria, at 57 percent in both. It receives the lowest endorsement in North Rhine-Westphalia (39 percent), Hamburg (40 percent), Rhineland-Palatinate (41 percent), and Bremen (45 percent). The example of Saxony-Anhalt shows once again Germans' ambivalence toward the country's federal system, since approval rates for the principle of competition are among the highest there, while Saxony-Anhalt is also the state with the highest level of respondents saying that solidarity within the federal system is necessary. This contradiction cannot be explained, even given an analysis of relevant correlative factors.

Conclusion

Even though the number of opinion surveys on the problems of Germany's federal system is rather low and the data already outdated in part, it seems clear that the public tends to favour uniformity, cooperation, and solidarity between federal partners. The corresponding values are relatively stable and are corroborated by a number of surveys.

It can therefore be established that the reform debates on the federal system and its financial structure have, for a long time now, not only been in a "disentanglement trap" but also decoupled from citizens' expectations (Benz 2007, 180). This is true because demands for a functional separation of powers between the federal and state orders of government have become—together with the debt-reduction paradigm—an end in itself and replaced a fundamental societal discussion on possible federal models. In the aftermath of the financial and economic crisis, simmering in the EU since 2008, one trend in the German federalism discussion, which had already been observed before the crisis, continues to intensify. The federal system and the fiscal politics of the federal and states levels have, with time, been ascribed a primarily market-serving function ("structure follows function"). In this way, a content wise "de-autonomization" (Trampusch 2009) of the discourse continues. After all, the question of which (social-integrative) functions of the federal state and its components should (still) be fulfilled in the future is only intermittently discussed in the current reform discourse, if at all. This leads to the fact that the self-perpetuating reform process—in spite of the dictum of being incapable of reform—changes the shape of the federal system gradually but fundamentally. Not without cause does former Federal Minister of Finance Wolfgang Schäuble (CDU) envision a trend toward a "cooperative centralized federalism" (Altenbockum 2014). Here, the problem consists less in the apparently unavoidable cooperation between levels than in the fact that states and communities continue to be allocated financial support by the federal government in order to fulfill basic tasks.

Because forms of cooperation between levels present a significant precondition for the adaptability of German states, both from the public's perspective and those of others, it seems necessary also that the basic theoretical assumptions behind federalism—such as competition among governments—that have previously dominated the reform debate are now being fundamentally questioned. From this point of view, a constitutional law promoting cooperation is conceivable. This would not nullify the nation's and states' claims to autonomy but instead would recognize that a federal state cannot survive without elements of intergovernmental negotiation. Normative reform debates emphasizing the need for a general division of tasks for its own sake without adequate remuneration in kind would be deprived of legitimacy. Such a form of cooperation requires institutional safeguards and consistency. Only then can nation and state meet each other eye to eye.

Of course, the gaps set out here between the attitudes of the federal elites on one hand and the broad population on the other side allow another reading, too. From a classical federalism theory perspective, which is arguing in favour of clearly separated constitutional and fiscal competences between the different jurisdictions, it could be argued that the people have to be convinced of the merits of such an order through an improvable communication of the political and academic elites. The present analysis had shown that these attempts at persuasion have not been fruitful. They rather imply the danger of undermining the legitimacy of the federal order. This is even more problematic because the political elites of the *Länder* themselves seem to be willing to transfer their own competences voluntarily to the federation. The reform of the financial equalization scheme between the federal government and the *Länder* in 2017 is the most recent example for this tendency.

References

Abromeit, Heidrun. 1993. *Der verkappte Einheitsstaat*. Opladen: Leske + Opladen.

Altenbockum, Jasper von. 2014. "'Harte Bretter' über Finanzen. Zentralstaat oder Autonomie?" In *Frankfurter Allgemeine Zeitung* (FAZ). http://www.faz.net/aktuell/politik/harte-bretter/harte-bretter-ueber-die-finanzbeziehungen-zwischen-bund-und-laendern-13260502.html.

Association for Canadian Studies. 2010. Survey.

Benz, Arthur, Jessica Detemple, and Dominic Heinz. 2015. *Varianten und Dynamiken der Politikverflechtung im deutschen Bundesstaat*. Baden-Baden: Nomos Verlagsgesellschaft.

Benz, Arthur. 2005. "Kein Ausweg aus der Politikverflechtung?—Warum die Bundesstaatskommission scheiterte, aber nicht scheitern musste." *Politische Vierteljahreszeitschrift* 46 (2): 207–17.

———. 2008. "Föderalismusreform in der Entflechtungsfalle." In *Jahrbuch des Föderalismus 2007*, edited by Europäisches Zentrum für Föderalismus-Forschung, 180–90. Baden-Baden.

Bertelsmann Stiftung. 2000. Entflechtung 2005—Zehn Vorschläge zur Optimierung der Regierungsfähigkeit im deutschen Föderalismus: Kommission "Verfassungspolitik & Regierungsfähigkeit." Gütersloh.

———. 2001. Neuordnung der Kompetenzen zwischen Bund und Gliedstaaten: Kommission "Verfassungspolitik & Regierungsfähigkeit." Gütersloh.

———. 2008. *Bürger und Föderalismus. Eine Umfrage zur Rolle der Bundes-*

länder. Gütersloh.

Bönker, Frank, and Helmut Wollmann. 2000. "Sozialstaatlichkeit im Übergang: Entwicklungslinien der bundesdeutschen Sozialpolitik in den Neunzigerjahren." In *Von der Bonner zur Berliner Republik. 10 Jahre Deutsche Einheit. Leviathan Sonderheft*, edited by Roland Czada and Helmut Wollmann, 514–38. Wiesbaden: Westdeutscher Verlag.

Broschek, Jörg. 2011. "Historical Institutionalism and the Varieties of Federalism in Germany and Canada." *Publius: The Journal of Federalism* 42 (4): 662–87.

Downs, Anthony. 1957. *An Economic Theory of Democracy*. New York: Harper & Brothers.

———. 1965. "Nonmarket Decision Making: A Theory of Bureaucracy." *American Economic Review* 55 (1/2): 439–46.

Fuest, Clemens. 2008. "Steuerwettbewerb unter den Ländern—wären die finanzschwachen Länder die Verlierer?" In *Föderalismuskommission II: Neuordnung von Autonomie und Verantwortung*, edited by Kai A. Konrad and Beate Jochimsen: 119–34. Frankfurt am Main: Peter Lang.

Greiffenhagen, Martin. 1998. *Politische Legitimität in Deutschland*. Bonn: Bundeszentrale für politische Bildung.

Grube, Norbert. 2001. "Föderalismus in der öffentlichen Meinung der Bundesrepublik Deutschland." In *Jahrbuch des Föderalismus 2001*, edited by Europäisches Zentrum für Föderalismusforschung, 101–14. Baden-Baden: Nomos Verlagsgesellschaft.

Hesse, Konrad. 1962. *Der unitarische Bundesstaat*, Karlsruhe: C. F. Müller.

Köcher, Renate, ed. 2009. *Allensbacher Jahrbuch für Demoskopie 2003– 2009*. Berlin: Walterde Gruyter.

Kronberger Kreis. 2000. "Die föderative Ordnung in Not—Zur Reform des Finanzausgleichs." In *Schriftenreihe des Frankfurter Instituts: Bd. 36*. Frankfurt/New York.

Lehmbruch, Gerhard. 2002. "Der unitarische Bundesstaat in Deutschland: Pfadabhängigkeiten und Wandel." In *Föderalismus—Analysen in entwicklungsgeschichtlicher und vergleichender Perspektive: Sonderheft Politische Vierteljahresschrift* 32 (200), edited by Arthur Benz and Gerhard Lehmbruch, 53–110. Wiesbaden: Westdeutscher Verlag.

Lehmbruch, Gerhard. [1976] 2000. *Parteienwettbewerb im Bundesstaat*. Opladen: Leske + Budrich.

Lhotta, Roland. 1993. "Der 'verkorkste Bundesstaat': Anmerkungen zur bundesstaatlichen Reformdiskussion." In *Zeitschrift für Parlamentsfragen* 24 (1): 117–32.

Musgrave, Richard A. 1969. *Finanztheorie*. Tübingen: Mohr Siebeck.

Noelle-Neumann, Elisabeth, and Renate Köcher, ed. 1997. *Allensbacher Jahrbuch der Demoskopie 1993—1997*. München: Verlag K. G. Saur.

———. 2002. *Allensbacher Jahrbuch der Demoskopie 1998—2002*. München: Verlag K. G. Saur.

Oates, Wallace E. 1972. *Fiscal Federalism*. New York: Harcourt Brace Jovanovich.

———. 1988. "On the Nature and Measurement of Fiscal Illusion: A Survey." In *Taxation and Fiscal Federalism: Essays in Honour of Russell Mathews*, edited by Geoffrey Brennan, Bhajan S. Grewal, and Peter Groenewegen, 65–82. Sydney: Australian National University Press.

Olson, Mancur, Jr. 1969. "The Principle of 'Fiscal Equivalence': The Division of Responsibilities among Different Levels of Government." *American Economic Review* 59 (2): 479–87.

Ostrom, Elinor. 1990. *Governing the Commons: The Evolution of Institutions for Collective Action*. Cambridge: Cambridge University Press.

Ottnad, Adrian, and Edith Linnartz. 1997. *Föderaler Wettbewerb statt Verteilungsstreit: Vorschläge zur Neugliederung der Bundesländer und zur Reform des Finanzausgleichs*. Frankfurt am Main: Campus Verlag.

Renzsch, Wolfgang. 1991. *Finanzverfassung und Finanzausgleich*. Bonn: Dietz.

Roller, Edeltraud. 2002. "Erosion des sozialstaatlichen Konsenses und die Entstehung einer neuen Konfliktlinie in Deutschland?" *Aus Politik und Zeitgeschichte* (29–30), 13–20.

Scharpf, Fritz W. 1985. "Die Politikverflechtungs-Falle: Europäische Integration und deutscher Föderalismus im Vergleich." *Politische Vierteljahresschrift* 26 (4): 323–56.

Scharpf, Fritz W., Bernd Reissert, and Fritz Schnabel. 1976. *Politikverflechtung: Theorie und Empirie des kooperativen Föderalismus in der Bundesrepublik*. Kronberg: Scriptor Verlag.

Scheller, Henrik. 2005. *Politische Maßstäbe für eine Reform des bundesstaatlichen Finanzausgleichs*. Lüdenscheid: Analytica Verlagsgesellschaft.

———. 2007. "Zu den langfristigen Implikationen von Verschuldungsverboten." In *Zwischen Reformidee und Funktionsanspruch*, edited by Martin Junkernheinrich, Henrik Scheller, and Matthias Woisin, 67–86. Lüdenscheid: Analytica Verlagsgesellschaft.

———. 2011. "Fiscal Governance in Zeiten der Krise—Vertikalisierung der Finanzverfassung infolge verfahrensrechtlicher Legitimitätsdilemmata?" In *Jahrbuch für öffentliche Finanzen 2011*, edited by Martin Junkernheinrich, Stefan Korioth, Thomas Lenk, Henrik Scheller, and

Matthias Woisin, 345-68. Berlin: Berliner Wissenschaftsverlag.

————. 2014. "Auf dem Weg zum fiskalischen Kontrollföderalismus? Leitbilder und Argumentationslinien als Verhandlungsrestriktionen im neuen Finanzausgleichsdiskurs." *der moderne staat (dms)* 7 (1): 137-56.

Scheller, Henrik, and Josef Schmid, ed. 2008. *Föderale Politikgestaltung im deutschen Bundesstaat—Variable Verflechtungsmuster in Politikfeldern.* Baden-Baden: Nomos.

Seitz, Helmut. 2008. "Föderalismusreform zwischen Anspruch und Wirklichkeit." In *Föderalismuskommission II: Neuordnung von Autonomie und Verantwortung,* edited by Kai A. Konrad and Beate Jochimsen. Frankfurt am Main: Peter Lang.

Trampusch, Christine. 2009. *Der erschöpfte Sozialstaat: Transformation eines Politikfeldes.* Frankfurt am Main: Campus.

Ziblatt, Daniel. 2004. "Rethinking the Origins of Federalism: Puzzle, Theory, and Evidence from Nineteenth-Century Europe." *World Politics* 57 (1): 70–98.

Index

bond markets, 9, 49-70
borrowing, 8-9, 49-56, 62-70
Brexit referendum, 314
British Columbia (BC), 60, 112, 183,
189, 191, 193, 209, 229, 232, 235, 311
Bush, George W., 164
Business, 24, 87, 89, 111, 144, 154, 164,
186, 191

Canada Assistance Plan (CAP), 231
Canada Child Benefit (CCB), 26, 103-
105, 109, 113-115, 118
Canada Elections Act, 307
Canada Health Act (CHA), 57, 86, 161
Canada Health and Social Transfer
(CHST), 196, 231-232, 247
Canada Health Transfer (CHT), 112
Canada Pension Plan (CPP), 5, 102,
114, 117, 165-166
see also Quebec Pension Plan
(QPP), pensions
Canada Revenue Agency (CRA), 109-
111, 116
Canada Social Transfer (CST), 105,
112, 115-116
Canada-Québec Accord Relating
to Immigration and Temporary
Admission of Aliens, 188
Canada-US trade agreement, 30
Canadian Alliance, 308
Canadian Census, 224, 234, 236
Canadian Election Study, 296, 301-302
Canadian Ethnocultural Council, 36
Canadian identity, 25, 34, 179, 181,
185
Canadian Labour Congress, 32 (n.10),
35, 178
Canadian nationalism, 292
Canadian Supreme Court, 168, 304
Carter Report, the, 107
CBC, 178
CCF, 23
centralization, 10, 61, 70, 86, 94, 131-
133, 135-136, 210, 215
see also decentralization
Centre d'étude sur la pauvreté et
l'exclusion (CEPE), 82
Charbonneau commission, 89

charter of Quebec values, 87, 90
see also Quebec
Charter of Rights and Freedoms, 14,
29, 35, 335
child
allowances, 35
benefits, 24, 34, 232
see also Canada Child Benefit
(CCB)
poverty, 29, 80, 82
childcare, 9, 26, 28, 33-35, 79, 85
see also daycare
citizenship, 2, 3, 11, 36, 179, 184, 196,
286, 303, 307, 329, 332
ceremonies, 267, 303-304, 309
regime, 11, 175-196
training, 179-180
Citizenship Act, 178
civic
culture, 285, 287
identity, 333
integration, 3, 335
civil rights, 138
groups, 134
movement, 131, 138
civil society, 20, 179-180, 184, 190
class, 1, 7-8, 17-20, 22-27, 31, 37-39, 75,
84, 87, 264, 266, 286, 324, 330
coalitions, 17-18, 27-28, 39
classical federalism, 5, 63, 69, 152, 208
Clinton, Bill, 140, 145, 158-159
Coalition avenir Quebec (CAQ),
88-90
collective
action, 75, 157
bargaining, 25, 32, 33, 35
identity, 334
solidarity, 266, 272
competitive state-building, 10, 153,
156, 168, 185, 206, 207, 213
complex diversity, 7, 17-39
conditional multiculturalist, 267, 291,
302-305
Conservative(s), 36, 63, 235, 308-309,
311
government, 25, 27-30, 36, 63, 204,
235, 293, 303-304
party, 90, 308, 311